D0848503

Brags and Boasts

Propaganda in the Year of the Armada

Calendar (Old Style) for 1588

January

Sun		7	14	21	28
Mon	1	8	15	22	29
Tue	2	9	16	23	30
Wed	3	10	17	24	31
Thu	4	11	18	25	
Fri	5	12	19	26	
Sat	6	13	20	27	

February

Sun		4	11	18	25
Mon		5	12	19	26
Tue		6	13	20	27
Wed		7	14	21	28
Thu	1	8	15	22	29
Fri	2	9	16	23	
Sat	3	10	17	24	

March

Sun		3	10	17	24	31
Mon		4	11	18	25
Tue		5	12	19	26
Wed		6	13	20	27
Thu		7	14	21	28
Fri	1	8	15	22	29
Sat	2	9	16	23	30

April

+

Sun		7	14	21	28
Mon	1	8	15	22	29
Tue	2	9	16	23	30
Wed	3	10	17	24	
Thu	4	11	18	25	
Fri	5	12	19	26	
Sat	6	13	20	27	

May

Sun		5	12	19	26
Mon		6	13	20	27
Tue		7	14	21	28
Wed	1	8	15	22	29
Thu	2	9	16	23	30
Fri	3	10	17	24	31
Sat	4	11	18	25	

June

Sun		2	9	16	23	30
Mon		3	10	17	24
Tue		4	11	18	25
Wed		5	12	19	26
Thu		6	13	20	27
Fri		7	14	21	28
Sat	1	8	15	22	29

July

Sun		7	14	21	28
Mon	1	8	15	22	29
Tue	2	9	16	23	30
Wed	3	10	17	24	31
Thu	4	11	18	25	
Fri	5	12	19	26	
Sat	6	13	20	27	

August

Sun		4	11	18	25
Mon		5	12	19	26
Tue		6	13	20	27
Wed		7	14	21	28
Thu	1	8	15	22	29
Fri	2	9	16	23	30
Sat	3	10	17	24	31

September

Sun	1	8	15	22	29
Mon	2	9	16	23	30
Tue	3	10	17	24	
Wed	4	11	18	25	
Thu	5	12	19	26	
Fri	6	13	20	27	
Sat	7	14	21	28	

October

Sun		6	13	20	27
Mon		7	14	21	28
Tue	1	8	15	22	29
Wed	2	9	16	23	30
Thu	3	10	17	24	31
Fri	4	11	18	25	
Sat	5	12	19	26	

November

Sun		3	10	17	24
Mon		4	11	18	25
Tue		5	12	19	26
Wed		6	13	20	27
Thu		7	14	21	28
Fri	1	8	15	22	29
Sat	2	9	16	23	30

December

Sun	1	8	15	22	29
Mon	2	9	16	23	30
Tue	3	10	17	24	31
Wed	4	11	18	25	
Thu	5	12	19	26	
Fri	6	13	20	27	
Sat	7	14	21	28	

Brags and Boasts

Propaganda in the Year of the Armada

BERTRAND T. WHITEHEAD

*Behold, I will send a blast upon him, and he
shall hear a rumour, and shall return to his
own land.*

2 Kings 19:7

ALAN SUTTON PUBLISHING LIMITED

First published in the United Kingdom in 1994
Alan Sutton Publishing Limited
Phoenix Mill · Far Thrupp · Stroud · Gloucestershire

First published in the United States of America in 1994
Alan Sutton Publishing Inc.
83 Washington Street · Dover · NH 03820

British Library Cataloguing-in-Publication Data

A catalogue record for this book is available from the British Library.

ISBN 0–7509–0613–8

Library of Congress Cataloging-in-Publication Data applied for

Typeset in 11/12 Garamond.
Typesetting and origination by
Alan Sutton Publishing Limited.
Printed in Great Britain by
The Bath Press, Avon.

CONTENTS

LIST OF ILLUSTRATIONS

Abbreviations: BL = British Library; NMM = National Maritime Museum, London.

ACKNOWLEDGEMENTS

Of the various people who have given me help and advice I should particularly like to thank the following, some of whom are no longer with us and none of whom must be blamed for any of my errors or opinions: Philip Brett, Leland H. Carlson, Gwladys M. Curtis, Fr Francis Edwards SJ, Howard M. Nixon, Geoffrey Parker and R.B. Wernham. I must also thank the helpful staff of the libraries I have consulted, particularly The Bodleian, the British Library, the Lambeth Palace Library, and the University of London Library.

Special thanks are due to the libraries and others who have given me permission to reproduce illustrations, some making their first appearance since 1588.

TO THE READER

This book is an attempt to describe the media of communication in the sixteenth century and how it was manipulated, in the context of a narrative of one year with whose events most readers will be reasonably familiar. I should therefore make it clear that it is not yet another history of how Drake drummed the Spanish Armada up the Channel long ago. Broadsides in this book are more likely to be the double folio sheets of paper that issued from hand-cranked printing presses rather than the salvoes from Drake's cannon.

The naval engagements, about which so much has been written, lasted barely two weeks in 1588, and the efforts of the English navy hardly came up to expectations. The Spanish and English propaganda campaigns continued over nine months, with results that have lasted over four hundred years. But those who put out the story of the defeat of the Spanish Armada had specific objectives in mind, now long forgotten, which have to be studied in context. They would perhaps be gratified to find that they had been successful in establishing a myth which still flourishes four centuries later. It must be admitted that the myth would have been very different if the Spanish Armada had been successful.

By November 1588, four months after the departure of the Armada, all the elements of the myth (apart from some mainly Victorian accretions, such as Drake's game of bowls) had been established. For example: that an ancient prophecy had predicted that 1588 would be 'a wonderful year'; that the Spaniards arrogantly called their Armada 'Invincible'; that Pope Sixtus V issued a bull deposing Queen Elizabeth and urging her subjects to support the invader; that Catholics fought loyally alongside Protestants in defence of their Queen and country; that David's small ships defeated the giant navy of Goliath; that God favoured Protestants by the weather; that the Spaniards wrecked in Ireland were massacred by the wild Irish.

Our own century is given to appeals to political and economic dogma rather than to God. But in the sixteenth century life expectancy was uncertain and usually short, while disasters like fire, tempest or flood were uncushioned by insurance. Hence religious practices and the salvation of souls took on the same importance which may now be applied to rates of interest, life insurance and economic theories. But we should not complacently forget that even now, in many parts of the world, including the United Kingdom, politics have not yet been disentangled from religion.

The Prologue is a selective sketch of the events, issues and beliefs which led up to the conflict of 1588 and were likely to be remembered at the time. Otherwise this book is not the sort of history which seeks to peer through the smudges, cracks and distortions in the window-pane to establish what actually happened; rather it is a study of the smudges, cracks and distortions. The reader should therefore beware that direct quotations from contemporary sources are often quite untrue. Sometimes there are several accounts of the same events, varying according to the medium, source, control or anticipated audience.

Not that the authors were always deliberate liars: sometimes they reported what they believed to be true at the time, sometimes they presented what they wanted to believe, and sometimes they deliberately distorted the facts to their own ends. Contemporary historians like Stow and van Meteren recorded what they had heard at the time and much of what they published was uncritically repeated for over three centuries. This book describes how some of their raw material was provided. From time to time I have tried to explain what actually happened.

Nowadays the media of radio and television continually invade our lives and our attention span is limited. Hence public relations practitioners tend to concentrate on the 'one-liner' or 'sound bite', usually provided by ghost writers, in the hope of attracting the attention of editors of news programmes or of headline writers. There were ghost writers too in the sixteenth century, though politicians were capable of preparing their own speeches if they had time. But the technique of persuasion was then influenced by rhetoric, a subject taught in every university. A sermon normally took up one hour, while political speeches were likely to last even longer. In market towns and villages, where news was dependent on rare visits from travellers or ballad singers, the audience was more patient and curious and its memory more retentive.

To extract 'one-liners' from the vivid Elizabethan speech would give a false impression. At the same time, it would be tedious to summarize a longwinded sermon or pamphlet. I have therefore compromised by quoting in paragraphs rather than in sentences, so as to provide the flavour of the technique without incurring indigestion.

In 1588 there were no newspapers (though an eighteenth-century forger obligingly supplied one called *The English Mercury*). Nevertheless a surprising amount of evidence remains of how news was transmitted. For example, the reports of spies in England, found in the Spanish archives, may or may not be true, but they do sometimes reflect contemporary gossip, particularly at Court. Even news hand-outs sometimes survive or can be reconstructed from their ultimate publication in different languages.

Moreover, those engaged in public relations communicated by letters, which survive, unlike modern practitioners who rely on the telephone or conversation at business lunches. As far as possible I have let them explain their techniques and intentions in their own words.

Until the mid-twentieth century there was no reliable method of assessing public opinion, so that propaganda could be no more precisely aimed than a sixteenth-century musket. But public relations existed long before opinion polls, just as warfare antedated the invention of the rifle, tank and bomber.

In the course of the book I have covered most of the media available, including rumours, assemblies, processions, plays, bells, beacons and bonfires, sermons and homilies, prayers, petitions, letters and forms of address, proclamations, demonstrations, books, pamphlets, and ballads, as well as show trials, public executions and other media no longer generally available. I have touched on electioneering and diplomatic procedure.

Private communications played an important part which can only be hinted at; the people who mattered and guided events were a small section (less than 5 per cent) of the three and a half million population, mostly related to each other, as I have occasionally reminded the reader. They did, however, have to keep a weather eye on 'the fearful multitude' of craftsmen, labourers, carriers and servants, who comprised about three-quarters of the population, very few of whom were literate. The remainder, merchants and tradesmen, could be relied upon to follow their own interests.

News could travel by word of mouth surprisingly fast on land, but normally (as a rough rule of thumb) at about twenty miles a day, the pace of a tinker's cart. The modern reader, used to instant communication from any part of the world, will have to remember that both at home and overseas news could be held up by adverse winds, rivers and mountains, poor roads, tired horses, and bandits, not to mention the censor. Hence it might be two or three months before people in Spain or Rome heard about events in England; this did not, however, stop them from making decisions as though they had happened yesterday.

In 1588 England was still using the Julian or Old Style calendar, which was ten days behind the New Style calendar introduced by Pope Gregory XIII into predominantly Catholic countries. To avoid unnecessary confusion, I have used Old Style for all dates, even altering dates in quotations from continental sources. Officially the year began on Lady Day, 25 March, but I have followed modern practice, used by some Englishmen, particularly astrologers, even at the time.

A hot dinner in a London inn cost sixpence in 1588, including wine or ale (see p. 120 for other price indices). What it will cost by the time this book appears in print is anybody's guess. To translate Elizabethan to modern values, allow forty hot dinners to the pound.

Spelling of quotations has been modernized, but I have seldom amended the original punctuation or the capitalization of important words. At a time when the spoken word was paramount, commas indicated pauses rather than syntax and capitals are often an indication of emphasis (the Queen's speech at Tilbury on p. 122 is probably close to her original manuscript). Capitalization also indicated respect, so that it can be significant whether an author writes 'Bishop' or 'bishop'.

THE ENTERPRISE OF WILLIAM ALLEN

> God knows it is not force nor might,
> Nor war nor warlike band,
> Nor shield and spear, nor dint of sword
> That must convert the land.
> It is the blood of martyrs shed,
> It is that noble train
> That fight with word and not with sword
> And Christ their capitain.
>
> Anon.: *On the Death of Edmund Campion* [1582]

1

The sea has long washed away the house in Rossall, Lancashire, where William Allen was born in 1532, the third son in a family of minor gentry. It was in that momentous year King Henry VIII finally lost patience over the reluctance of the Pope in Rome to annul his marriage to his Spanish queen, Catherine of Aragon. Events moved swiftly after the death in August of the Archbishop of Canterbury, the King's main obstacle to divorce through the English ecclesiastical court and marriage to Anne Boleyn.

In October Thomas Cranmer, a former chaplain to the Boleyn family, was summoned back from Mantua to be the new Archbishop of Canterbury. By January Anne Boleyn was pregnant and secretly married; the King was certain he would have a son and heir. In May divorce proceedings were begun under a new Act of Parliament; Cranmer declared the marriage to Catherine annulled and Anne's lawful. The new Queen of England was crowned on 1 June.

In July came the reaction from Rome. The annulment and the King's new marriage were both declared invalid. Archbishop Cranmer and his associates were excommunicated. So, two months later, was the King himself. The breach with Rome was complete.

On 7 September 1533, when William Allen was about a year old, the new Queen's child was born at Greenwich Palace. It was a daughter, who was given the name Elizabeth. The King did not attend her christening. Before she was three, her mother, having failed to produce a son, was sent to the scaffold and she was declared illegitimate, like her half-sister Mary. The day after Anne's execution, the King married Jane Seymour, who died giving birth to a son, Edward.

King Henry VIII felt justified in retaining his title of Defender of the Faith, awarded by the Pope for a tract against Martin Luther. While monasteries were dissolved and their lands sold off to bear the expenses of the state, little change was noticeable in the ceremonies of the Church. The Mass was still said or sung in Latin, the old feast days continued, and the familiar parish priest usually remained. The most profound innovation, the widespread distribution of the printed Great Bible in English, was almost inadvertent. Nevertheless it was allowed to be read only by men of the rank of yeoman upward and by women of noble degree.

Although it became a treasonable offence not to accept the King's supremacy as Head of the Church in England, on the remote coast of Lancashire William Allen was tutored at home in the Catholic faith. At the age of fifteen, he was sent to Oriel College, Oxford, still a bastion of papalism. He was slightly older than the normal university entrant, but his education must have been up to grammar school standards if he was able to understand the lectures, which were always given in Latin.

Allen arrived in Oxford in 1547, the year in which the young Edward VI succeeded to the throne. Under the regency of the Duke of Somerset, more radical changes were introduced into the services of the Church. The missal was replaced by a Book of Common Prayer in English, at first little more than a translation by Cranmer of the Mass. But a second version, two years later, introduced a Protestant liturgy where the sacraments became symbolic and the priests became ministers. A *Book of Homilies*, read in place of a sermon, instructed the congregation in their duty to God and the King. The printed word began to be more venerated than the images of saints.

Allen obtained his BA degree in only three years rather than the usual four, and four years later was awarded his MA. By this time Queen Catherine's daughter Mary had succeeded to the throne and was setting about restoring the Catholic religion with rigorous suppression of heresy. Allen's career began to blossom. He was appointed Principal of St Mary's Hall, then a University proctor, and in 1558 was made a canon of York.

In contrast, Queen Mary's reign was a perilous time for the young Princess Elizabeth. When Mary determined to marry Philip of Spain, only son of the Emperor Charles V, Anne Boleyn's daughter became the focus both of those who feared a foreign king and of the opponents of papal supremacy, even when Elizabeth conformed, at least outwardly, to the Roman faith. In the first year of Mary's reign she was thought to be implicated in the unsuccessful rebellion of Sir Thomas Wyatt and sent to the Tower. Close associates such as Sir Nicholas Throckmorton and Sir James Croft gave no evidence which might convict her. Elizabeth was removed to Woodstock to live under close supervision while Mary married Philip, who was allowed the title of king but not the ceremony of coronation. He returned to Spain on his father's abdication in 1555 and only once revisited his English queen. Elizabeth spent most of the rest of the reign under the suspicious scrutiny of her sister.

Early in November 1558 the Count of Feria arrived in London as ambassador for Spain to convey King Philip's congratulations to Queen Mary on her rumoured pregnancy. He found her dying and without delay sought an interview with the twenty-five-year-old Princess Elizabeth. His report to his king suggests a difficult meeting, but his comments though hostile were both shrewd and prescient:

She is a very vain woman but a very acute one. She evidently has great admiration for the King her father and his way of doing things. I greatly fear that in religion she will not go right, as I perceive her inclined to govern by men who are held to be heretics . . . She is much attached to the people and is very confident that they are all on her side, which is indeed true; indeed she gave me to understand that the people had placed her where she now is. On this point she will acknowledge no obligations either to your Majesty or to her nobles, although she says that they have one and all of them sent her their promise to remain faithful . . . I am told for certain that Cecil, who was secretary to King Edward, will be her secretary also. He is said to be a prudent and virtuous man albeit a heretic.

2

Queen Mary died in the early hours of 17 November 1558, followed by her Archbishop of Canterbury. Elizabeth was proclaimed Queen at noon, but had already appointed Sir William Cecil, the future Lord Burghley, her Secretary of State.

The Parliament called in January 1559 took less than six months to pass the legislation required to re-establish the Protestant Church of England. An Act of Supremacy declared the Queen 'Supreme Governor' of the Church and ordered clergy and teachers to take an oath of allegiance; the nobility were exempted. An Act of Uniformity restored the second Prayer Book of Edward VI and required all the Queen's subjects (except the nobility) to attend the service at their parish church every Sunday and holy day or pay a 12d. fine for each offence, collected by the churchwardens for the poor of the parish.

Like all Queen Mary's bishops but one, William Allen did not subscribe to the oath of allegiance but in 1560 resigned his Principalship of St Mary's Hall. In the following year he left Oxford for Louvain in Flanders, then a Spanish province. By the time he returned to Lancashire in 1562 the process of reformation was almost complete. Many churches were closed, often through the lack of a parish priest. By 1563 a revised Book of Common Prayer was being used at the compulsory church services, a compromise between the first and second, more Protestant, prayer books of Edward VI. To the Great Bible in English, found in every church, there was added a copy of Foxe's *Acts and Monuments of the English Martyrs*, updated to include descriptions of the persecution of Queen Mary's reign; it was particularly influential (over three centuries) for its vivid illustrations designed for a largely illiterate population. The *Book of Homilies* was revised and reprinted. The clergy, unless licensed to preach, were charged to read one homily each Sunday and holy day in order. So the congregation, literate or not, would be indoctrinated in their duty to their Queen and protector:

For our Saviour Christ and St Peter teach, most earnestly and agreeably, obedience to kings, as to the chief and supreme rulers in the world next under God; but the bishop of Rome teacheth, that they that are under him are free from all burdens and charges of the commonwealth and obedience towards their prince, most clearly against Christ's doctrine and St Peter's. He ought therefore

756.   The Image of the true Catholicke Church of Chrift.

🙏 The proude primacie of Popes paynted out in Tables, in order of their riſyng vp by little and little, from faythful Byſhops and Martyrs, to become Lords and gouernours ouer Kyng and kyngdomes, exaltyng themſelues in the Temple of God, aboue all that is called God.&c. 2.Theſſal. 2.

Pſalmes and Hymnes together. In all ſo which their dreadfull daungers, and ſorowfull afflictions, notwithſtandyng the goodnes of the Lord left them not deſolate : but the more their outward tribulations did increaſe, the more their inward conſolations did abound: and the farther of they ſeemed from the ioyes of this lyfe, the more preſent was the Lord ſoith them ſoith grace and fortitude to confirme and releaſe their ſoules. And though their poſſeſſions and riches in this ſoorld ſoere loſt and ſpoyled: yet ſoere they enriched ſoith heauely giftes and treaſures from aboue an hundreth fold.

Foxe's *Book of Martyrs* was the most widely read book in England after the Bible and described the cruelties of the Roman Catholic Church towards heretics with vivid illustrations for the illiterate

to be called Antichrist and the successor of the Scribes and Pharisees, than Christ's vicar or St Peter's successor.

In 1564 William Allen paid a last, brief, and secret visit to Oxford, moved on to Norfolk and the protection of the Catholic Duke of Norfolk's family, and in the following year left England to study for the priesthood in Mechelen. The English authorities appear to have lost track of him, for in 1568 his name was included in a list of Lancashire Catholics sought by the Privy Council. But by this time he was on his way back from his first visit to Rome and about to embark on what was to be his life's work.

From Pope Pius V he received dispensation to establish an English College at Douai in the Spanish Netherlands. It was the first to be founded after the Council of Trent had decided that every diocese should have a seminary for the training of priests.

Allen realized that the policy of Queen Elizabeth's government was to allow the old Catholic faith to wither away as the priests of Queen Mary's time died or lapsed into heresy. The aim of his college was to recruit sons of well-to-do families, train them for the priesthood, and send them back to England to administer the sacraments, to hear confessions, and to reconcile the English to the Catholic faith.

Students could be expected to be well grounded in Latin before they embarked on their seven year course, but they had also to study Hebrew and Greek. On Sundays and festivals the more advanced students were encouraged to preach in English. Mass was said every day at 5 a.m. There were fast days twice a week, but food was at all times in short supply, partly as ascetic discipline, but mainly through lack of funds.

Allen insisted to his students that their mission was peaceful conversion of their native country; they were not to meddle in politics but to confine themselves to the cure of souls. But three related events transformed his own attitude, and possibly that of his students, if they read his books.

In 1568 Mary Queen of Scots fled to England, where she was taken under protective custody by Queen Elizabeth; to Allen and most other English Catholics she was the rightful heir to the throne. Moreover she was a member of the powerful Guise family of France, who themselves had pretensions to the French throne.

The following year came the 'Rising in the North'. In September the Earls of Westmorland and Northumberland began to gather armed bands to rescue Mary Stuart from her prison at Tutbury in Yorkshire and marry her to the Duke of Norfolk. In November they advanced towards Tutbury, but received little support. Mary had already been removed to Coventry and an advance party of the Queen's forces under Lord Hunsdon was approaching from the south. By December, without a battle, the rebellion was over and the earls had fled into exile over the Scottish border. Their less fortunate supporters were hanged from gibbets throughout the northern counties as a deterrent to others. *A sermon against wilful rebellion* was added to the *Book of Homilies*.

Then came the belated intervention of the Pope. Although the two earls had written to ask for papal support on 7 November, their letter did not arrive in Rome until February 1570. But Pope Pius V had already heard of their intentions and had opened proceedings against Elizabeth for heresy. After she had been found guilty, a bull, *Regnans in Excelsis*, was published by the papal chancery on 25 February. It first listed the crimes of 'the pretensed queen of England' against the Church, then declared her to be excommunicated and deprived of her pretended title. Her subjects were absolved forever from any oaths they had sworn to her, and charged not to obey her orders and laws or be likewise excommunicated.

No provision had been made to enforce the bull and the Catholic princes of Europe had not even been informed of the Pope's intention. Both the Emperor Maximilian and King Philip of Spain protested to Queen Elizabeth that they had had no hand in the Pope's hasty action. Maximilian even tried to get the bull rescinded.

Three months after the northern rebellion had ended, the news of its failure had still not arrived in Rome. It took as long for the bull to arrive in England. On the

S. D. N. PII PAPAE V.

Sententia declaratoria contra Elisabeth prætensam Angliæ Reginam, & ei adhærentes Hereticos.

Qua etiam declarantur abſoluti omnes ſubditi a iuramento fidelitatis & quocunque alio debito

Et deinceps obedientes Anathemate illaqueantur.

PIVS Epiſcopus Seruus ſeruorum Dei, Ad futuram rei memoriam.

EGNANS in excelſis,cui data eſt omnis in cœlo,& in terra poteſtas,vnam ſanctam Catholican, & Apoſtolicam Eccleſiam , extra quam nulla eſt ſalus , vni ſoli in terris videlicet Apoſtolorum Principi Petro,Petriq.ſucceſſori Romano Pontifici,in poteſtatis plenitudine tradidit gubernãdam. Hunc unum ſuper omnes gentes,& omnia regna principem conſtituit,qui euellat,deſtruat,diſsiper, diſperdat,plantet, & ædificet : vt fidelem populũ mutuæ charitatis nexu conſtrictum,in unitate ſpiritus cõtineat;ſaluumq. & incolumem ſuo exhibeat ſaluatori.Quo quidem in munere obeundo, nos ad prædictæ Eccleſiæ gubernacula Dei benignitate vocati,nullũ laborem intermittimus,omni opera contendentes,ut ipſa unitas,& Catholica religio (quam illius author ad probandam ſuorum fidem,& correctionem noſtram, tantis procellis con flictari permiſit) integra conſeruetur. Sed impiorum numerus tantum potentia inualuit,ut nullus iam in orbe locus ſit relictus,quem

Heading of the Bull of 1570 by Pope Pius V declaring Queen Elizabeth excommunicate and deprived of her throne

morning of Corpus Christi day, 15 May, Londoners coming to St Paul's Churchyard found a copy of the bull fixed to the gates of the Bishop of London's palace, opposite the Great West Door of the cathedral. John Felton, a wealthy Norfolk man, had obtained it from the Spanish ambassador and placed it the night before. He was captured at his house in Southwark, racked to obtain information without success, and hanged at the scene of his crime on 8 August.

No attempt was made to suppress the contents of the bull. Queen Elizabeth reportedly expressed her indifference. Catholics understandably kept their counsel. The more extreme Protestants, as usual, took the bull as another proof of the Catholic international conspiracy organized at the Council of Trent. But the main reaction was ridicule: a pamphlet was printed entitled *A Disclosing of the Great Bull and certain Calves that he had gotten: and especially the Monster Bull, that roared at my Lord Bishop's Gate.*

3

At the same time, Queen Elizabeth's peaceful religious compromise came under another threat. In 1570 Thomas Cartwright, Lady Margaret Professor of Divinity in the University of Cambridge, electrified his undergraduate audience with a series of lectures on the first two chapters of the Acts of the Apostles.

He demonstrated that the early Christian Church had been governed by deacons, elders and presbyters, elected by their congregations, and concluded that there was no justification in Scripture for the Church of England hierarchy, with its archbishops and bishops appointed by the Queen, archdeacons to carry out their will, and priests ordained to administer the sacraments but rarely licensed to preach. The proper course was to abolish the offices of archbishop and bishop and to place the government of the Church in the hands of officials chosen by their congregations, as was the custom of Calvin's church in Geneva and of the Scottish kirk of his disciple, John Knox.

Cartwright was deprived of his professorship by John Whitgift, the Vice-Chancellor of the University, but had powerful protectors like the Earl of Leicester and his brother, the Earl of Warwick. His followers soon became a political force who found the new fear of papal militancy a useful weapon to further their cause. Queen Elizabeth remained adamant that religion was a matter for the royal prerogative or the bishops in Convocation, but in successive parliaments the puritans succeeded in imposing more stringent penalties on Catholics who refused to attend Church of England services.

Meanwhile on the continent of Europe the stage was being set for future conflict. On 1 April 1572, forbidden by Queen Elizabeth to enter English ports, the 'Sea Beggars', the piratical remnants of the first Dutch revolt against Spain, captured the Netherlands port of Brill. From this base they advanced through Zealand, pillaging churches on their way, then moved on to Holland. By the end of the summer both provinces were in their hands and William of Orange returned from exile in Germany to resume his leadership of the Netherlands revolt.

The next scene took place later in the year in Paris, after the wedding arranged by the Queen Mother, Catherine de Medici, of her daughter Margaret to the Protestant King Henry of Navarre. In the early hours of St Bartholomew's Day, 24 August, some two or three thousand of his Huguenot supporters in the city were massacred. Anti-Protestant frenzy spread through France until the Huguenots were fighting for their lives. In La Rochelle on the Bay of Biscay they secured a base from which to form an alliance with disaffected nobles, Catholic as well as Protestant, and a semi-independent state in the south of France.

To William Allen, probably the most important event of 1572 was the death in May of Pope Pius V and his succession by Hugo Buoncampagno, who took the title of Gregory XIII. In August 1572 Allen wrote to the new Pope about his project of restoring England to the Catholic faith and of removing the 'excommunicated pretensed Queen' and her tyrannical council of obscure men, and urged him to complete the work begun by his distinguished predecessor. The new Pope assisted Allen in the most practical way, granting a subsidy of a hundred crowns a month to the English College in Douai. The first four priests were sent to England in 1574.

In December 1575 William Allen was summoned to advise the Pope on the founding of an English College in Rome. After a journey of ten weeks, he arrived in the company of Sir Francis Englefield, an English Catholic exile in the service of Spain, who had been a privy councillor in Mary's reign. Pope Gregory had by this time come to the conclusion that England would have to be converted by force rather than by moral persuasion but had been disappointed by the inactivity of the King of Spain and of the Holy League in France.

Allen and Englefield outlined a plan to liberate Mary Queen of Scots and place her on the throne of England. They proposed that five thousand soldiers should sail from Italy and land in Liverpool, where they could be sure of the support of the local population. 'There can easily be found some Englishmen, men of trust and prudent, chiefly priests, who will cross over into England secretly from Flanders, and covertly prepare certain gentlemen in England, useful in this affair.'

Nothing came of the project because the Pope decided on an invasion of Ireland, and the commander of the expedition, Sir Thomas Stukely, was diverted by King Sebastian of Portugal to an invasion of Morocco, where they both perished with their army of twenty-two thousand men. King Philip of Spain was enabled to add Portugal to his empire.

By the end of July 1576 Allen was back in Douai, where the number of students had grown to about 120. He was soon involved in a plan for invasion of England by the new governor of the Netherlands, Don John of Austria, who would then marry Mary Stuart. But despite the revenue from the silver mines of the Indies, King Philip had gone bankrupt in 1575, and the governor did not even have the resources to pay his troops, who mutinied and sacked the towns and countryside. French troops and German mercenaries financed by Queen Elizabeth added to the confusion. The plot therefore came to nothing and in any case Don John died in 1578. He was succeeded by his able deputy, Alexander Farnese, Duke of Parma, who patiently began the task of recapturing towns for his uncle the King of Spain.

The situation in the Netherlands deteriorated so badly that Allen was forced to move his college to Rheims in France, with the aid of a grant of 500 crowns from Pope Gregory and the patronage of the Duke of Guise.

In 1579 Allen made his third journey to Rome, this time to sort out the problems of the English College he had helped to found, which had been beset by quarrels between the English and Welsh students. His main purpose, however, was to strengthen his English mission by the appointment of bishops. In this he was unsuccessful, but the Pope did agree to send a mission from the new and powerful order of the Society of Jesus.

Pope Pius V's bull deposing Queen Elizabeth had made it too easy for the English government to convict captured priests of treason. As a measure of protection Pope Gregory XIII provided the new Jesuit mission with an 'explanation' of the bull, which in effect stated that it did not apply to Catholics, 'as things now stand', but only when the sentence of deposition was put into effect. Catholics might thus freely declare their allegiance to the Queen without incurring mortal sin.

Allen had already left for Douai before the two Jesuit priests selected for the mission arrived in Rome. Robert Parsons and Edmund Campion (one of Allen's early students) set off at Easter 1580 after an audience with the Pope. But it was not until they arrived in Louvain that they heard that a papal expedition, under the leadership of Nicholas Sanders, the papal nuncio, and Edward Fitzgerald, had landed in Ireland with eighty men and four priests. Instead of the expected uprising, they were joined by only three hundred Irishmen and four captains. The local English garrison was quite sufficient to withstand the invasion and Fitzgerald was killed; Sanders evaded capture but eventually died of his privations. Spanish reinforcements belatedly sent in 1580 surrendered soon after they landed.

When Parsons and Campion arrived in England in June 1580, circumstances could hardly have been less auspicious for a peaceful mission of conversion.

By this time Allen had already sent over a hundred seminary priests to England, but the effect of the Jesuit mission far outweighed its numbers. Both Campion and Parsons continued to elude capture, moving their separate ways from refuge to refuge, mostly in houses of the nobility. They were soon publishing pamphlets, purportedly printed in France, but in reality on secret printing presses in England. In June 1581 500 copies were printed of *Decem Rationes*, in which Campion justified his mission to the Privy Council; copies were left on the seats of the Oxford University church of St Mary's by William Hartley, one of Allen's seminary priests.

Shortly afterwards Campion was captured and tortured to try to extract information about his colleagues. He was offered preferment in the Church of England if he was prepared to recant, and was allowed to debate his case with learned divines. Together with other captured priests he was condemned after a show trial under the 1352 Treason Statute of Edward III. In his last statement to the court, he declared: 'The only thing that we have now to say is, that if our religion do make us traitors, we are worthy to be condemned; but otherwise are, and have been, as good subjects as ever the queen had.' A rather different version was published in an account

Richard Verstegan (aka Rowlands) illustrated the persecution of Catholic priests in England and other Protestant countries in his *Theatrum Crudelitatem*, published on the Continent in 1587

of the execution by Anthony Munday, 'sometime the Pope's scholar, allowed in the Seminary at Rome'. Munday was one of several agents of the English government who had infiltrated Allen's English College in Rome. The following year, in *The English Roman Life*, he published a colourful account of his experiences at the seminary and the preparation of its students for martyrdom.

Meanwhile, the war of words from the Continent intensified. Robert Parsons escaped to France after Campion's capture and soon set up a printing press in Rouen, whose products were smuggled into England; a favourite method was to pack pamphlets in wine casks, which could not all be inspected without spoiling the wine.

Although many of these publications were devotional rather than political in nature, possession of them remained a treasonable offence. One such work, *The First Book of the Christian Exercise, pertaining to resolution*, was written by Parsons himself (identified only as 'R.P.'). It was edited by Edmund Bunny, a Protestant Yorkshire vicar and freely published in England, purged of its 'Catholic errors and corruptions', achieving great popularity particularly among puritans. But the Rheims *New Testament* in English, fulfilling an early ambition of Dr Allen, drew a more hostile response. It contained polemical notes which drew many Protestant commentaries; the puritans had used the same technique in their own 'Geneva Bible', first produced in exile during Queen Mary's reign, which even sometimes included the prohibited presbyterian order of service.

In 1582 William Allen, by now Nicholas Sanders's acknowledged successor as leader of the English Catholics in exile, published *An Apology and True Declaration of the Two English Colleges*. He argued, as Campion had done at his trial, that neither the Jesuits nor the seminary priests had the Pope's authority 'to move sedition or to deal against the state or temporal government: but only . . . to do such duties as be required for Christian men's souls, which consist in preaching, teaching, catechising, ministering the Sacraments and the like'. Nevertheless in the same book Allen maintained that the [Catholic] Church 'hath right to correct the temporal and to procure by all means possible that the terrene kingdom give no annoyance to the state of the Church', even to the point of excommunicating or deposing 'apostate princes'.

This was no mere academic exercise. Allen was then involved in a plan to depose Queen Elizabeth and to free Mary Queen of Scots by means of a simultaneous invasion by Esmé Stuart, the Earl of Lennox, from Scotland and his cousin, the Duke of Guise, from France. Details of the plan fell into the hands of the English government after the capture of William Creighton, a Jesuit priest, on his return from a visit to Scotland, and Francis Throckmorton, an English recusant. Their evidence revealed the complicity, not only of Mary Queen of Scots, but of Don Bernardin de Mendoza, the Spanish ambassador in London.

Such evidence, following on the papal invasion of Ireland, made it impossible for the English government to accept that the mission of the priests was as entirely spiritual as Allen maintained. Yet again Queen Elizabeth refused to take action against Mary, despite clear evidence of her complicity, but Don Bernardin de Mendoza was expelled from the country. He was promptly appointed Spanish ambassador in Paris, where he resumed his intrigues with English Catholic refugees and Mary's cousin the Duke of Guise.

Lord Burghley (left), Queen Elizabeth's Lord Treasurer, engaged in a pamphlet war against Dr William Allen (right), leader of the English Catholic exiles, which extended well into 1588

Concerned about criticism from abroad of their treatment of Campion, the seminary priests, and English recusants, the English government published in December 1583, a brief, anonymous pamphlet of twenty pages called *The Execution of Justice in England.* It was also printed in French, Italian and Latin. The author was in fact Lord Burghley himself, who argued that Catholics who remained in England as peaceful subjects had not been persecuted for their faith, as Protestants had been in Queen Mary's time. The government's concern was with seditious Catholics who had fled abroad and tried to stir up foreign princes to make war on their native land, who also set up 'certain schools which they called seminaries, to nourish and bring up persons naturally disposed to sedition' and sent them secretly into England and Ireland 'but yet so warily they crept into the land, as none brought the marks of their priesthood with them.'

These were, Burghley maintained, political agitators rather than religious men and deserved the penalty of treason. Even so, 'not above three score' had been executed in the twenty-five years of Queen Elizabeth's reign, compared with almost four hundred Protestants in the five years' reign of Queen Mary.

William Allen's reply, also published anonymously, was a 250 page book called *A True, Sincere, and Modest Defence of English Catholics*, printed in Rouen on Robert Parsons' press. He maintained that, on the contrary, many priests and other Catholics had been persecuted, tortured, condemned and executed merely for upholding their religious beliefs. Their denial that the Queen was head of the Church had been made a treasonable act by Parliament, not by any universal law. He pointed out that they had not hesitated to declare their loyalty to the Queen, despite the bull of Pope

Pius V, but avoided mention of Pope Gregory's 'explanation', to which Burghley had referred.

A large part of Allen's book dealt with the much debated question of when it was lawful to depose a ruler. The orthodox view, like the *Book of Homilies*, demanded the subject's unquestioning loyalty to those set over him. But after citing examples from the Bible, the Church Fathers, and even noted Protestants, Allen concluded 'that in the case of heresy the sovereign loseth his superiority and right over his people and kingdom, which cannot be a lawful Christian state or commonwealth without due obedience to Christ and to the Church's laws.' He went on to claim that given a free choice, two out of three Englishmen 'are inclined to Catholic religion in their hearts and consequently are discontented with the present condition of things'.

4

It was but a short step from lawful deposition to lawful assassination. In 1580 King Philip of Spain had offered a reward to anyone who succeeded in killing William of Orange. In July 1584 an assassin at last succeeded at his home in Delft. For a whole generation William had been the leader and unifier of the Dutch struggle for independence. The official report of his death related that 'in the whole town there is such great sorrow that the little children are crying in the streets.'

Coming soon after the discovery of the Throckmorton plot, the assassination caused increased alarm in England for the Queen's safety. A 'Bond of Association' signed by thousands of her subjects vowed to prevent the succession of a Catholic, particularly Mary Stuart, whose easy-going gaoler, the Earl of Shrewsbury, was replaced by the dour Sir Amyas Paulet. Parliament resolved to take even more stringent steps against Catholics and eventually enacted that any priest ordained by Rome since the Queen's accession should be given forty days to leave the country. If he remained or returned thereafter he would be guilty of high treason. Anyone who should 'receive, relieve, comfort or maintain' such priests would be guilty of felony and could be sentenced to death.

While Parliament was still sitting, one of their members, Dr William Parry, was found to have been engaged in a plot to assassinate the Queen. In his confession he claimed to have been influenced by Dr Allen's book against *The Execution of Justice in England* which 'taught that princes excommunicate for heresy were to be deprived of kingdom and life'. He was executed for treason in February 1585.

A month before the assassination of William of Orange the Duke of Anjou died, of tuberculosis rather than poison as rumoured. He had been Queen Elizabeth's last suitor for marriage and the last surviving brother of the childless King Henry III of France. His death left the Protestant King Henry of Navarre with the strongest claim to the succession. The King of Spain took steps to obstruct a Protestant heir. Allen and his associates were closely involved in the negotiations for his secret treaty, signed in December 1584, with the Duke of Guise, promising to provide the revived Holy League with 50,000 crowns a month to ensure the recognition of Navarre's uncle, the Cardinal of Bourbon, as heir to the throne.

Queen Elizabeth heard of the treaty in April. A few weeks later, King Philip seized

English and Dutch shipping in Spanish ports; the crews, it was reported, were treated with the utmost cruelty. Meanwhile the Duke of Parma was besieging Antwerp, still the financial centre of western Europe. By September, too late to save Antwerp, the Queen reluctantly accepted that there was no alternative but to send English troops to the Netherlands.

A *Declaration of the Causes* of her intervention, jointly written by Burghley and Walsingham, was printed for foreign consumption in Dutch, Italian and French as well as English. She claimed that her purpose was not to gain sovereignty nor to establish religion, but only to restore the ancient liberties of self-government that the provinces had enjoyed under Burgundian rule. Four months later the Earl of Leicester, whom the Queen had appointed to command her troops, accepted the title of Governor-General, against her express wishes, and began to behave like a viceroy. Indeed the Earl proved himself as inept at finance and generalship as he was lacking in political acumen. The costs of intervention mounted but failed to hold back the Duke of Parma's inexorable progress in regaining his king's lost territory.

England had more success at sea. Sir Francis Drake, who had been unleashed on the Spanish treasure fleet, which he missed only by a few hours, came back from sacking the West Indies ports of Santo Domingo and Cartagena with ships laden with booty.

5

In August 1585 William Allen was taken seriously ill and nearly died. While convalescing in Spa a few weeks later, he was joined by the Jesuit Robert Parsons, with whom he set out on 16 September on his fourth and last journey to Rome.

Pope Gregory XIII had died the previous April, to be succeeded by Pope Sixtus V. Before he left Spa, Allen prepared for the new Pope a 'brief memorial on the present state of the English, from which may be discerned the ease and opportunity of the holy enterprise'. A copy was sent for information to the King of Spain.

Allen repeated his claim that at least two out of three Englishmen 'are at heart inclined to the Catholic faith and interest, although many, through fear of the royal power, do not publicly avow their faith'. The Queen and her adherents were much more afraid of the latter, 'because they cannot deal severely nor be on their guard against them when the time of divine chastisement comes'.

Most of the nobility could be counted on to support an invasion sanctioned by the Pope, together with their servants and those engaged in agriculture, particularly in the north. Moreover, the Catholics, now far more numerous, only obeyed the Queen through fear, 'and that fear will be removed when they see the foreign forces.'

Allen and Parsons thought that the whole operation could be carried out by fifteen thousand trained soldiers, helped by the Catholic inhabitants after 'the sentence of excommunication and deposition should be seen to be renewed.'

King Philip II thought differently. As early as 1582 he had contemplated an invasion of England from Spain. His admiral the Marquis of Santa Cruz reckoned that it would require a fleet of 500 ships carrying an army of sixty thousand men, more than even King Philip could afford. He had come to the view that the best course was an invasion by his nephew the Duke of Parma from the Netherlands under the protection of a fleet sent from Spain. On the other hand, he was reluctant to undertake such an enterprise simply to place a French queen on the throne of England, still less her heretic son King James of Scotland. Count Olivarez, his ambassador in Rome, therefore had the delicate task not only to persuade the Pope to provide financial assistance and spiritual endorsement but also to acknowledge King Philip's claim to the succession after Mary Stuart. William Allen and Robert Parsons had been summoned from Rheims to help him in this task.

In November, when they arrived in Rome, they found Pope Sixtus V a very different proposition from his predecessor. Of peasant stock, Felice Peretti's skill in preaching had brought him to the attention of Pope Pius V, who made him Vicar General of the Franciscans with instructions to reform the Order, a task he performed with ruthless efficiency. But he and Hugo Buoncompagno had early formed a mutual antipathy on an embassy to Spain and when the latter became Pope Gregory XIII he had to contain his restless energy during seventeen years of enforced inactivity. On his unexpected elevation as Pope he embarked on an ambitious programme to rebuild Rome, to reform papal administration and finance, even to revise the Vulgate. Always ready to take an opposite view to his predecessor, he was suspicious of the motives of Philip of Spain and treated his ambassador to the Holy See, Count Olivarez, with ill-concealed contempt. He had hopes of reconciling, if not Queen Elizabeth, at least King James of Scotland to the Catholic faith.

During 1586 news began to come in from England of the discovery of another plot to murder Queen Elizabeth. This time Sir Francis Walsingham, by intercepting her correspondence, had taken steps to ensure that the complicity of Mary Stuart could be proved beyond question. Sir Anthony Babington and his fellow conspirators were executed with the full rigours of the law of treason. Mary was tried and found guilty by a distinguished court of both Catholic and Protestant nobles, and Parliament was summoned to determine her fate. In both Madrid and Rome the result was regarded as a foregone conclusion. By December Count Olivarez, not without difficulty, had secured the Pope's agreement in principle to Philip's right of succession, to a contribution of a million ducats towards the cost of the invasion, and to William Allen's election to the College of Cardinals.

The sentence of death on Mary Queen of Scots was published before Christmas 1586, but months went by while Queen Elizabeth balked at the responsibility of executing an annointed Queen. Allen wrote on 9 March 1587 to the King of Spain advising that it would 'be well to say nothing for the present, either to the pope or any one, about your majesty's succession'. After victory, Parliament would decide on his claim to the throne and the papal legate, the Archbishop of Canterbury, would be able to convince the bishops and Catholic peers. Allen himself, of course, was to be the legate and new Archbishop. But there was need for haste. 'While you linger, souls are perishing, friends are murdered, and the enemy grows strong.'

Five days later the news of the execution of Mary Queen of Scots arrived in Rome. Without delay, William Allen wrote to King Philip, formally acknowledging his right to the throne of England and signing his letter 'your devoted servant and subject'. But it was over a month before he heard that the King of Spain had at last made up his mind to undertake the Enterprise of England.

The irascible and impetuous Pope Sixtus V (left) was suspicious of the motives of King Philip II of Spain (right), but nevertheless agreed conditionally to subscribe one million gold ducats to the Enterprise of England and to make Dr Allen a cardinal

He employed the time in writing a new pamphlet, justifying the action of William Stanley and Rowland York, two English Catholics in the service of the Earl of Leicester, who had surrendered two forts in the Netherlands with their garrisons to the enemy. In his conclusion he recalled the suggestion of another 'Gentleman and Captain',

> that as we had certain Seminaries and Colleges for preservation or restitution of the Clergy, when the time should come to serve God in our country, so . . . there were some companies of English soldiers also, to be trained up in Catholic and godly military discipline, for the help of our said country in that kind likewise.

Allen arranged for Count Olivarez to send his manuscript to the Duke of Parma in Flanders to be printed and smuggled into England.

Sometime in the early summer of 1587 Allen and Parsons sent a further confidential letter to Madrid on matters requiring the King's urgent decision. Allen realized the crucial importance of timing for the success of the Enterprise. If the invading army was to have the support of English Catholics, there must be no such tardy announcement as in 1570 of the Pope's sentence depriving 'the pretensed queen' of her crown. After pointing out the need to send reliable agents secretly into Scotland and Ireland to prepare the ground, Allen came to 'the book which is to be written to announce and justify the enterprise'.

We shall point out the multiple bastardy of Queen Elizabeth, her wicked mode of life, the injuries she has done to all Christendom and to his Majesty in particular, her excommunication and deposition by the common law and by the Bulls of various Pontiffs, and at the same time it will be very amply demonstrated to all who are subject to the English crown that they will derive immense advantage from the good success of this enterprise; as also to the Christian [i.e. Catholic] princes elsewhere that it will not result in prejudice to any of them.

Meanwhile Count Olivarez had at last succeeded in securing the written agreement of the Pope to contribute a million gold ducats towards the cost of the Enterprise, to renew Pope Pius V's sentence of excommunication and deposition, to declare a jubilee conferring on the Enterprise the status of a crusade, and to create Dr William Allen a cardinal in readiness for the re-establishment of the Catholic Church in England.

Allen was duly elected a cardinal in July 1587. The Venetian ambassador, who attended the consistory, commented: 'He speaks Latin very well, but does not venture on Italian. He is handsome, about forty years of age [he was in fact 55] and although not of the noblest blood is still wellborn.'

The Pope, however, immediately expressed his regret to the King of Spain because 'as soon as it was known in Rome, they at once began to say that we are now getting ready for the war in England, and this idea will now spread everywhere.' He was also annoyed to hear that King Philip intended to reserve the right to appoint the new bishops and archbishops in England, just as he did in Spain. 'I have shed many tears over this great sin of yours,' he wrote, 'and I trust that you will amend it, and that God will pardon you. The Vicar of Christ must be obeyed without reply in questions of salvation, and I therefore hope that you will submit.'

Both in letters and through the Spanish ambassador, he continued to impress on the King the need for haste in accomplishing the Enterprise. Furthermore he made it plain that his promises were conditional on the invasion actually taking place. Not one gold ducat was to be paid until a Spanish soldier set foot on the shore of England.

CHAPTER ONE

THE YEAR OF WONDERS

Tausend fünfhundert achtzig acht
  Das is das Jahr das ich betracht.
Geht in dem die Welt nicht under,
  So g'schicht doch sonst gross merklich wunder.

Fifteen hundred and eighty-eight
  That is the year I contemplate.
If then the world do not go under
  There'll else be great events and wonder.

Anon. (quoted by Regiomontanus;
Leovitius: *Ephemeridum*, 1557)

1

Elizabethans kept notes of their appointments and business transactions in diaries called almanacs, which also contained useful information for travellers about the tides, phases of the moon, and dates of fairs and feast days. To assist sales, printers of almanacs usually spiced them with prognostications of the year to come, rather as popular newspapers and magazines print horoscopes today.

In the autumn of 1587, as printers prepared their almanacs for the Christmas trade, there was every reason for them to anticipate bumper sales. The coming year of 1588 was the subject of a notorious prophecy attributed to Regiomontanus, otherwise Johann Müller of Königsberg in Franconia, a noted astrologer who had calculated, a century before, the astronomical tables used by all the famous navigators, including Christopher Columbus on his voyage to the Indies and Ferdinand Magellan in his circumnavigation of the globe.

Johann Müller may have been fond of reciting the four lines of German doggerel, quoted above, during his university lectures, but it is unlikely that he was responsible for an expanded Latin version which was first published in 1564 by a Bohemian astrologer called Cyprian von Leowitz (or Cyprianus Leovitius) and subsequently rendered by an English translator as follows:

When after Christ's birth there be expired
  Of hundreds fifteen, years eighty and eight,
There comes the time of dangers to be feared,
  And all mankind with dolours it shall freight.   [load]
For if the world in that year do not fall,

> If sea and land then perish ne decay:
> Yet Empires all and Kingdoms alter shall,
> And man to ease himself shall have no way.

The English version came in a translation by Thomas Rogers of a book, also in Latin, by a Flemish scholar, Sheltoo a Geverin, called *Of the end of this world, and the second coming of Christ*. The calculations of Leovitius had shown that there would be an unusual conjunction of the planets Saturn and Jupiter in 1583 and 1588. The evidence of the scriptures and numerology indicated that 1588 and 1593 were the years 5550 and 5555 since the Creation. With proper scientific caution, Sheltoo a Geverin hesitated to predict which year would prove to be the end of the world, or something almost as awful. But his own fancy was suggested by his quotation of the Latin verses of Leovitius, which he mistakenly attributed to Regiomontanus.

Thomas Rogers' translation was first printed in 1577, when the appearance of a comet had aroused widespread interest in the significance of celestial bodies. Such was the popularity of prophecies of doom that it ran to three editions before the first critical year of 1583. But on the whole it was mainly read by professional people and medical students, for whom astrology was a required subject.

One such student at Cambridge University was Richard Harvey, the second of three sons of a prosperous ropemaker of Saffron Walden. In 1582 he wrote *An Astrological Discourse upon the great and notable Conjunction of the two superior planets, Saturn and Jupiter, which shall happen the 28 day of April, 1583*. There was an eclipse of the sun in 1582, which made him certain that 1583 would bring, if not the end of the world, at least 'many fierce and boisterous winds then suddenly breaking out' which would cause 'great abundance of waters and much cold weather, much unwonted mischiefs and sorrow'.

The book aroused controversy which spread far beyond the cloistered walls of Cambridge. Knowledge of the prophecy spread even to 'the common sort of people' who could not read, let alone understand, the arguments of the *Discourse*.* So it was that at high noon on 28 April 1583, the very hour which Richard Harvey had prophesied, a large number of people looked 'for some strange apparition or vision in the air' or even prepared themselves for the Last Trump. Nothing, of course, happened except that Richard Harvey found himself the laughing-stock of Cambridge and London. He was satirized on the London stage and mocked in popular ballads. Nevertheless, the popularity of his book had given wide circulation to his description of 'that old and common prophecy touching the year 1588', in which he even improved on Leovitius:

> That year hath many hundred years ago been specially foretold, and much spoke
> of amongst Astrologers, who have as it were, *Unanimi consensu*, prognosticated,
> that either a marvellous fearful and horrible alteration of Empires, Kingdoms,

---

* Approximately 20 per cent of men and 5 per cent of women in 1588 could write, but probably over twice as many could read to some extent.

Seignories and States, together with other wonderful, and very extraordinary Accidents, as extreme hunger, and pestilence, desperate treasons, and commotions shall then fall out, to the miserable affliction, and oppression of huge multitudes: or else that an utter and final overthrow, and destruction of the whole world shall ensue.

How seriously the prophecy was taken varied, of course, from person to person. The editor of the new edition of Holinshed's *Chronicles*, the popular history book which came out in 1587, described the commotion over Richard Harvey's *Astrological Discourse* and remarked in a marginal note: 'The great year of 1588 is more talked of than feared.'

A sophisticated young lawyer like Francis Bacon could think that prophecies and the like 'ought to serve but for winter talk by the fireside. But,' he added, 'the spreading or publishing of them is in no sort to be despised. For they have done much mischief.'

With this view the Queen's Privy Council was in full agreement. If 1588 was to be a year of wonders, 1587 had been a year of rumours. In January a spate of rumours had swept the country that Mary Queen of Scots had escaped from prison, that the Duke of Guise had landed in Sussex with a French army to rescue her, that there was rebellion in the north and a plot to kill the Queen, that the Scots had invaded England, even that the Queen was dead. The historian William Camden, then a schoolmaster at Westminster, had no doubt that these rumours were deliberately spread by 'such as bore a mortal hatred against the Queen of Scots . . . to hasten her death'. Certainly they led Queen Elizabeth to sign Mary's death warrant; her Privy Council took it upon themselves to order the execution to take place.

After Mary's execution, rumours with more substance began to come in of the preparation by the King of Spain of a huge fleet in Lisbon and other Atlantic ports. In April Sir Francis Drake sailed from Plymouth with a small squadron of ships to raid Cadiz and the ports of Portugal. After his daring destruction of some twenty-four Spanish ships in Cadiz harbour, he wrote to Sir Francis Walsingham: 'I assure your Honour the like preparation was never heard of or known as the King of Spain hath and daily maketh to invade England.' On his return in June to England, his flair for publicity brought not only rejoicing at how he had 'singed the King of Spain's beard' but uneasy speculation about the intentions of the most powerful king in Europe.

In August a rumour swept around southern England that a fleet of 200 Spanish ships had been sighted off the coast. Coast-dwellers fled inland, while the well-to-do came up to rent houses in an already overcrowded, but well fortified London. The Queen had to issue a proclamation ordering them to return to their homes, while her new Lord Chancellor, Sir Christopher Hatton, lectured the judges and lawyers assembled in the Star Chamber in White Hall on the need for calm.

But the rumours were taken seriously enough for the Queen to order a 'stay of ships in ports'; armed merchant vessels would provide a reserve for the Queen's ships if it came to war. The Queen's subjects applied themselves vigorously to arms drill and the arts of war. London printers looked to future trade with military and medical treatises such as Niccolo Tartaglia's *Art of shooting* and Franciscus Arcaeus' *Most excellent method of curing wounds*.

There was quite enough anxiety about already without risking commotions like those of 1583 and talk of 'miserable affliction and oppression of huge multitudes'. Astrologers who arrived at their almanac printers with their prognostications for 1588 therefore found that a complete ban had been imposed on references to Regiomontanus and the like. One astrologer, Walter Gray, reached print with a reference to the two eclipses of the moon, due on 3 March and 26 August 1588, but commented: 'what the influence of these may be (within this year to happen) . . . I purposely omit to set down, more than this, that there is likelihood of an Earthquake, with fear of the Plague and pestilence to scourge the people.' That was the sort of prophecy one could read any year.

John Harvey, younger brother of Richard and recently qualified as a physician, discussed in the preface to his almanac how far prophecies 'are to be valued or

It took two men to operate a sixteenth-century printing press, one to apply the ink, the other to load the paper, which was first dampened, then hung up to dry after printing. Typesetting (in background) was slow but skilled

credited'. He concluded that the science of astrology was too inexact to be taken literally, and failed to mention the famous prophecy of 1588.

It was not a difficult task for the Privy Council to prevent publication of matter which might disturb the peace of the realm. Regulation of printing had been codified in a Star Chamber Decree of July 1586, which restricted printing to the university presses of Cambridge and Oxford and the members of the Stationers Company of London. Anything the latter printed had to be passed by a member of the Privy Council or by the Bishop of London, whose palace was conveniently situated opposite the west door of St Paul's, almost next to Stationers Hall. In practice, members of the Stationers Company censored themselves; good behaviour could bring the reward of valuable monopolies of certain classes of books, while there was no profit in matter held up by the censor. The Master and Wardens of the company were zealous in hunting down unauthorized printing presses which, besides being illegal, threatened their prosperity. Furthermore, the company operated its own system of copyright: any member could register a book or pamphlet before publication, a fee of sixpence giving him the exclusive printing or publication rights. Authors, of course, had no such protection.

A word of warning from the office of Sir Francis Walsingham, Principal Secretary of State, or from John Whitgift, Archbishop of Canterbury, was enough to spread the news among the printers and booksellers in St Paul's Churchyard that certain subjects were currently unwelcome. Publication could not legally proceed without the signed authorization 'seen and allowed' on the back of the manuscript, but the censor was seldom offered a work he might reject.

Sometimes the Privy Council might go further. After his almanac was printed, John Harvey was encouraged by someone unnamed (but possibly indicated by the dedication of his book to Sir Christopher Hatton, Privy Councillor and Lord Chancellor) to write a supplement 'especially in abatement of the terrible threatenings, and menaces, peremptorily denounced against the kingdoms, and states of the world, this present famous year, 1588, supposed the Greatwonderful, and Fatal year of our Age'. Although he completed his supplement by 14 January, it was not for the time being committed to print.

2

Just before Christmas Sir Francis Walsingham informed the Queen that the King of Spain's fleet was expected to sail from Lisbon any day with the object of invading England. On the face of it, the information was unlikely. Prudent kings like Philip II did not commit their fleets to sail in midwinter through the uncertain weather and treacherous waters of the Atlantic Ocean. But the Queen had learned to trust the intelligence her Principal Secretary garnered from his network of agents in Spain, Portugal, Italy and France; she had even allowed an increase in his secret service fund to £3,300, for which he did not have to account in detail. It had been from Walsingham's agents in Lisbon that she had learned, the previous August, that the Spanish fleet was not ready to sail, despite the rumours, and they had been proved right. Reluctant as she may have been to incur the expense of paying ships' crews, she gave Lord Howard of Effingham, her Lord Admiral, authority to order the immediate mobilization of all available fighting ships. Lord Howard had only just been appointed commander-in-chief of the Queen's naval forces and took a justifiable pride at the speed at which ships in ports from Gravesend to Plymouth were placed in readiness, whether Queen's ships or armed merchantmen.

If Walsingham took less than his usual care to verify the information about the fleet in Lisbon, it may have been due to the encouragement of his former patron, the Earl of Leicester, who had returned at the beginning of December from active service in the Netherlands. He had finally relinquished his command of the army the Queen had sent to support the Dutch in their struggle for independence from the rule of Spain. He was a strong advocate of thorough preparation for war and of an aggressive foreign policy, but when he resumed his seat on the Privy Council he found that arrangements were well advanced to negotiate a peace treaty with Spain through King Philip's nephew, governor and military commander in the Spanish Netherlands, Prince Alexander Farnese, Duke of Parma.

The overtures had been resumed shortly after the execution of Mary Queen of Scots, at a time when the Queen had been ruling virtually alone while most of her privy councillors were in disgrace for authorizing the execution without her knowledge. Andrea de Loo, an ambivalent Flemish merchant with Italian connections, was the go-between. He had assured the Queen that the Duke of Parma was sincere in his desire to end the war of attrition which was devastating the Low Countries and to restore the provinces to their former prosperity. Matters had by now reached the stage where peace commissioners were to be appointed on either side to negotiate terms.

The news had broken on an astonished public in November, just as they had been reconciled to the prospect of war. Philip Gawdy, a young lawyer and courtier, on whom his relations in the country depended for news from the capital, sent a letter on 11 November to his brother by the common carrier:

> Some speech there is both at the court and at London that certain commissions should go over to Flanders about a peace. These that be nominated be my Lord of Derby, my Lord Cobham, Sir James Croft and Doctor Dale. But whether any such news will hold or no is to me uncertain.

With the arrival of the Earl of Leicester, meetings of the Privy Council became more frequent and heated. The majority of councillors were suspicious of the sincerity of the Duke of Parma and were concerned that a dishonourable peace would lead to a false sense of security and inadequate preparations for defence. Others, encouraged by the example of Sir Francis Drake, thought war would be profitable. A minority, led by Sir James Croft, Comptroller of the Queen's Household, favoured a negotiated peace; since the Queen herself was determined to negotiate, their importance outweighed their numbers.

On 26 December a despatch arrived from the Duke of Parma granting safe conduct to the English peace commissioners while they were in Spanish territory. The Earl of Derby, the Queen's cousin and Lord Chamberlain, was summoned from his home in

Lancashire to head the delegation, which was to start without delay.

That evening in Greenwich Palace, where the Queen and her court were spending Christmas, a play was performed by her own company of actors, the Queen's Men, watched by both the Queen and the Earl of Leicester. The Master of the Revels, whose duty it was to arrange the performance, entered in his account book the name of the company and what they were paid, but saw no need to record the name of the play or its author.

It cannot be more than speculation, therefore, that the play was *The Cobbler's Prophecy*, written by Robert Wilson, one of the founder members of the Queen's Men when the company had been created out of the Earl of Leicester's players. The part of the Cobbler seems to have been written with a fellow actor in mind, Richard Tarlton, a Shropshire comedian who dressed in the baggy clothes of a country bumpkin and who was renowned for his brilliant mime and extempore doggerel verse. Moreover the play bears unmistakable signs of having been devised for a private performance, rather than the public theatre.

A play was not infrequently the thing used to catch the conscience of the Queen. The Earl of Leicester, her Lord Steward and former patron of the Queen's Men, was ideally placed to have had a hand in its selection or to have suggested additions or alterations. He was the foremost advocate of active preparation for war.

We should imagine a long banqueting hall, with the Queen's high table at one end and two long tables for members of the Court facing each other down the sides. At the far end, two doors were used by the serving men to bring in and clear the various courses. Once the banquet was over, the Queen moved down from the high table, accompanied by the Earl of Leicester and her ladies-in-waiting, to sit opposite a platform erected between the two doors.

Through one of the doors, as musicians played, there entered a procession of actors, dressed to represent the gods and goddesses of Ancient Greece. As they moved across the back of the stage, to exit by the other door, Ceres and Mercury came forward to explain the circumstances of the play.

The gods had been sitting in council, considering the position of Boeotia, a country which had grown complacent after years of peace:

> Know that security, chief nurse of sin,
> Hath bred contempt in all Boeotia.
> The old are scorned by the wanton young,
> Unhallowed hands, and hearts impurer far
> Rend down the Altars sacred to the Gods.

The gods had decided to teach Boeotia a lesson. Mercury was to appoint a warning messenger and to endow him with the gift of prophecy. Ceres withdrew, throwing 'comfits' (sweetmeats) to the audience, leaving Mercury to search out his prophet. His choice fell upon Ralph, a poor cobbler, hen-pecked by his wife. Not only was Ralph told to prophesy, but his wife was to go mad until she had committed a murder — though Ralph protested that she was mad enough already.

The Cobbler's Prophecy is an actor's play, little concerned with coherent plot, whose characters include gods and goddesses, figures from the old-fashioned morality plays like Contempt (who masquerades as Content), and types like the rack-renting Country Gentleman and the impractical Scholar. Then there is Ennius, the ambitious courtier, who aims to marry the Duke of Boeotia's daughter, and Sateros, the soldier, whose warnings and abilities are neglected. Ralph's prophecies mocked the gloom and banality of almanacs:

> But he that lives to ninety-nine
> Into the hundreds shall decline.
> Then shall they speak of a strange time:
> For it will be a wondrous thing
> To see a carter lodge with a king.
> Towns shall be unpeopled seen,
> And markets made upon the green.
> This will be true I tell ye all
> As Cobblers use the thread and awl.

The climax of the play was reached when Ennius the courtier attempted to assassinate the noble Duke of Boeotia. But he was prevented in the nick of time by Ralph's wife, who killed him, thereby recovering her sanity. Meanwhile, however, the gods had decided that Boeotia needed an even sterner lesson. As Ennius's corpse was borne away, a messenger arrived to bring the Duke 'ill tidings to your quiet state':

> The Argives and the men of Thessaly,
> With mighty power are come upon your coast,
> They burn, waste, spoil, kill, murder, make no spare
> Of feeble age, or harmless infant youth,
> They vow to triumph in Boeotia,
> And make your Honour vassal to their will.
> They threaten mightily, their power is mighty,
> The people fall before them as the flowering grass
> The mower with his scythe cuts in the mead;
> Help your poor people, and defend your state,
> Lest you, they, it, will soon be ruinate.

The Duke was faced with the consequences of his failure to prepare for war. Ralph the cobbler had been thrown into prison for his troublesome prophecies. The warnings of Sateros the soldier had gone unheeded.

But now Sateros came into his own. He was called upon to 'muster up the people with all speed'. The Scholar offered to fight with his pen. Ralph and other prisoners were released and promised their freedom for their loyalty. Even the Country Gentleman was pressed into service, though he first tried to hire Sateros to act in his place. The Boeotians, united in arms, repulsed the invaders and Sateros was duly thanked and rewarded by the Duke.

We know from the account of a courtier watching the play performed on 26

December that it ended at eleven o'clock and was followed by a furious argument between the Queen and the Earl of Leicester. The Queen declared that it was essential to be friendly with the King of Spain 'because I see that he has great preparations made on all sides. My ships have left to put to sea, and if any evil fortune should befall them, all would be lost, for I shall have lost the walls of my realm.'

Leicester, trying to calm her, argued that the King of Spain's fleet was not as powerful as people said. In any case, it was much inferior to hers, which had been shown last year by Drake with quite a small force. The Queen retorted that Drake had never fought yet, and she did not see that he had done much damage to the enemy, except to scandalize him at considerable loss to herself. Whereupon Leicester told her to do as she pleased; he could only give his opinion as he understood the situation.

The courtier who witnessed this exchange was a Portuguese in the entourage of Don Antonio of Crato, the exiled pretender to the throne of Portugal. He also happened to be in the employ of Don Bernardin de Mendoza, the Spanish ambassador in Paris, who was responsible for the King of Spain's intelligence service in England. Like most spies of the time, he was not above embroidering a tale to please his paymaster. Equally, the Queen and the Earl of Leicester were quite capable of putting on a performance at Court to confuse any foreign informer who happened to be present.

3

Early in January another play was performed before the most influential member of the Privy Council, Lord Burghley, the Lord Treasurer. This time the play was performed, not by professional actors, but by a group of lawyers from Grays Inn. As usual, we know nothing about the play, except that the subject was Catiline.

It may have been a revival of Stephen Gosson's old play, *Catiline's Conspiracies*, whose object, the author said, 'was to show the reward of traitors . . . and the necessary government of learned men, in the person of Cicero, which foresees every danger likely to happen, and forestalls it continually ere it takes effect.' It would be an appropriate choice to present to an important member of the government who, like Cicero, was regarded as one of the foremost orators of his day.

What is certain is that the play was intended as encouragement to take firm measures against those potential traitors, the English Catholics, who might prove to be loyal to the Pope rather than the Queen if invasion came. Since the execution of Mary Queen of Scots there seemed to be signs of a false sense of security. Although Catholic priests still entered the kingdom secretly, when captured they were no longer executed for treason, but merely deported or imprisoned. Recusants, Catholics who refused to attend Church of England services, were not always fined, as the law demanded, but allowed to remain at liberty. To zealous Protestants of Grays Inn, the issue was simple: all Catholics were potential traitors who should be locked up before they created any more mischief.

Lord Burghley had, in fact, already taken steps to forestall the 'danger likely to happen'. The previous autumn, he had asked all the bishops to send lists of justices of the peace in their dioceses who were suspected of being sympathetic to the Catholic cause. On receiving the lists, it was a simple administrative action for the Privy Council to withdraw their commission and to appoint more reliable justices in their place. At the same time, Sir Francis Walsingham was compiling a list of well-to-do recusants throughout the country 'that there be such order taken with them as they may do no harm nor be any comfort to the enemy'.

On 4 January orders were issued for all known recusants to be placed under arrest, the nobility and gentry in bishops' palaces or in houses of assured loyalty, the commoners in prison. The purge of justices of the peace helped to ensure that these orders were carried out. But there were still Catholics about who were not known to the authorities.

4

The Hilary law term ended on 12 February. According to tradition, all lawyers who were in London assembled in the Star Chamber of the Queen's palace of White Hall in Westminster. The assembly included not only members of the Privy Council, but all the judges from the courts in Westminster, the assize judges who were about to go on circuit, a large number of justices of the peace from all parts of the country, and many other 'gentlemen of sort and quality' who had come up to London to plead their causes.

It had become the custom for the Lord Chancellor to address the assembly at the end of each law term on some topic of state importance. The message would then be spread through the country as the audience dispersed to their various homes or duties. The previous November, Sir Christopher Hatton had castigated those coast-dwellers who had fled in panic to London on the rumours of invasion. He had also talked of the success of King Henry of Navarre in defeating the forces of the Catholic Holy League at Coutras with his Huguenot army, and praised the King of France for steadfastly maintaining his alliance with England against the blandishments of Spain and the threats of the Holy League. Since then, talk of almost certain war had largely been supplanted by discussion of the Queen's preparations to negotiate peace with Spain.

The Earl of Derby had arrived in mid-January to head the peace commission, which now consisted of two privy councillors besides himself, Lord Cobham and Sir James Croft, and two lawyers, Dr Valentine Dale and Dr John Rogers, who were both fluent in Italian. The Lord Admiral wrote to Walsingham that

> there was never, since England was England, such a stratagem and mask made to deceive England withal as this is of the treaty of peace. I pray God . . . that we do not curse for this a long grey beard with a white head, witless, that will make all the world think us heartless [lacking in courage]. You know whom I mean.

Walsingham knew that he meant Sir James Croft, who, apart from Dr John Rogers, was the only member of the commission who ardently desired success.

If the assembly in the Star Chamber expected the Lord Chancellor to say something about the peace negotiations they were due for a disappointment. Instead, he spoke to them of a subject of equal concern to the Queen, whose 'earnest meaning is without delay to have a speedy reformation of this great intolerable abuse, grown to an unmeasurable disorder', about which she had already given instructions to the Lord Steward of her Household, to her Lord Chamberlain, and to the Lord Mayor and aldermen of the City of London at a special audience.

The subject was 'disordered excess of apparel', which had led not only 'to the confusion of degrees of all estates' but also to the 'daily bringing into the [realm] of superfluity of foreign and unnecessary commodities'.

It was a subject familiar to everyone assembled in the Star Chamber, for none could have escaped the homily against excess of apparel which was read at regular intervals at compulsory church services on Sundays and holy days. The homily enjoined that

> every man behold and consider his own vocation, inasmuchas God hath appointed every man his degree and office, within the limits whereof it behoveth him to keep himself. Therefore all may not look to wear like apparel, but every one according to degree, as God hath placed him. Which if it were observed, many [a] one doubtless should be compelled to wear a russet coat [who] now ruffleth in silks and velvets, spending more by the year in sumptuous apparel than their fathers received for the whole revenue of their lands.

Not only should every man know his place, but he should show it by the clothes he wore. A farm labourer or common tradesman was to wear only russet English cloth and a woollen cap, which he was expected to doff to a yeoman with silk in his hat, who would in turn recognize his superior in a knight wearing a plumed hat and clothes embroidered with gold, silk, or silver. Anyone wearing scarlet, like the robes of a judge or privy councillor, would be instantly recognized as being in the service of the Queen; even the Queen's Men had a scarlet livery. The Queen herself wore the most sumptuous and elaborate clothes to demonstrate her unique position at the top of the hierarchy.

But despite the homily and no fewer than seven proclamations on the subject in the twenty-nine years of the Queen's reign, the regulations were not being observed even, the Lord Chancellor pointed out, 'in the universities of Cambridge and Oxford, where this infection was seen to have made an entry among the youth'. To leave no room for doubt, an eighth royal proclamation on excess of apparel, complete with schedules of what could be worn by each degree and vocation, was issued shortly after the assembly dispersed. It was rather carelessly drafted; perhaps the Solicitor General's clerks did not have their hearts in their work. It was not long before there were renewed complaints that the proclamation was not being observed.

5

The peace commissioners had set out for Dover at the beginning of February. Just as they were leaving, news arrived of the death of Admiral the Marquis of Santa Cruz, who for the past year had been assembling the King of Spain's fleet in Lisbon. The

Though fashions changed, regulations about what the classes and professions should wear continued into the reign of Queen Elizabeth's successor. The Queen's elaborate dress was not an indication of vanity but symbolized her position as the head of the hierarchy

omens for peace never looked better. But after over a fortnight they were still awaiting a favourable wind to carry them across the Narrow Seas to Flanders. On 22 February Sir James Croft took the opportunity to write a warning letter to the Queen:

> Those that recommend war recommend it for sundry respects: some for war's sake, as I should do perhaps if I were young and a soldier; others for religion; others for spoil and robbery, whereof your Majesty feeleth too much. They are all inclined to their particular interests, caring nothing for the Prince's treasure, the impoverishment of the subject, and the overthrow of trade. It is my duty to remind your Majesty that if you do not stand fast in what is best for the whole estate and commonwealth, many practices will be used to persuade you against yourself.

One of these practices was already in preparation. Eight gentlemen, all lawyers of Grays Inn, had offered to put on a play for the Queen's entertainment at Greenwich Palace. The performance took place on 28 February. Most unusually, we know not only the date and place of the performance, the name of the play and of its author, but even the names of the actors who took part. All these details appeared in the printed text which was published less than a month later, another unusual event.

The play was called *The Misfortunes of Arthur*, written by Thomas Hughes, a member of Grays Inn since 1579 who had also been a member of parliament for Lyme Regis in 1586–7. That means he probably had the patronage of the Earl of Warwick, Leicester's elder brother, and a zealous Protestant. A new introduction to the play had been provided by Nicholas Trotte, a family friend of the Bacons, whose widowed mother was a staunch supporter of the Earl of Leicester and also a zealous Protestant. There were two new speeches by William Fulbecke, a puritan lawyer who had just published *A Book of Christian Ethics*. Two choruses in the first and second acts were written by Francis Flower, an associate of the puritan Robert Beale, a Privy Council clerk, in searching out dissident Catholics; he may also have been a member of parliament for Huntingdon.

Each act of the play was preceded by a dumb show, which explained the plot and pointed its moral. One of those who helped to devise the dumb shows was Christopher Yelverton, a senior member of Grays Inn. As long ago as 1562 he had participated in an earlier play performed before the Queen called *Gorboduc*, which had not pleased her; she took it as a veiled criticism (as it undoubtedly was) of her failure to marry and produce an heir to replace Mary Stuart. He was assisted in producing the dumb shows by Francis Flower and John Lancaster, another senior member of Grays Inn, and also by Francis Bacon, the twenty-eight-year-old son of the late Lord Keeper of the Great Seal and already twice a member of parliament. Francis Flower and John Lancaster also directed the play, assisted by John Penruddock, a member of the politically active Penruddock family who had the patronage of the puritan Earl of Pembroke, married to Sir Philip Sidney's sister Mary. Such close collaboration ensured that praise or blame would have to be shared equally between all eight well-connected gentlemen, whose ages ranged from the early twenties to over fifty.

The performance began with Nicholas Trotte's introduction. Three Muses came on the stage leading the other five gentlemen captive, dressed in their lawyer's gowns. They had been captured so easily, one Muse explained, because they had decided to forsake their legal vocation to present her Majesty with the fruits of Poetry. One of the lawyers replied:

> We well perceiv'd (I say) your mind to be
> T'employ such prisoners, as themselves did yield,
> To serve a Queen, for whom her purest gold
> Nature refin'd, that she might therein set
> Both private and imperial virtues all.

After this disarming introduction came the first dumb show.

> Sounding the music, there rose three furies from under the stage apparelled accordingly with snakes and flames about their black hairs and garments . . . Whiles they went masking about the stage, there came from another place three Nuns which walked by themselves . . . Then after a full sight given to the beholders, they all parted.

The somewhat obscure mime was followed by William Fulbecke's speech, delivered in the character of the ghost of Gorlois, who described how the curse on the line of Uther Pendragon brought death to King Arthur and his ambitious son Mordred, and civil war and ruin to Britain.

It was at last time to come to Thomas Hughes' play. Hughes took his plot from Malory's *Morte d'Arthur* and Geoffrey of Monmouth's *History of the Kings of Britain*, both standard reading for an educated Elizabethan. About a third of his lines are a direct translation of passages from Seneca and Lucan, equally required reading. What with his colleagues' contributions, this leaves little room for originality and is possibly a sign that the play was composed in a hurry. But where Thomas Hughes most departs from his sources he best reveals his purpose.

The first act described King Arthur's return from nine years of war on the Continent to find that his bastard son Mordred and his wife Queen Guenevora had been lovers. The Queen fled to a convent, but Mordred attempted to seize the throne, only to be defeated by Arthur in the first battle.

In the second dumb show, three nymphs (played presumably by the younger gentlemen) approached a king with peace offerings, which he scornfully rejected. On to the stage came 'a man bareheaded, with long black hair shagged down to his shoulders, apparelled with an Irish jacket and shirt, having an Irish dagger by his side and a dart in his hand'. He chased the king offstage, away from the peace offerings.

The mime might be thought to represent the offers of peace currently being made to the King of Spain. The wild Irishman who drove the king to reject them might represent the militant and superstitious Church of Rome. On the other hand, the dumb show might simply represent the plot of the second act, in which, as the printed text carefully explains, Mordred rejected 'through revenge and fury' the peace offered by King Arthur.

The third dumb show started with two peacemakers setting a table with incense and a banquet. Two soldiers entered and laid their swords on the table. 'Then there came two sumptuously attired and warlike, who, spying this preparation, smelled the incense and tasted the banquet.' They were interrupted by a messenger bearing letters, which they perused and then 'furiously flung the banquet under feet, and violently snatching the swords unto them, they hastily went their way'.

Now this could be interpreted to mean the Spaniards' pretence of talking peace was only to distract attention from their preparations for war. But the published version of the play innocently explains that the first four characters were the servants of peace and war, the last two were Arthur and his minister Cador, while the messenger was bringing letters of defiance from Mordred.

It is in the first two scenes of the third act that Thomas Hughes begins to depart significantly from his sources. There is a strange difference between the Arthur of his play and the warrior king of Malory or Geoffrey of Monmouth. In the original story, Arthur did not hesitate to engage Mordred in battle, but in the play he showed himself reluctant to shed his son's blood even when he was in his power. His minister, Cador, warned him that such indulgence ill befitted a king and soon undid a kingdom:

> Rough rigour looks outright, and still prevails:
> Smooth mildness looks too many ways to thrive . . .
> Let sword, let fire, let torments be their end.
> Severity upholds both realm and rule.

Arthur still hoped that wounds might be healed through mildness and forgiveness, but Cador warned him that such trust would be betrayed.

> What then for minds, which have revenging moods,
> And ne'er forget the cross they forced bear?
> The t'one secure, whiles t'other works his will.
>   Attonement sield defeats, but oft defers   [seldom]
> Revenge: beware a reconciled foe.

King Arthur's inaction gave Mordred time to gather an army of 'sluggish Saxons crew, and Irish kerns, And Scottish aid, and false redshanked Picts'. Britain was plunged into civil war.

In the fourth dumb show, four soldiers attacked a lady and killed her child, then set on a king and 'cast his crown in pieces under feet'. This was explained as symbolizing 'the fruit of War, which spareth neither man woman nor child'. The crown was supposed to be Mordred's.

As the civil war began in the fourth act, Cador bewailed his failure to persuade his stubborn king.

> And as for Mordred's desperate and disloyal plots
> They had been none, or fewer at the least,
> Had I prevail'd: which Arthur knows right well.

Mordred was killed in the final battle, but both Arthur and Cador were mortally wounded.

The fifth and last dumb show was the most elaborate of all, showing 'the dismayed and unfortunate victory of Arthur'. Four gentlemen in black bore symbols of hollow victory. A king staggered on stage, 'leaning on the shoulders of two heralds in mourning gowns and hoods'. The last to enter was a page with a shield 'whereon was portraited a Pelican pecking her blood out of her breast to feed her young ones, through which wound she dieth, . . . signifying Arthur's too much indulgence of Mordred, the cause of his death'.

William Fulbecke's second speech closed the performance. Again in the character of Gorlois' ghost, he warned of the dangers of mildness towards conspirators against the state. He looked to the future, when the same dangers would occur through priests sent secretly into the realm from the seminaries of Rome:

> Britain, remember, write it on thy walls,
> Which neither time nor tyranny may raze,
> That rebels, traitors and conspirators,
> The seminary of lewd Catiline,
> The bastard covey of Italian birds,
> Shall feel the flames of ever-flaming fire,
> Which are not quenched with a sea of tears.

But he was diplomatic enough to end on a note of flattery to the most important member of the audience:

> Vaunt, Britain, vaunt of her renowned reign,
> Whose face deters the hags of hell from thee,
> Whose virtues hold the plagues of heaven from thee;
> And with foresight of her thrice-happy days,
> Britain, I leave thee to an endless praise.

Criticism of the Queen's foreign policy was a very hazardous undertaking, however well wrapped in allegory. Her displeasure could blight a promising career, if not worse. Hence the particular care taken, in the text that was quickly printed, to emphasize the indissoluble contribution made by each and every member of the cast and to explain the dumb shows wholly in terms of the plot. *Littera scripta manet*. The good lawyers of Grays Inn were at pains to ensure that what they set down could not be used in evidence against them.

6

By the time *The Misfortunes of Arthur* was performed, the Queen's peace commissioners had at last crossed the Narrow Seas from Dover. Sir James Croft was the first to arrive on the other side. He landed at Dunkirk, in Spanish territory. The Spanish governor entertained him before sending him the next day along the coast to join his colleagues, who had in the meantime arrived at the English garrison town of Ostend, to be greeted by Andrea de Loo. The five peace commissioners met on 26 February and immediately sent word of their arrival to the Duke of Parma.

CHAPTER TWO

THE GODLY
UNDERGROUND

Two sorts of Recusants are in this land; the one
Popish, the other Anabaptistical. They give out that we
have no ministry, no Sacraments, no visible Church.
                    Robert Some: *A Godly Treatise*, 1588

1

Paul's Cross was an open pulpit on the north-east side of St Paul's Cathedral, where every Sunday a sermon was preached to the most important congregation in England. The Bishop of London appointed the preacher, but his choice required the express approval of the Queen. Not infrequently, the Privy Council suggested a matter of public interest as the subject of the sermon, which was normally attended by the Lord Mayor and aldermen of the City, the masters and wardens of the livery companies, and many other distinguished citizens.

On Sunday 21 January, after the sermon, arrangements had been made for Anthony Tyrell, a captured seminary priest from the English College in Rome, to deliver a public recantation of his faith. As Tyrell was brought by his guards to Paul's Cross, the preacher recited Psalm 6:

> O Lord, rebuke me not in thine indignation, neither hasten me in thy displeasure. Have mercy upon me O Lord, for I am weak. O Lord, heal me, for my bones are vexed.

Tyrell was lifted above the heads of the crowd to a platform just below the pulpit. He rose to his feet and began to speak:

> I have come before this assembly, dearly beloved, in order that I may abjure that ancient faith which I sucked in with my mother's milk and which I have reverenced since my tenderest years. But what I do now so vehemently bewail is that other faith which so long and wickedly I made pretence of, knowing that it was false; and what I now proclaim and embrace with all my heart is the religion of the Roman and Catholic Church, from which by the instigation of the devil I fell away. To her I now return, and in her defence I am ready by God's help to die, counting myself happy if by this pain I might cancel the heavy burden of my sins.

Paul's Churchyard, the media centre of London and the nation. Paul's Cross, the open pulpit, is on the north-east corner. The Bishop of London's palace is opposite the Great West Door of the cathedral, by the tree

Something had gone wrong! The Lord Mayor rose to his feet, the aldermen all cried out together, and Richard Young, the Middlesex justice, came rushing up with his pursuivants to snatch Tyrell from his perch and bear him off through the excited crowd to Newgate prison. But they could not reach him before Tyrell had torn up his recantation and scattered the pieces among the crowd, together with some other writings which he had concealed in his doublet. Such a crowd followed him to Newgate and stayed shouting outside, that two hours later he had to be conveyed secretly to another prison, the Counter in Wood Street.

This was not, in fact, the first time that Tyrell had withdrawn a recantation and he knew what was in store for him. Of Justice Richard Young he had written to the Queen, two years before:

> I cannot but say, although I abide all the torments that he can procure me, if ever I come again under his hands, that he is a most cruel bloodsucker, a destroyer of your people, and a great abuser of your majesty . . . For such as he cannot destroy both in body and soul (as he hath done me) he will be sure to prefer unto the gallows.

Tyrell had been encouraged to withdraw his recantation this time by Richard Leigh, another seminary priest, who was actually present at Paul's Cross. Helped by a

Catholic lawyer, he gathered up some of Tyrell's papers and arranged for them to be copied and even printed for wider circulation. Richard Leigh was confessor and frequent visitor to the Earl of Arundel in the Tower of London, where he had been kept in custody since 1585 for declaring his conversion to the Catholic faith and attempting to flee to France.

An account of Tyrell's demonstration was sent by one of the three Jesuits in England, Robert Southwell, to the General of the Jesuits in Rome, Claudio Aquaviva. He was then secretly lodged in the household of the Countess of Arundel, also a Catholic convert. His 'post office' was the French embassy in London where the ambassador, M. de Chateauneuf, was a notorious supporter of the Guise party and the Holy League. (When Londoners had celebrated the execution of Mary Stuart, the year before, with their customary bonfires, some of them had knocked on the door of the French embassy to ask for wood.)

In the same letter, Southwell reported a meeting with William Weston, the former Superior of the Jesuit mission, who had been captured in 1586 and was being moved with other Catholic priests to the former Bishop of Ely's palace at Wisbech in Cambridgeshire. Southwell's Superior, Henry Garnet, who also sent regular reports to the Jesuit General, was absent on a tour of the Midlands.

2

By 1588 Richard Rogers had spent nearly fourteen years of his life in the small village of Wethersfield in Essex as a 'preacher of the word of God'. He had worked his way through Cambridge University as a 'sizar' or college servant and now existed on the contributions of his parishioners, in the absence of the official minister. He kept a diary, a rare enough practice at the time, which was intended to record not his daily life and doings but his spiritual problems. We must be thankful for a unique record which was intended to impress nobody but its author. On 31 March he wrote that he was 'unsettled at study through going from home' and continued:

> For besides the great fear of wars at hand, the departure of sundry godly
> brethren of late, which hath cooled my heart toward the world in some measure,
> I do with indifferent feeling contemn the glory of this deceivable world. This
> day I spent the half by myself to good purpose, but at noon cut off.

In a marginal note he added: 'Mr Field was buried March 26th, 1588.' It is a laconic reference to the death of the organizing secretary of the presbyterian movement to which Richard Rogers belonged. Possibly his 'going from home' was to attend the funeral in St Giles, Cripplegate, in London, but it was dangerous to record such activity on paper.

The movement seems to have grown out of the conferences of puritan ministers who wished to introduce the Calvinist 'discipline' into the organization of the Church of England. They had enjoyed the support of Archbishop Grindal, but he had therefore been effectually deprived of office by Queen Elizabeth and had died in 1583. When John Whitgift, Thomas Cartwright's old enemy, was appointed his successor as Archbishop of Canterbury, the movement went underground, surfacing from time to time when their supporters among the landed gentry were summoned to attend a parliament.

There were local conferences which secretly sent delegates to regional conferences, usually held in market towns at times of fairs, when a sudden influx of strangers would not be noticed. Rogers himself had attended a conference at Cambridge the previous September at the time of Stourbridge Fair. But the more difficult questions were commonly referred to 'our brethren in London' and it was John Field's 'apostles' or roving preachers who went round the countryside to knit the organization together. As one London minister put it, it was remarkable that John Field died in his bed, his clandestine activities unknown to the authorities.

On 10 April the regional conference was held at Coventry, probably for the convenience of Thomas Cartwright, the intellectual leader of the movement, who lived under the protection of the Earl of Leicester at Warwick. One of its main purposes was to approve a final draft of the *Book of Discipline* or manifesto of the movement, of which manuscript copies had been circulated to local conferences for comment. No progress could be made because many had not yet got around to discussing it, while others were content to leave it to their leaders. The delegates did agree the unlawfulness of popish ceremonies like using the sign of the cross in baptism, the invalidity of ministers who read from the *Book of Homilies* rather than preaching their own sermons, and the illegality of bishops (rather than congregations) appointing ministers or forbidding them to preach. Pending the adoption of the Discipline, they agreed to observe outwardly the forms of the Church of England while discreetly introducing presbyterian practices.

But in London there were hot-headed supporters of John Field's more militant policy. Possibly when many preachers were gathered at the time of his funeral, there seems to have been open discussion of the introduction of the Discipline. It may have been stimulated by Archbishop Whitgift's relentless campaign to impose conformity. Since most preachers were inclined towards further reformation on Calvinist lines, sermons were regarded with suspicion by the ecclesiastical authorities and many preachers were being threatened with withdrawal of their licences.

3

Henry Smith, like Richard Rogers, was a preacher chosen and supported by his congregation at St Clement Danes in the Strand in London. There was standing room only at his sermons and some of his audience took shorthand notes so that they could pass their contents on to their friends. But a less friendly note-taker reported him to John Aylmer, Bishop of London, for preaching against the Book of Common Prayer. Smith was brought before Whitgift's High Commission at Lambeth and deprived of his licence to preach, despite his protestations of innocence. He sought the help of Lord Burghley, his stepmother's brother, to regain his licence.

Richard Rogers himself, returning to Wethersfield after ten days in London, recorded in his diary on 16 April: 'Since my return I have been somewhat troubled in thinking I am like to lose my liberty.' Once already he had been deprived of his licence to preach for refusing to wear the surplice and to subscribe to the restrictive articles imposed by Archbishop Whitgift; he regained it through the intervention of Sir Robert Wroth, the High Sheriff of Essex and a member of the powerful and puritan Rich family. But churchwardens were now being asked during the archdeacon's annual visitation to enquire whether their ministers kept strictly to the service and sacraments prescribed by the Book of Common Prayer, and whether they used 'the ornaments appointed by the laws'.

On that same day, John Wolfe, the beadle of the Stationers Company, rode down to Archbishop Whitgift's country house in Croydon to obtain a warrant to search the premises of his fellow stationer, Robert Waldegrave. Probably he suspected Waldegrave of printing an unlicensed pamphlet by a young Welsh preacher, John Penry, called *An exhortation unto the Governors and people of her Majesty's country of Wales, to labour earnestly to have the preaching of the Gospel planted among them*. That afternoon, with two other stationers, he searched Waldegrave's premises in St Paul's Churchyard where he found another unlicensed pamphlet being printed. He seized all the copies and two cases of type.

The full title of that pamphlet was *The State of the Church of England laid open in a Conference between Diotrephes a Bishop, Tertullus a Papist, Demetrius a Usurer, Pandochus an Innkeeper, and Paul a Preacher of the word of God*. It was exceptionally entertaining for a puritan pamphlet. It was also surprisingly candid about the attitude of the ordinary man to puritans and of puritans to the ecclesiastical authorities and bishops in particular.

Diotrephes the bishop and Tertullus the papist, both in disguise, stop at an inn on their way back from Scotland where they have been inspecting the Calvinist kirk. Pandochus the innkeeper tells them of an awkward guest who is staying under his roof.

Diotrephes: Why mine host, what are his qualities, that you dislike so much?
Pandochus: What? I will tell you, as soon as ever he lighted, my man took his horse, chanced but to swear by God, and he was reproving of him by and by, and a gentleman cannot come all this evening, in any place where he is, but he is finding fault with him for one thing or another: and when he should go to supper with other gentlemen, sitting at the lower end of the table, he would needs say grace (forsooth) before and after supper, and so stay them that were hungry, and from their meat the longer, and from their sleep afterward: but one wiser than the rest, served him in his kind, for he started up, saying my father had no grace before me, neither will I have any.
Diotrephes: I perceive he is one of these peevish Puritans, that troubled the Church, when my friend and I went into Scotland; have not the bishops yet suppressed them, neither by countenance, nor by authority?
Tertullus: Suppressed? No my Lord, a friend of mine writ unto me, that one of their Preachers said in a pulpit, he was persuaded that there were 10,000 of them in England, and that the number of them increased daily in every place of all estates and degrees.

The ſtate of the Church of England, laide open in a conference betweene *Diotrephes* a Byſhop, *Tertullus* a Papiſt, *Demetrius* an vſurer, *Pandochern* an Inne-keeper, and *Paule* a preacher of the worde of God.

PSAL. 122,6.
Pray for the peace of Hieruſalem, let them proſper that loue the Lorde.

REVEL. 14.9,10.
And the third Angel followed them, ſaying with a loud voyce, if any man worſhip the beaſt and his image, and receiue his marke in his forehead, or on his hande, the ſame ſhall drinke of the wine of the wrath of God.

The anonymous dialogue (attributed wrongly to John Udall) usually referred to as *Diotrephes*, seized by the searchers of the Stationers Company on Robert Waldegrave's premises in Paternoster Row. It was subsequently reprinted secretly at a private house in East Molesey

Pandochus fetches his unwelcome guest to meet Diotrephes.

> *Diotrephes*: You are welcome my friend, I was desirous to speak with you for that I perceive you came from London; I pray you can you tell us any good news?
> *Paul*: No surely, for I am a very ill observer of such things.
> *Diotrephes*: You seem to be a minister; can you tell me what good success my Lords the bishops have in their proceedings?
> *Paul*: They have too good success; they wax worse and worse, they grow even to the height of their iniquity, so that I hope their kingdom will not stand long!
> *Diotrephes*: Why sir, what do they, that they offend you so grievously?
> *Paul*: They stop the mouth of the shepherds, and set at liberty the ravening wolves, and turn the foxes among the lambs.

Diotrephes later has a much more comfortable discussion with Tertullus the papist, who works on him to suppress the more notable preachers in London, to allow only conformists to preach at Paul's Cross, to ensure that only conforming chaplains are allowed near the Queen, and to try to get more bishops onto the Privy Council. Although there is no law in England compelling preachers to wear the surplice, the bishops should continue to proceed as if there were. They should 'also still accuse their exercises to be unlawful assemblies, and conventicles to breed sects and schisms, and your authority will bear you out in all this and more too'. They should pretend to desire a learned ministry by making ministers learn 'some part of Master Nowell's Catechism, or of Bullinger's Decades by heart'. Finally Tertullus urges that Catholics in prison should be given 'the liberty of the prison, and their friends to come to them, and when any of them come before you, that you would deal favourably with us'.

Before his case came up, Robert Waldegrave continued to live at his premises in Paternoster Row and on 13 May even went to Stationers Hall to register a publication 'whereof he is to bring the title'. Perhaps he was warned, for on the very same day the Master and Wardens of the company ordered his press to be destroyed, his type to be defaced, and all the copies of his books to be burned. Before a warrant was issued for his arrest, Waldegrave vanished from the scene, leaving his wife and six children to be looked after by charitable fellow stationers. What the authorities did not know was that Waldegrave had already conveyed his second printing press to a house at East Molesey in Surrey, where he was to spend the next five months in hiding, printing new and enlarged editions of Penry's *Exhortation*.

4

Penry's *Exhortation* had suggested that the cause of the lack of preaching in Wales was 'the ecclesiastical government now established among us . . . for it is foreign and Antichristian for the most part.' It drew not only attempts at suppression by the Stationers Company but an official reply printed by George Bishop, Deputy to Christopher Barker, the Queen's Printer. On 6 May was published *A Godly Treatise containing and deciding certain questions moved of late in London and other places touching the Ministry, Sacraments and Church*. The author was Dr Robert Some, vicar of Girton, near

Cambridge, who had earned the respect of puritans for daring to criticize Archbishop Whitgift's high-handed methods. But in his attack on the extreme puritans he did not mince his words:

> Two sorts of Recusants are in this land; the one Popish, the other Anabaptistical. They give out that we have no ministry, no Sacraments, no visible Church. These men labour of diseases: the one is of great pride, the other gross ignorance. Their pride appears in their behaviour, which is void of humility: their ignorance is in their Arguments, which hang together like a sick man's dream.

He was prepared to agree with John Penry about the need for a learned ministry in Wales or elsewhere, but he argued that any subject of the Queen who refused to accept her established Church, 'whatever faults it might have', was guilty of encouraging disunity and dissension which imperilled the state:

> The greatest enemies of the English nation are the sins of the English nation: but if we desire and obtain pardon for our sins at God's hands, and shall serve our God, and sanctify his Sabbath more carefully than we have done, the Lord will go forth with our armies, our captains and soldiers shall amaze and vanquish our Popish enemies, . . . and our gracious God will cover both Prince and people with the shield of his Justice, and defend us with the sword of his Judgement.

The author of *A Buckler against a Spanish Brag*, dedicated to 'the right virtuous Lady M. P.' (Mary, Countess of Pembroke, Sir Philip Sidney's sister), quoted Dr Some with approval and called for unity of the people: 'there must be a mutual concord, a correspondence of affection, and they must be all as it were linked together in one band.'

But his chief concern was the English Catholics,

> so much infected with popery, as they stand very ill affected to their prince . . . They deal secretly; they practise in the dark; they conspire in corners; and therefore must be well looked unto . . . Enemies abroad, enemies at home, foreign enemies, domestical enemies, open enemies, secret enemies, yea swarms of both sorts; chiefly such as will fleer in our faces, and wish for opportunities to cut our throats; such as have honey in their mouths, and gall in their hearts . . . such as enter into our Synagogues like the *Pharisees*, into our churches and congregations like the *Scribes* and *Hypocrites*, when indeed they abhor us and our religion: whose prayers are not for the state of the true church . . . but for the setting up of idolatry, for the restoring of the mass, for the utter extirpation of the word of the Lord, and subversion of the present state of the land.

The pamphlet may have been held up by the censor as too severe on uncommitted Catholics. When it was eventually published in September, the author revealed that his pamphlet was 'penned when the rumour of the Spanish invasion was first dispersed; which I then did forbear to publish for some particular causes'.*

5

By April Henry Garnet, the Superior of the Jesuit mission, had returned from the Midlands to escape 'the efforts of the adversaries' and to rejoin his colleague, Robert Southwell, in London. Writing to Claudio Aquaviva, the General of his order in Rome, he anxiously awaited the time when 'their efforts would be relaxed a little so that a wider field for our excursions may be hoped for.'

'I have remained in London since Easter [7 April],' he continued, 'both to await those for whom we long so much, and because during the rumours of war with which everything has been full it was hardly safe to wander about, but there can be no more rewarding place to be than London.'

He was not referring to the Spaniards, but to the arrival of the promised reinforcements of his tiny mission, who had, in fact, not yet even left Rome when he wrote. The organization he envisaged bore a close resemblance to John Field's underground movement. As soon as things quietened down again, he planned to travel round the kingdom to set up a network of refuges where priests would carry out their work undisturbed. When more Jesuits arrived, two would be stationed in London or the suburbs, while the remainder would each be put in charge of a province or county with a roving commission to organize missionary work in conjunction with seminary priests.

* On 3 June Archbishop Whitgift appointed nine censors of the press. Probably this only ratified existing practice.

CHAPTER THREE

DIPLOMACY AND DEFENCE

If your hearts be weakened at any time with the
reports of our enemies' preparation against us, know
this for a surety that whensoever you are dismayed
therewith, that day ye begin to proclaim and show
yourselves void of true faith.

Edmond Harris: *A sermon preached at Brocket*
Hall before the Right Worshipful Sir John Brocket, and
other gentlemen there assembled for the training of
soldiers, January 2 and 3 [1588]

1

Every able-bodied Englishman between the ages of sixteen and sixty was obliged to turn up at his local muster, usually held weekly, with his weapons (pike, longbow, or the more modern caliver or musket) and armour, if any, to demonstrate that they were in working order and that he knew how to use them. If his equipment did not 'pass muster' he could be fined or otherwise punished. He also had to undergo training, which was becoming more and more necessary in the changing conditions of modern warfare. Officers were recruited from the local gentry and the organization and efficiency of the musters were the responsibility of the Lord Lieutenant of the county, though in practice these duties were usually delegated to a Deputy Lieutenant. Weapons had to be provided at the expense of the county and were now a much greater financial burden than in the days when every subject could provide his own bow or billhook.

From time immemorial, beacons consisting of logs covered with pitch had been erected at prominent points along the coast. From the beginning of March until the end of October, each beacon was guarded, twenty-four hours a day, by two men. At the first sign of an invader, the beacons would be lit and the men from the musters were expected to rush to the nearest part of the coast, under the command of the local nobility and gentry. It was a system of defence which had changed little in essentials from the time when, as one could read in Holinshed's *Chronicles*, the Ancient Britons met Julius Caesar and sent him packing.

2

On 25 February a special committee of the Privy Council met to discuss England's defence problems. It consisted of the Earl of Leicester, the Queen's Captain General, Lord Burghley, her Lord Treasurer, Sir Christopher Hatton, the Lord Chancellor, and

The Earl of Leicester, from a Dutch engraving probably of 1587

John Wooley, the Latin Secretary. Burghley seldom threw anything away and therefore, among his papers, an *aide mémoire* which he prepared for the meeting survives. Burghley, unlike Leicester, had always sought to avoid war with Spain. It should not be assumed that this document represents his support for an aggressive policy. More likely it is a private document illustrating his wiles in dealing with committees. In the Earl of Leicester he was up against a formidable opposition.

First in his memo he considered the military and naval resources of the King of Spain, whom he regarded as 'the mightiest enemy that England ever had'. He anticipated that there would be a simultaneous invasion of England and Ireland, as well as an attempt to induce 'devoted papists and sworn enemies' to invade the north of England from Scotland. Then he turned to an appreciation of the strengths and weaknesses of England's defences.

> The first and last Comforter for her Majesty to take hold on is the Lord of hosts, for whose cause only her Enemies are risen with might and fury to overthrow the Gospel of Christ and the professers thereof . . .
> The Realm of England cannot from Spain or the low Countries be assailed but by sea.
> Therefore her Majesty's special and proper defence against the Enemy's Navy must be by ships. And her defence against them which shall land must be by power on land.

So much was unlikely to be contradicted. Burghley felt that so long as they made contact with the enemy, the Queen's ships were powerful enough to prevent a landing, particularly if they had the support of the armed merchantmen and the navy of Holland and Zealand. He was confident that, in the event of open war, the King of France would withdraw all aid from Spain, 'as of victuals into Spain and mariners into Flanders'.

The English navy, he continued, should be deployed in two parts, one in the east in the Narrow Seas and the other in the west towards Ireland and Spain, 'by which means the Spanish Navy shall not be able to come to the Low Countries to join with the Flemish navy [under the Duke of Parma], for the English [western] fleet shall follow them if they come to the east, and they shall be intercepted by the English East Navy.'

Then he turned to the strategy which some of his colleagues on the Privy Council had been arguing, as well as Sir Francis Drake, that attack was the better form of defence. Burghley proceeded to show what such tactics might involve.

There should be a naval expedition to Portugal, he proposed, as soon as the Spanish fleet left Lisbon, to land Don Antonio, the Portuguese pretender, and so place the King of Spain's crown at risk. Yet another fleet should be prepared to intercept the Spanish treasure fleet from the Indies at the Azores, since it could prove 'very profitable for the maintenance of the charges of the wars and the report of the intention to put such a Navy in readiness in the name of Sir Francis Drake may be an occasion to diminish the number of the King's shipping against England or percase a diversion of his purpose against England.' These expeditions would require large quantities of 'powder, sails, masts, cordage' and a stay of all ships in English ports.

Burghley gave little attention to land defence. After a brief reference to the problems of training the musters and defending the coast, he came to the question of finance. He estimated that the cost of maintaining an augmented navy, an army to defend the coast, another army to defend the Queen's person, and the continuation of the war in the Netherlands would amount to something more than a quarter of a million pounds over a period of three months. This was in itself more than the Queen's total annual revenue and took no account of the proposed expeditions to Portugal and the Azores.

The Lord Treasurer made no suggestion how such a sum could be raised. But if he merely wished to dampen the ardour of the Earl of Leicester and other supporters of an aggressive policy, like Sir Francis Drake, he seems to have succeeded. For the time being, the concept of a Portugal expedition was abandoned.

No decision was made about the deployment of the navy, which continued to operate in three fleets, one in Plymouth under Sir Francis Drake, the other two in the east under the Lord Admiral and his cousin, Lord Henry Seymour. The subject of land defence was referred to another committee of professional soldiers under the chairmanship of the Earl of Sussex.

The Lord Treasurer, rather than the Captain General, seems to have had the last word.

3

The Earl of Sussex reported a month later, recommending a radical reorganization of England's land defences. Instead of attempting to defend the entire coastline, with the aid of the local musters, effort and expenditure should be concentrated on the most likely five of sixteen possible places where the enemy might land. Special precautions should be taken to prevent an enemy fleet from entering the Thames estuary.

Defence should be entrusted to trained soldiers who, at the first news of invasion, should concentrate on the new fortified strong points, so that they could meet the enemy in force. If the invading armies proved overwhelming, they could retire in good order, laying waste the countryside, until reinforcements were brought up. Only as a last resort were they to call up the untrained musters, who 'in times of alarm and trouble are for the most part given rather to run up and down amazed, than to follow their necessary work and labour'.

The counties on the south and east coasts of England were to be divided into three groups, each under a professional soldier who would have power to overrule even a Deputy Lord Lieutenant. The report concluded:

> when it shall be bruited in Spain that there are at Plymouth and other places such a number of armed soldiers, under ensigns and leaders, the number will be reported double or treble, so as the King of Spain, upon good probability, may conceive that those soldiers and such as are in other places upon the coast in like readiness are determined to land in Portugal or the Indies: the same opinion

being fortified by the preparation of so many ships as are given in charge to be made ready in those parts by Sir Francis Drake.

The concept of an expedition to Portugal to attack the Spanish fleet before it came out had been reduced to a rumour to be spread. But Drake was not content with bluff alone. He wrote to the Privy Council on 30 March:

> My very good Lords, next under God's mighty protection, the advantage and gain of time and place will be the only and chief means for our good: wherein I most humbly beseech your good Lordships to persevere as you have begun, for that with fifty sail of shipping we shall do more good upon their own coast, than a great many more will do here at home; and the sooner we are gone, the better we shall be able to impeach them.

Drake did not get his way. The Queen was still reluctant to lose 'the walls of her realm', nor would she jeopardize the peace negotiations. But so far as land defence was concerned, the Earl of Sussex's report was accepted in full. Sir John Norris in the south-east, Sir Thomas Leighton in East Anglia, and Sir Richard Grenville in the south-west began to inspect and reorganize the whole system of defence and training.

4

The Privy Council had no qualms about the superiority of the English navy, whose ships were maintained and some even designed by John Hawkins, one time pirate and slave trader, and now Treasurer of the Navy. In his attempts to reform the administration of the admiralty dockyards he came up against the shipwrights, who, finding their contracts less profitable, criticized Hawkins' specifications and claimed that his ships were unseaworthy. They even succeeded in having him brought before a committee of inquiry of the Privy Council.

Hawkins was fortunate in having a staunch ally in Lord Howard of Effingham, the Lord Admiral and an enthusiastic sailor. On 3 March a favourable wind gave Howard an opportunity to put into the Dutch port of Flushing in the *Elizabeth Bonaventure*, which happened to be commanded by one of Hawkins' sternest critics, Sir William Winter. Unfortunately, through an error of the pilot, the ship was grounded on a sandbank at the entrance of the harbour and could not be floated off until next day.

> The next tide [Howard wrote to Lord Burghley] by the goodness of God and great labour, we brought her off, and in all this time there never came a spoonful of water into her well. My Lord, except a ship be made of iron, it were to be thought impossible to do as she hath done; and it may be well and truly said there never was nor is in the world a stronger ship than she is . . . And this is one of the ships which they would have come into a dry dock, now before she came out. My Lord, I have no doubt but some ships which have been ill-reported of will deceive them as this ship doth.

While still in Flushing, he received a letter from his brother-in-law, Sir Edward Stafford, the Queen's ambassador in Paris, stating that Don Bernardin de Mendoza, the Spanish ambassador, was spreading rumours that all the Queen's ships were rotten and unfit to put to sea. Howard replied with vehemence that one of his ships was ready to take on five of the King of Spain's and that he was glad that the Spanish ambassador sent his master such news as this; he was only sorry that the peace negotiations prevented him from coming to close quarters with the Spanish fleet. He enclosed a list of the twenty-one fighting ships and nine pinnaces in his own fleet, with details of their tonnage, guns and crew, and the reminder that Sir Francis Drake had nineteen ships at Plymouth while a further fifteen with Lord Henry Seymour were patrolling the Narrow Seas.

Stafford published the Lord Admiral's letter and list in Paris, possibly in print. The list was forwarded to King Philip by the Spanish ambassador, who disclaimed responsibility for the rumours about the Queen's rotten ships; they had come from the English Catholic exiles in Paris. The figures for tonnage and crews were accurate enough, but it was another matter when it came to the guns. Martin Frobisher's 1,100 ton *Triumph*, it is true, was shown correctly as carrying twenty-four guns each side, six cannon at the prow, and four long-barrelled culverins at the stern. But if some of the other ships were carrying the weight of armament reported in Howard's list, their sea-going qualities would have been seriously impaired. One small pinnace, of 6 or 7 English tons displacement, was listed as carrying two guns each side and a culverin, which would itself have weighed about 2 tons, at the prow. Appropriately, it was called the *Fantasy*.

Also while in Flushing, the Lord Admiral met a Dane who had just come from Lisbon. He confirmed the death of the Marquis of Santa Cruz, but maintained that the preparation of the fleet had not slackened. Later that week Martin Frobisher spoke with two other ships from Lisbon, who told him that the King of Spain's fleet would certainly leave for Corunna on 5 March. 'Sir,' wrote Howard to Walsingham, 'there is none that comes from Spain but brings this advertisement.'

Another informant came to Howard from Spanish-held Dunkirk and assured him that 'on Wednesday last there came a Scottish gentleman out of Spain to the Duke of Parma, and brought a packet [of letters] from the King and declared that the Spanish forces by sea are for certain to part from Lisbon the 20th of this month with the light moon.' He said the Spanish fleet consisted of 210 sail with 36,000 soldiers on board.

Not long after the return of the Lord Admiral and his sailors from Flushing, London was filled with rumours as alarming as those of the previous autumn. Perhaps this was why John Harvey's book was eventually published about 'the terrible pretended prophecy, even now notoriously in *Esse*, concerning the imagined mighty and wonderful casualties and hurliburlies of the present year 1588'. The Archbishop of Canterbury sent instructions to all ministers of the Church 'for fasting and daily prayer, in view of the danger from invasion'. According to a Spanish agent, preachers in London frequently repeated that 'the king of Spain . . . swears that if he enters England by force of arms he will leave no English person alive between the ages of seven and seventy.'

The navy was still operating in three squadrons, two in the east based on Margate and one in the west based on Plymouth. But in mid-April the Lord Admiral moved his own fleet to Portsmouth, leaving his brother-in-law, Lord Henry Seymour, to patrol the Narrow Seas. He appointed a council to advise him consisting of his nephew, Lord Sheffield, his cousin, Lord Thomas Howard, four professional seamen, Sir Francis Drake, John Hawkins, Martin Frobisher and Thomas Fenner, and one professional soldier, Sir Roger Williams.

5

The Privy Council could no longer put off the problem of finance. It was a costly business to maintain three fleets continually at sea. No further taxation was possible without calling a new parliament and it was difficult to make further demands on the counties and corporate towns who were already having to finance their own armaments and musters. It was decided to resort to a forced loan.

It was the task of Lords Lieutenant to arrange for the justices of the peace in their counties to assess each man of property for his contribution. The Lord Privy Seal then provided signed and sealed letters to be completed and delivered by the justices. The letters began with the civilities of the time and left the unpleasant part to the end:

> Trusty and well-beloved, we greet you well – whereas for the better withstanding of the intended invasion . . . we are now forced . . . to be at infinite charges both by sea and land . . . we have therefore thought it expedient, having always our good and loving subjects most ready upon such like occasion to furnish us by way of loan of some convenient portions of money, agreeable with their estate (which we have in mind always to repay) to have recourse unto them in like manner at this present.
>
> And therefore, having made choice in the several parts of our realm of a number able to do us this kind of service, . . . amongst the number we have also particularly named you — —, for your ability and goodwill you bear to us and our realm, to be one; wherefore we require you to pay unto our use the sum of — pounds. . . .

To raise funds for the navy, an entirely new type of levy was devised, without the sanction of Parliament. Each port town was assessed for the number of ships it was able to supply and maintain. The Privy Council then sent letters to the mayors and burgesses demanding the ships as their local contribution to national defence.

The response was almost unanimous. Kingston upon Hull replied that they were unable to furnish the two ships and a pinnace as directed by their Lordships, since all their best ships were at present abroad. King's Lynn complained that the neighbouring towns had refused to subscribe. Colchester asked that nearby Coggeshall, Dedham and East Bergholt should not be excused their contribution. Southampton blamed the decay of their town and poor trade for their inability to furnish the two ships demanded. Lyme Regis had no ship of 60 tons but had fitted out a 40 ton ship. Barnstaple regretted their inability to supply two ships and a handsome pinnace because trade had suffered so badly through the restrictions imposed by the King of Spain.

It was not until a number of mayors and aldermen had been summoned to appear before the Privy Council that all the towns began to meet their obligations. Some, however, such as Exeter, were prompt from the start in furnishing the ships demanded. London even offered to supply a greater number of ships. The gesture did not go unnoticed.

On 28 April Sir George Bond, the Lord Mayor of London, received a summons to Court at White Hall in Westminster. He arrived with some of his aldermen in the afternoon and was asked to wait in the Lord Chancellor's chamber. In due course the Earl of Leicester and Lord Burghley came to welcome them and to convey the gratitude of the Queen for the 'charges and travail' which they and the citizens of London 'so willingly showed and performed'. What was more, the Queen herself wished to speak to the Lord Mayor.

Sir George was ushered into the Privy Council Chamber and then into the adjoining Presence Chamber. He knelt down as the Queen entered and seated herself on the throne. Gesturing towards him, she began:

> My Lord Mayor, you are heartily welcome to us. We greatly thank you in the name of all our faithful and good subjects of our City of London for your and their diligent forwardness and willing expedition, together with their liberal contribution towards our necessary affairs so lavishly done to us, in setting forth and so well furnishing their sixteen ships and four pinnaces and other great charges so willingly and diligently expedited.
>
> And I pray you, my Lord Mayor, tell them that I thank them all for it, and desire them to pray for me and I will pray for them, and I would be sorry mine enemies should have the like subjects, for I think no Prince in Christendom hath the like or can have better, for whom I am greatly bound to God. And I assure you the same shall be employed for the wealth and honour of my country.

At this point the Queen noticed that Sir George was old and stiff in the joints and had been kneeling for a long time. Holding out her hands towards him, she asked one of her lords to assist him to his feet and even came forward herself as though to help him. Sir George was almost overwhelmed by her kind words and gracious actions, but he struggled to find a reply which would be worthy of the occasion. He became involved in a metaphor of the Queen's subjects being the hairs of her head, of which the loose ones should be cast into the fire.

If the Queen's hair was thinning beneath her chestnut wig, Sir George Bond was clearly unaware of it. He reminded her how Samson was able to overcome a thousand men when he had 'his hair fast on his head', but lost his strength when it was taken away. He trusted that the Queen would take her people through the forthcoming trials as Amphonus and Astrophe carried their aged father through the flames of Catania and as Aeneas carried his father Anchises from burning Troy.

The following Saturday all the liverymen of the City companies assembled in the Guildhall to hear the story of their Lord Mayor's audience with the Queen recounted in detail by the Common Serjeant 'in a loud voice'. The proceedings ended with a prayer as requested by the Queen herself, that God 'long bless, keep and preserve her, the mother of his children, and give her Highness the victory over all His and her enemies. Amen.'

6

The peace commissioners in Ostend had received strict instructions on the procedure they were to follow. First, of course, they had to arrange a suitable place to meet the Spanish commissioners. Secondly, they had to see the commission from the King of Spain show to what extent the Duke of Parma had authority to negotiate. Thirdly, they had to arrange an armistice or 'cessation of arms' not only on land but also at sea. Only when these three conditions were fulfilled could they proceed with negotiating the terms of the peace treaty.

Dr Valentine Dale went off to see the Duke of Parma in Ghent. He arrived on 12 March and was received in audience. Following instructions, he proposed that the negotiations should take place in Ostend. The Duke replied that his king could not agree to a meeting in one of his own towns which was occupied by foreign troops. He suggested Antwerp as an alternative. This was a matter which Dr Dale would have to refer back to London.

As it turned out, the Queen would not agree to a meeting in Antwerp and it was necessary to seek a compromise. This time Dr John Rogers went to see the Duke in Ghent. On 27 March he suggested a first meeting in Ostend, for the sake of appearances, and then further meetings in Spanish territory. The Duke sent one of his own commissioners, Jean Richardot, to Ostend to discuss this proposal in more detail. Eventually it was agreed to hold a meeting in tents just outside Ostend. The two commissions met for the first time on 11 April, six weeks after the English delegation had arrived in Ostend.

The Spanish commission consisted of the Count of Aremberg, nominally their head, two professional diplomats, Richardot and Champigny, and two junior officials to make up the numbers. The English commissioners opened the discussion by asking for the Duke of Parma's powers to negotiate. The Spanish commissioners had brought no such document with them but argued that since the meeting was only to discuss the site of a more permanent meeting-place, the Duke's powers as Governor of the Netherlands were quite sufficient.

After three weeks of fruitless discussion Sir James Croft became impatient. Without a word to his colleagues he set off alone to see the Duke of Parma, now at Bruges, where he arrived on 27 April. He announced that he had a better knowledge of the intentions of the Queen of England than any of the other commissioners and asked for an audience. The Duke kept him waiting for the rest of the day and saw him the following morning.

Croft first asked to see the Duke's commission, although he himself had not brought any powers of negotiation with him. He was shown a document which satisfied him and then proceeded to propose twelve articles of peace. These included a complete cessation of arms between Spain and England, the return of Holland and

Zealand to the Spanish Empire, an amnesty for the rebels, religious toleration in the two rebel provinces so far as the King 'may in safe conscience and honour' permit, the return by the Queen of the 'cautionary towns' of Ostend, Brill, Flushing and Bergen, compensation to the Queen for the return of these towns, and the establishment of peaceful relations between Spain and England.

Croft spoke no Italian and the Duke no English, so all discussions were carried out through an interpreter. Croft left, a day or so later, under the impression that the Duke was prepared to accept all his proposals, with the possible exception of the religious issue. In his haste to return to Ostend in triumph he did not wait for confirmation of the agreement in writing.

On his arrival in Ostend he sent his younger son, John Croft, back to England with a report of his achievement to Lord Burghley. Burghley was at his country house at Theobalds, suffering from an attack of gout, when the messenger arrived. He took the despatch immediately to the Queen at Greenwich.

The Queen was interested but sceptical. Such an important despatch should not have been entrusted to such a junior messenger and not even enciphered. There were other shortcomings. Sir James Croft had gone off to see the Duke of Parma without permission or authority to negotiate. He had not brought back a copy of the Duke's commission. He had also neglected to enclose a copy of his proposed articles of peace with his report.

The peace commissioners in Ostend were therefore instructed to send one of their number to verify Parma's commission and agreement to Croft's proposals. Significantly, there was no comment on the proposals themselves; probably they were a fair indication of the lengths to which the Queen was prepared to go to secure peace.

Dr Valentine Dale was sent to the Duke in Antwerp where he arrived on 5 May. He was told the Duke was 'taking physic' and could not see him. He was finally received on the morning of 7 May. He immediately asked to see the King of Spain's authority for the Duke's powers of negotiation. Parma acknowledged his right to see it but unfortunately did not have it with him; his secretary Champigny finally produced it in the afternoon. It seemed to be in order, but Dr Dale noticed that it was dated 7 April, a full six weeks after the English commissioners had arrived in Ostend. He asked to have a copy to retain, but the Duke replied abruptly that it was enough he was satisfied. Parma was not prepared to provide confirmation of the terms agreed with Croft, but promised to have it ready soon.

Dr Dale's report, written on his return to Ostend two days later, drew further displeasure from the Queen. Not only had there been six weeks of spurious negotiation, but Dr Dale had failed to secure copies of either the Duke's commission or his confirmation of the terms. The latter however, was brought to Ostend by Richardot on 13 May. The official summary, dated 30 April, did nothing to bear out Croft's impression that he had secured a basis of settlement. On the question of the return of Holland and Zealand to Spain, there was a demand for the Queen's promise of assistance, in writing. Liability to compensate the Queen for the return of the cautionary towns was firmly denied. Replies to the other proposals were equally negative or equivocal.

As soon as she received the official summary, the Queen ordered Sir James Croft to return to England in disgrace. Croft begged to be allowed to stay, to save his dignity. Surprisingly, the Queen agreed; probably she remembered his loyalty to her in Queen Mary's reign when she was in the Tower. Croft remained with the commissioners but took no further part in the negotiations. He continued to write to Lord Burghley, criticizing his colleagues and complaining that he was not being kept informed. The Spanish commissioners encouraged him in his belief that his proposals were acceptable to the Duke of Parma.

But at least with the sight of the Duke of Parma's commission, the first step in the negotiations had at last been achieved. In comparison, the next was accomplished with astonishing speed. In a matter of days agreement was reached to hold the meetings at Bourbourg, a small town near Gravelines, further along the coast in Spanish territory.

7

The French embassy in London was the first to hear, at midnight on 1 May, the news that the Duke of Guise and the Holy League had successfully occupied Paris and that the King of France had fled from his own capital. A day or so later, the Privy Council received Sir Edward Stafford's account of the events leading up to the abrupt departure of the King with six or seven of his councillors, 'some without boots, some without spurs, some upon foot cloths, and going over St Cloud bridge went to Trappes, where he rested awhile, and within three hours after went to horse again, and is gone to Chartres yesterday to dinner'.

To Queen Elizabeth, early in May, it must have seemed that her foreign policy was falling in ruins. After over two months her peace commissioners had made no progress towards a treaty with Spain. In April her staunch ally King Frederick II of Denmark, who had been organizing a conference of German Protestant princes, had suddenly died, leaving his eleven-year-old son as heir. Holland and Zealand, disgruntled at the peace negotiations, had flatly refused to allow their ships to join forces with the English navy in patrolling the Narrow Seas. Now the King of France, whose alliance and friendship she had so long and carefully cultivated, had been driven from his capital and might any day be deposed by the Holy League. The Spanish fleet, expected to sail from Lisbon in mid-May, would find the entire sea coast from Cadiz to Norway in the hands of her enemies or undefended.

The only good news was that the King of Scots had rejected Spanish offers of support and was ready to resume diplomatic relations. The Queen wrote to the young king:

> I have millions of thanks to render you, that so frankly told Carey [Robert Carey, Lord Hunsdon's son] such offers as were made you, which I doubt not but you shall ever have cause to rejoice that you refuse; for where they mean to weaken your dearest friend, be you assured they intended to subject you and yours.

Her first priority was a message to the King of France, written in French in her own hand, and sent to Chartres by a special messenger, Thomas Bodley. She lamented his failure to heed her warnings and expressed her sympathy for his misadventure, 'such that a Prince in the world will not suffer without apert punishment':

> In the name of God, stop your ears to those who frighten you with shadows when you must set yourself in the clear light of the sun. You could hardly believe that I am of another party than your own. And please God that all who seem to be yours are the same. I beg you, do me the honour to read this yourself, without a secretary, and give favourable audience to this bearer as secretly as will seem good to you. And be assured that he is trustworthy and wise and discreet. Unwilling to be a cause of your grief, I shall pray to the Creator with clasped hands that he preserve you for many years.
>
> Your very Sure good sister and cousin,
>
> Elizabeth R.

So discreet was Thomas Bodley that even in his memoirs, written some fifteen years later, he would not reveal any details of his mission. He returned almost immediately from Chartres with the King's reply, which 'found more kindness in his good sister the Queen of England than in all the Princes, his friends and allies besides'. Henry expressed his gratitude 'for those particular offers of succour and help' but had no doubt that he would be sufficiently able to chastise his enemies with his own force and power, 'and in the end, the world shall perceive that he would not put up unrevenged so manifest indignities.'

Clearly the Queen had offered troops, probably German or Swiss mercenaries, which the King's pride prevented him from accepting. All he had done so far was to send letters to the principal cities of his realm calling on them to support him and prevent civil war. The Duke of Guise followed with letters from Paris, justifying his action and urging the cities to support the Catholic cause. None of these letters much altered attitudes.

Just as the French situation was at its worst, Sir Francis Drake arrived at Court from Plymouth to argue his case for attacking the Spanish fleet before it left home waters. In his letters to the Privy Council, Drake had been less than precise about his plans. He did not know the strength of the enemy and would not be confident of 'the resolution of our people' until he was at sea. The fact that his ships were not yet ready was of no account: those that followed could bring 'with them victuals sufficient for them and us, to the intent the service be not utterly lost for the want thereof'. The Lord would take care of logistics and strategy, 'for this I surely think: there was never any force so strong as there is now ready or making ready against your Majesty and true religion: but the Lord of all strengths is stronger and will [defend] the truth of his word for his name's sake; unto the which God be all glory given.'

Drake was a man of action rather than words and proved more convincing in person than he had been on paper. All the indications were that the Spanish fleet would shortly be sailing from Lisbon, while the peace negotiations were not even begun. If the Spaniards were to be attacked in their own waters, there was no time to lose. The result was that Lord Howard of Effingham was at last authorized to sail with the main fleet to Plymouth. Pausing only to bandy words with the Duke of

Aumale, who was besieging Boulogne on behalf of the Holy League, he set sail for Plymouth. Drake sailed out with the western fleet to greet him when he arrived on 21 May. The following Sunday, which was Whit Sunday, the Lord Admiral and his Vice-Admiral rode to church together 'in a friendly manner to receive the sacraments', so putting paid to the rumours that Drake was reluctant to relinquish his command in Plymouth.

Four days later, by the first favourable wind, the combined fleet of over fifty ships sailed towards Spain. They only got as far as the Scilly Isles, where they caught a glimpse of fourteen Spanish ships; almost immediately the wind changed and they were driven back by storms. It was not until they made port again that they heard the news that was already spreading throughout England, that the King of Spain's fleet had sailed from Lisbon.

CHAPTER FOUR

THE MOST HAPPY FLEET

O Catholic island, once the temple strong
Of faith, and now the shrine of heresy.
Field of Mars, Minerva's school, for long
A realm where noble brows bore worthily
That royal diadem of shining gold
Which now is foully overgrown with weeds.
Blessed mother, handmaiden of old
To Arthur, Edward, Henry, by whose deeds
Of valour could their strength of faith be told.
But now eternal shame is thy reward
  For her in that royal seat
  Who rules with hands more meet
To spin than wield the sceptre and the sword.
Step-daughter of many, at many a lover's call,
O harlot queen, in fact no queen at all
  But a wild she-wolf on heat.
Upon thy head may fire from heaven fall.
(Trans. from Spanish) Luis de Gongora y Argote:
On the Armada that sailed for England 1588

1

All winter Pope Sixtus V had been urging the King of Spain to launch his invasion of England before Queen Elizabeth and her government were ready. At the beginning of March, during his weekly audience with the Venetian ambassador to the Holy See, he referred to a rumour that had been spreading round Europe that the Turk was preparing a great fleet and that the Queen of England had promised 300,000 ducats if he would send it out against Spain. 'She is a great woman,' declared the Pope, 'and were she only a Catholic she would be without her match, and we would esteem her greatly. She omits nothing in the government of her kingdom, and she is now endeavouring, by way of Constantinople, to divert the King of Spain from his enterprise.'

The rumour had its origin in a petition (in Latin), presented on 9 February by Sir William Harborne, the Queen's ambassador in Constantinople, urging Sultan Murad III to take up arms against their mutual enemies Spain and the idolatrous Church of Rome:

[If] your Highness, in concert with my mistress, will wisely and bravely, without delay, send a war fleet to sea . . . then will the proud Spaniard and the

55

false Pope, with all their followers, be not only hurled down from their hope of victory, but will receive full punishment for their temerity.

Although the Sultan shortly afterwards began to fit out a fleet, it turned out to be in preparation for a war against Persia. But someone gave a copy of the petition to the Venetian ambassador in Constantinople; it was only a matter of time before the information spread through the efficient Venetian diplomatic network.

A week later the Pope again took up the theme of the Queen of England with the Venetian ambassador to the Holy See. Himself a Venetian, he surely knew, like Sir William Harborne, that his remarks would eventually reach Spanish ears.

> The king has prepared his Armada, it is true, but he is so slow in resolution that we have no idea of when he will carry his project into effect. Nor do we see what he can do, for the Queen has one hundred and forty ships on the sea. She is supported by Denmark and Saxony. She is fortified, and has had every opportunity to fortify . . . We do not know what will be the outcome.
>
> She certainly is a great Queen, and were she only a Catholic she would be our dearly beloved. Just look how well she governs; she is only a woman, only mistress of half an island, and yet she makes herself feared by Spain, by France, by the Empire, by all. She enriches her kingdom by Spanish booty, besides depriving Spain of Holland and Zealand.

Pope Sixtus V had a reputation for being garrulous and outspoken. But he took care not to reveal that he had heard through the Jesuits (though surely not Cardinal Allen's associates) that the Queen of England was disposed to return to the Catholic faith. He had sent his nuncio to Paris on a secret mission to ask the King of France to act as intermediary, promising the Queen that, 'if she became a convert, we would, notwithstanding the "depriving act" of Pius V, recognise her as Queen, would give her every concession which she might desire, protect her against her subjects and the King of Denmark . . . and, in fact, would grant her everything.' The nuncio carried out his instructions, but King Henry III, who had a better knowledge of Queen Elizabeth's mind on religious matters, did nothing about it. Of course the Spanish ambassador in Paris eventually heard of these overtures and duly reported them to Madrid.

These aspirations, or the Pope's growing doubts about the success of the Enterprise, may account for the bombshell that he delivered to the Spanish ambassador in Rome. On 8 March, Count Olivarez reported to King Philip that the Pope had withdrawn, 'on the most absurd pretext in the world', his promise of a jubilee when the Armada set sail, which was to have been a public acknowledgement of the papal blessing. The ambassador could think of no rational explanation; perhaps His Holiness was out of his mind. The Pope also expressed his regret at having made William Allen a cardinal, on the palpably untrue grounds of the expense. 'He is also', added the ambassador, 'talking about his rights over the English bishoprics.'

2

At about the same time, early in March, the new commander of the Armada arrived in Lisbon. The Marquis of Santa Cruz, who had spent a year trying to assemble a fleet fit to go to sea, weakened by his exertions died on 30 January. King Philip had already decided on his successor. As soon as he heard of his admiral's death he wrote to Don Alonso de Guzman el Bueno, Duke of Medina Sidonia and Captain General of Andalusia:

> Dear Duke and cousin,
> I have decided to confer on you the office of my Captain General of the Ocean. Your first action will be to take charge of the Armada which I have ordered to assemble in Lisbon, and as speed is particularly important, if within eight or ten days you find that you are able to set out with the galleons provided with their full complement of sailors and soldiers, I charge you to embark and to proceed straight to the mouth of the river at Lisbon without loss of time. The general opinion here lately has been that it would be as well to spread abroad the report that the galleons are bound for the Indies, so as the more easily to recruit personnel, particularly seamen.

The Duke of Medina Sidonia was an able administrator but had no experience of naval command. Nevertheless, his position as head of the most ancient and noble family in Castile meant that none of the seasoned commanders in the Armada would object to serving under him. Moreover he was one of the few great nobles of Spain who were acceptable to the Portuguese. His lack of experience in generalship was no disability; as soon as the Armada reached the coast of Flanders he was to hand over his command to the Duke of Parma.

The Duke had, however, little faith in the project. He could not, of course, refuse the appointment outright, but had to protest his unfitness for the task. His small experience of the sea, he said, had shown that he was always seasick. He had no knowledge of navigation, fighting at sea, nor of the detailed plans of such a vast Enterprise. He begged for someone more qualified to be appointed in his place. His further objections to the enterprise were suppressed by the King's advisers.

The King had already anticipated this reaction. In his reply, he put the Duke's reluctance down to an excess of modesty. In any case, he had already allowed the appointment to be made public in Spain and had written to Portugal and Flanders. The Duke could not in honour withdraw, but he held out for a month for higher pay.

When he eventually arrived in Lisbon he found almost total chaos. No system had been laid down for arming or supplying the fleet. Captains and crews had therefore scrambled for what they could get, with the result that some ships were overloaded while others were almost empty and unarmed. The crews' and soldiers' quarters were so appalling that desertions almost exceeded recruitment.

As a first step, the Duke appointed a council of the three ablest commanders to advise him: Dons Pedro de Valdez, Miguel de Oquendo, and Juan Martinez de Recalde. He selected competent staff officers to supervise the distribution of rations, cannon, ammunition, and cordage more equitably. The number of officers' servants was restricted according to rank and more berths were thus made available for the seamen and soldiers. The casks of provisions and ammunition were recorded as they were stowed away. Slowly, too slowly for the King of Spain, the ships lying in the harbour of Lisbon began to be organized into a fleet fit to put to sea.

3

On 10 April, in his rooms near St Peter's in Rome, Cardinal Allen completed the book he had proposed to justify the Enterprise and to rally all Catholics to assist the invading armies. It cannot have taken long to write. For the most part it was merely a question of updating material which had been prepared years before. This time it was no *Apology* or *Defence*, but *An Admonition to the Nobility and People of England and Ireland, concerning the present wars made for the execution of his Holiness' Sentence, by the high and mighty King Catholic of Spain. By the Cardinal of England*. It followed very closely the synopsis of the previous summer (see p. 16 above).

First he demonstrated the 'multiple bastardy' of Queen Elizabeth, the product of an illegitimate union between Anne Boleyn and Henry VIII, and how she had usurped the throne and ruled 'without the lawful consent of the nobility, clergy, and people'. He announced that the Pope now intended to remove her from her throne and launched into a catalogue of the 'pretensed Queen's' crimes.

She had broken her coronation oath, abolished, persecuted and looted the Catholic Church, advanced base and impure persons and heretics and rebels, oppressed her people with taxation, taken bribes, sold offices, licences and pardons. 'She hath exalted one special extortioner [the Earl of Leicester] only to serve her filthy lust . . . and made her Court as a trap . . . to entangle in sin and overthrow the younger sort of the nobility and gentlemen of the land.'

She had refused to allow her successor to be named, 'dallied and abused by dissembly all the great personages of Europe', and dealt with the 'cruel and dreadful Tyrant and enemy of our Faith the Great Turk himself'. She had 'caused the annual day of her coronation to be sacredly kept and solemnised, with ringing, singing, shows and ceremonies'. She had tortured famous religious men and holy bishops and last year had 'murdered the lady Mary of famous memory, Queen of Scotland . . . and by law and right the true owner of the crown of England'.

This list of crimes, which would have taken a prominent place at a trial after the conquest (and in subsequent history), took up about a third of Allen's book. He went on to justify, by both common and canon law, the right of the Pope to depose Queen Elizabeth, with precedents drawn from the Bible, Church history, the fathers of the Church, and English history. Much of the material was taken with little alteration from his earlier *Modest Defence of the English Catholics*.

Finally Allen came to the crux of his discourse in a monumental sentence of over six hundred words: the 'holy father Sixtus the fifth', determined on 'chastisement of that wicked woman', had especially sought the help of the King Catholic of Spain, who, moved by 'his own unspeakable zeal and piety, . . . also not a little by my humble and continual suit', had at last consented to undertake 'your delivery (my good brethren) from the yoke of heresy and thralldom of your enemies'.

Allen warned his countrymen not to be deluded by their enemies the heretics. He assured them that, 'by my honour, and in the word of a Cardinal', neither the Pope nor the King of Spain intended 'the conquest of the land, dispossessing the English, destruction of Catholics, ruin of ancient houses, abolishing our old laws liberties or customs', except what was agreed with a reformed Parliament for the restoration of the Catholic religion and the 'punishment of the pretended'.

To this end, the King had appointed as commanders on the one hand 'a Prince, no less renowned for his piety, mercy and clemency . . . than for his valour and manifold victories', and on the other 'one of the worthiest peers of Spain, for valour, virtue and sweetness of nature'. With the latter was coming 'a great number of the flower of that nobility, who . . . are appointed for your succour, that if by your fault or mishap, the matter should come to a battle, they might after the victory overrule and restrain the fury of the common soldiers, lest they should ruin and sack the whole country.'

As an additional safeguard, Allen continued, the Pope

hath also, not for my deserts, but of special care and love for our nation preferred me, being of your flesh and blood, to this high function, intending to send me as his Legate . . . for the sweeter managing of this godly and great affair, and with them [the Pope and the King of Spain] to deliberate of all the best means, how with least damage of our country . . . this godly purpose of restoring the Catholic religion, and putting the realm in order . . . may be achieved.

And so

His Holiness confirmeth, reneweth and reviveth the sentence declaratory of Pius Quintus of blessed memory . . . against the said Elizabeth . . . And dischargeth all men from all other obedience, fealty, and fidelity towards her . . . commanding under pain of excommunication and other penalties of the law . . . that all and everyone, . . . immediately upon intelligence of his Holiness' will, by these my letters or otherwise, or at the arrival of his Catholic Majesty's forces, be ready to join to the said army, with all the powers and aids they can make, of men, munition, and victuals.

Catholics were assured of the support of all the saints in heaven, the virtuous priests, God's holy Angels, and 'our blessed Saviour himself in the sovereign Sacrament'. They would have nothing to fear from those who were 'indifferent, of neither, or no religion', who would 'never adore the sun setting, nor follow the declining fortune of so filthy, wicked, and illiberal a creature, or her base and dishonourable leaders'.

Allen ended his book by reminding his countrymen of the honourable behaviour of those who had deserted wicked leaders like Richard III in the past, and of the unbroken series of Catholic victories over the previous fifty years. He expressed his impatience to be among them after so many years of banishment and asked God's blessing on an action entered upon 'to his glory, our country's good, and your own honour and salvation'.

He signed it: 'The Cardinal'.

Allen had mentioned, though hardly stressed, that the renewal of the sentence of Pope Pius V only took effect when the Spanish armies had arrived in England or 'upon intelligence of his Holiness' will or otherwise'. The publication of his book in England would give effect to a bull which Allen assumed or hoped that Pope Sixtus V would have ready on receiving confirmation of the invasion. But while the book would provide useful material for future sermons and declamations in an England reconciled to the Catholic faith, it was hardly likely to be perused in the heat of the battle, if it should come to a battle. Something shorter was required for rapid and general distribution as soon as Spanish troops landed.

Allen therefore provided a summary of the salient points in the form of a proclamation, which he entitled *A Declaration of the Sentence and Deposition of Elizabeth, the usurper and pretensed Queen of England*. It began:

> SIXTUS the fifth, by God's providence the universal pastor of Christ's flock, to whom by perpetual and lawful succession appertaineth the care and government of the Catholic Church, seeing the pitiful calamities which heresy hath brought into the renowned countries of England and Ireland . . . inspired by God for the universal benefit of his Church, moved by the particular affections which himself and many his predecessors have had to these nations, And solicited by the Zealous and importunate instance of sundry the most principal persons of the same, hath dealt earnestly with divers Princes, and specially with the mighty and potent *King Catholic of Spain* . . . that he will employ those forces which almighty God hath given him, to the deposition of this woman, and correction of her complices, so wicked and noisome to the world; and to the reformation and pacification of these kingdoms, whence so great good, and so manifold public commodities, are like to ensue.

After a summary of Elizabeth's crimes and misdemeanours which made her unfit to reign, it declared His Holiness' renewal of his predecessors' sentence of excommunication and deposition of Queen Elizabeth absolving her subjects 'from all Obedience, Oath, and other band of Subjection unto her, or to any other in her name'. The *Declaration* concluded:

> To prevent also the shedding of Christian blood, and spoil of the country . . . Be it known by these presents, that it shall not only be lawful for any person . . . to arrest, put in hold, and deliver up unto the Catholic party, the said usurper, or any her complices, but also holden for very good service and most highly rewarded . . . And finally by these presents, free passage is granted to such as will resort to the catholic camp, to bring victuals, munition, or other necessaries; promising liberal payment for all such things, as shall be received from them for the service of the army.

Such helpers would also be granted 'Plenary Indulgence and pardon of all their sins'.

A translation of the *Declaration* into Italian was prepared for the Pope's consideration. The English version, together with the *Admonition to the Nobility and People of England and Ireland*, was sent to the Duke of Parma in Flanders by the Spanish diplomatic bag.

4

In Flanders, meanwhile, the Duke of Parma had grown as impatient as the Pope at the Armada's delay in setting sail. Since his capture of the port of Sluys the previous August, all his plans for the reconquest of the remaining provinces of the Netherlands had had to be subordinated to the Enterprise of England. He had dug miles of canals as lines of communication to the channel ports of Sluys and Dunkirk, trying at the same time to convey the impression that he was planning an attack on the island of Walcheren. While the Dutch quarrelled among themselves and with their English allies, and their garrisons mutinied over lack of pay, Parma was forced to keep his veteran army idle in camp and wasting from disease. Of the twenty-eight to thirty thousand men he had had ready to invade England the previous September, only seventeen thousand were fit for battle by the beginning of March.

On 10 March, just after hearing of the arrival of the English peace commissioners, he wrote to the King of Spain:

> I should be failing in my duty if I did not inform your Majesty that the general opinion is that if the English proceed straightforwardly, as they profess to do, and if their alarm at your Majesty's armaments and great power really compels them to incline to your Majesty's interests, it would be better to conclude peace with them. By this means we should end the misery and calamity of these afflicted States, the Catholic religion would be established in them, and your ancient dominions restored; besides which we should not jeopardise the Armada which your Majesty has prepared, and we should escape the danger of some disaster, causing you to fail to conquer England, whilst losing your hold here . . . But things are not as we intended; and not only have the English had time to arm by land and sea, and to form alliances with Denmark and the Protestants of Germany and elsewhere, but the French also have taken measures to frustrate our aims, as they certainly will do to the extent of their ability.

While he waited for a reply, he appointed his own peace commission to treat with the English. His two secretaries, Richardot and Champigny, were the only members of any importance, and could be relied upon to keep discussion going without committing him to any agreement.

The King's reply arrived in less than two weeks: despite his general's warnings, in no circumstances was he prepared to postpone the Enterprise. Parma answered with the irony that those on active service reserve for their chairborne masters:

Since God has been so pleased to defer for so long the sailing of the Armada from Lisbon, we are bound to conclude that it is for His greater glory, and the more perfect success of the business, since the object is so exclusively for the promotion of His holy cause. The enemy have thereby been forewarned and acquainted with our plans, and have made all preparations for their defence; so that it is manifest that the enterprise, which was at one time so easy and safe, can now only be carried out with infinitely greater difficulty, and at a much larger expenditure of blood and trouble.

He felt sure that the King must have taken all the necessary steps to protect his troops, by means of the Armada, in their passage across to England. His troops were ready to embark as soon as the Armada arrived, which he hoped would not be long. The Earl of Morton and Colonel Sempill had already arrived in Flanders to arrange a diversion in Scotland at the time of the invasion. Meanwhile, he was keeping the English peace commissioners occupied with discussions of a possible meeting-place.

Just as he was completing his despatch, he heard of the arrival of one of the English commissioners, Dr John Rogers, who proposed the compromise of a first meeting in Ostend followed by further discussions in Spanish territory. Although he sent Richardot off to Ostend to prolong the negotiations, Parma realized that he could not delay a formal meeting much longer, when he would be asked to show the commission from the King, which he did not yet possess, giving him authority to negotiate. He asked the King to send such a commission 'in due and ample form'.

Three weeks later, while he was in Bruges, he heard of the unexpected arrival of Sir James Croft, the English peace commissioner best disposed towards Spain. At about the same time he received a bundle of despatches from the King of Spain, forwarded by Don Bernardin de Mendoza in Paris. He was thus able to show Croft, on 30 April, the King's commission conferring plenipotentiary powers. He sent Croft away satisfied, describing him later as being apparently of seventy years of age, 'well disposed but of little wit and easily taken in'.

Among the despatches was an announcement that the Armada would be departing from Lisbon any day and that he should keep his forces in instant readiness for the forthcoming invasion. Mendoza also warned him that troops were being assembled by the Duke of Epernon in Picardy to protect England, on the orders of the King of France, but that a 'demonstration' had been arranged with the Duke of Guise which would effectively prevent the French king's interference with the Enterprise.

It was not until 3 May that the Duke of Parma had time to reply to all these despatches. He was able to report that the Earl of Morton and Colonel Sempill had been safely landed from a fishing vessel on the Scottish coast, ready to create a diversion in Scotland. The operation had gone very smoothly; it was a sign, he commented to the King, of divine favour with regard to the Scots.

He acknowledged receipt of the King's peace commission, which he undertook would 'only be used under the circumstances and in the way stated by your Majesty; the object of the power being to keep the negotiations on foot as long as possible, and not for the purpose of being used for concluding any arrangement'. He was ready to keep the negotiations going even after hostilities commenced, in England if necessary, should the English commissioners decide to return.

In another despatch the same day, he promised the King to take all due care over 'the rumour that your Majesty orders to be spread at the invasion that our object is the reform of religion, and that Cardinal Allen is coming with the apostolic authority to absolve them'.

> The Count Olivarez [he continued] has sent me from Rome a discourse and declaration drawn up in English by Allen, with the object referred to, in order that it may be printed and spread over England at the time of the invasion. It shall first be translated, so that we may see whether there is anything to suppress or add to it, and it shall then be printed in the form of a short proclamation, containing the principal heads of the discourse, as Allen himself agrees. I have no doubt that Allen's aid, both in the important religious questions, and in other political affairs, will be extremely advantageous, seeing his present influence among the Catholics, and his goodness, efficiency, and learning.

5

Meanwhile in Paris, Don Bernardin de Mendoza, though he supplied most of their funds, was having difficulty in keeping the Holy League in check. The League controlled most of eastern France, had a substantial standing army, and was openly supported by many of the French nobility. In Paris, however, governed by a *politique* Parliament sympathetic to King Henry, it was largely a clandestine movement. Each department of the city had a committee, elected by the tradesmen and small businessmen who supported the League, which met in secret and whose members communicated with each other through the churches. A representative of each committee sat on a central coordinating Committee of Sixteen.

From their point of view, the King of France had refused to accept their demands that he declare war on heresy and had forbidden their leader, the Duke of Guise, to enter the capital. The Spanish ambassador could hardly explain that the plot he had discussed with them so thoroughly was merely part of a larger Enterprise. He did not even dare describe his plans fully to the King of Spain, for his despatches ran the risk of being intercepted and decoded when they passed through Huguenot territory.

On 4 April he wrote,

> If the project in question is carried out as planned the king [of France] will have his hands so full that it will be impossible for him, either by words or deeds, to give aid to the English queen. It is for this reason that I have thought it wise to delay the execution of the project until the moment Your Majesty's Armada is on the point of departure.

The delay should have given King Henry the opportunity to secure his position. One of his own agents had succeeded in working his way into the Committee of Sixteen and had learned of the plot. But the King did not heed his warnings. He merely sent two of his councillors to the Duke of Guise at Soissons to reaffirm his banishment from Paris. Both his representatives and his offers to come to an understanding were treated with contempt. Only then did he send his most trusted supporter, the Duke of Epernon, to consolidate his position in Normandy and summoned his Swiss mercenary troops to assemble outside Paris.

On 22 April Don Bernardin de Mendoza received from the King of Spain the despatch that he had so eagerly been awaiting:

> The Armada I have assembled in Lisbon being now ready to sail, and only awaiting a fair wind, I wish to say that it may be that some of the ships, especially the galleys and galleasses, may enter French ports, although they will endeavour to avoid doing so. In such case you will be on the watch and will arrange that they shall be supplied with what they require in the ports and be allowed to put to sea again at once.

Couriers were sent post-haste with the despatches to the Duke of Parma in Flanders. Another was on his way to the Duke of Guise in Soissons.

Six days later the Duke of Guise rode into Paris, in defiance of the King's orders. At the sound of a howling mob of Holy League supporters outside the palace, the King took no action even when the Duke came to confront him in the Louvre. It was not until dawn on 2 May that his Swiss troops began to enter the city and take up positions at the gates and other strategic points. All was quiet in the city except in the Latin Quarter on the Left Bank, where students, egged on by priests and preaching friars, began to demonstrate and erect barricades in the streets.

Later that morning more barricades began to be set up in streets on the Right Bank. It happened so suddenly that onlookers thought it spontaneous, not pausing to consider how barrels filled with stones and linked by chains should be so conveniently at hand. A rumour began to spread that the Swiss troops had come to massacre the Catholic leaders and their supporters. Suddenly, a mob of students, priests, and other Holy League supporters burst across an unguarded bridge from the Left Bank. At the same time, the cathedral bells rang out, summoning the citizens of Paris to arms.

The Swiss troops found themselves isolated from each other by the barricades and surrounded by a hostile mob attacking them with cobble-stones and even firearms. The King had forbidden them to fire on his subjects. When no countermanding orders came, they laid down their arms and began to withdraw from the city.

The Queen Mother, Catherine de Medici, was escorted under guard to the Hotel de Guise to learn the Duke's terms. He demanded to be appointed Lieutenant Governor of France, that Henry of Navarre be excluded from the succession, that the King's personal guard be disbanded, that the Duke of Epernon be deprived of his office of Governor of Normandy and banished from Court, that members of the Holy League or other good Catholics be appointed to the principal government posts, and that a meeting of the States General be called to ratify these demands irrevocably. While negotiations went on, King Henry III slipped out of Paris with a few courtiers through an unguarded gate and rode furiously to Chartres.

Mendoza's report to the King of Spain betrayed his satisfaction at a complex operation successfully accomplished. The escape of the King he thought a matter of little importance; the Duke of Guise was effectively 'King of Paris'. The Duke of Guise himself was more concerned. King Philip had promised him that as soon as King Henry was in his hands, Spain would break off diplomatic relations with the French government and recognize Guise as head of a provisional government. But until King Henry was actually deposed, such recognition, and the assistance of necessary arms and subsidies, was not likely to be granted.

6

Rather than the eight or ten days which his king had allowed him, the Duke of Medina Sidonia had taken as many weeks to make the Armada assembled in Lisbon ready to set sail. Nevertheless, he had accomplished more in the short time since his appointment than the Admiral de Santa Cruz in over a year. On 25 April, just before the Duke of Guise entered Paris and Sir James Croft started his negotiations with the Duke of Parma at Bruges, the first ships of the Armada began to move down the River Tagus from the harbour of Lisbon. The arms, ammunition and provisions had been collected, counted, and stowed away. The guns, for which all King Philip's dominions had been scoured, had been divided more equitably among the ships. The living quarters had been properly allocated. Each squadron had its set of navigational charts and its own pilots in case it became separated from the others. An elaborate system of communication between the ships had been devised to take account of almost every conceivable condition of weather or war. All the twenty-seven thousand soldiers and sailors on board had confessed their sins and been shriven. Detailed instructions had been issued as to how they were to conduct themselves on this holy Enterprise.

It must have been with a sense of relief as well as satisfaction that the Duke sent King Philip a detailed summary of the ships that made up 'the most Happy Fleet [*La Felicissima Armada*] which His Majesty has ordered to be assembled in this Port of Lisbon: together with the Soldiers, Sailors, Pilots, Munitions, Provisions, and other necessaries therein, and the period of time for which the said provisions will last'.

The Duke had commandeered a printing press in Lisbon and arranged for his submission to the King to be printed and distributed among the fleet. Carefully tabulated, the summary first listed the ships in each squadron, named almost invariably after saints, together with the names of their commanders, their tonnage, their complement of soldiers and mariners, and the number of guns and cannon-balls. Then followed a consolidated summary of the total.

The hulks were troop transports, with little defensive armament. The pinnaces were small fast ships used for scouting and communication. The galleasses were a hybrid type of ship, propelled partly by sail and partly by oars. The galleys were shallow draft fighting ships propelled entirely by the oars of their galley-slaves.

The summary then listed the names of the *aventureros*, gentlemen who had volunteered to serve without pay; there were 124 in all, with 456 servants. The 238 *entertenidos*, paid volunteers, were also listed by name; they brought 163 servants. The 165 gunners were listed by trade rather than by name; they had their own physician and apothecary, 92 artillery men, their mules, and 22 boys.

The hospital ship held 85 men, including 5 physicians, 5 surgeons, and 5 assistants. There were 180 religious men, listed according to their order. The 5 regiments of soldiers were divided into 171 companies, making a total of 19,295 men. Including the admirals, the total numbers came to 28,687 men and 2,088 slaves. There were provisions for six months of biscuit, wine, bacon, rice, beans and white pease, olive oil and vinegar. There was sufficient fish for four months and enough cheese and water to last three months. The summary concluded with a list of arms carried by the soldiers, which included 7,000 guns, 1,000 muskets, 10,000 pikes, 1,000 halberds, and 6,000 half-pikes.

Because the printer provided fitting embellishments it has been assumed that this printed summary was intended as a propaganda exercise. It was, however, simply an example of the Duke's adoption of the new technology, and was probably only circulated to the captains of the Armada. Printing ensured that they each received accurate information without the errors of manuscript copyists.

	Ships	Tons	Soldiers	Mariners	Total	Guns	Cannon-balls
Squadron of Portugal	12	7737	3330	1293	4623	347	18450
Squadron of Biscay	14	6567	1937	863	2800	238	11900
Squadron of Castile	16	8714	2458	1719	4171	384	23040
Squadron of Andalusia	11	8762	2325	780	3105	240	10200
Squadron of Guipisque	14	6991	1992	616	2608	247	12150
Squadron of Levant	10	7705	2780	767	3523	280	14000
Hulks	23	10271	3121	608	3729	384	19200
Pinnaces	22	1221	479	574	1093	91	4550
Galleasses of Naples	4		873	468	1341	200	10000
Galleys of Portugal	4			362	362	20	1200
TOTAL	130	57868	19295	8050	27365	2431	123790

An Address to the Captains and Men on the Armada, on the other hand, had more of an eye to security; it was distributed among the Vice-Admirals of the squadrons in manuscript. Like Cardinal Allen's *Admonition to the Nobility and People of England and Ireland*, it was intended for use as soon as the invasion was under way; it contained similar abuse of Queen Elizabeth and an assurance that the majority of the people in England were Catholics who could be expected to assist the invaders. It concluded with these words:

❧ SVMARIO ❧
GENERAL DE TODA
EL ARMADA.

	Numero d̃ Nauios	Toneladas	Gête d̃guerra.	Gête d̃mar	Numero d̃ todos.	Pieças de artilleria.	Peloteria.	Poluora	Plomo qui tales.	Cuerda qui tales.
¶ Armada de Galeones de Portugal.	12.	7.737.	3.330.	1.293.	4623.	347.	18450.	789.	186.	150
¶ Armada de Vizcaya d̃ que es General Iuan Martinez de Ricalde.	14	6.567.	1.937.	863.	2.800	238.	11.900.	477.	140.	87
¶ Galeones de la Armada de Castilla.	16	8714.	2.458.	1.719.	4171.	384.	23.040.	710	290.	309
¶ Armada de naues del Andaluzia.	11.	8.762.	2.325.	780.	3.105.	240.	10.200.	415.	63.	119
¶ Armada de naos de la Prouincia de Guipuscua.	14.	6.991.	1992.	616.	2.608.	247.	12.150.	518.	139.	109
¶ Armada de naos leuantiscas.	10.	7.705.	2.780.	767.	3523.	280.	14.000.	584.	177.	141
¶ Armada de Vrcas.	23.	10271.	3.121.	608.	3729.	384	19.200.	258.	142.	215
¶ Pataches y zabras.	22.	1.221.	479.	574.	1.093.	91.	4550.	66.	20.	13
¶ Galeaças de Naples.	4.		873.	468.	1.341.	200.	10.000.	498.	61.	88
¶ Galeras.	4			362.	362.	20.	1.200.	60.	20.	20.
	130.	57.868.	19295.	8.050.	27365.	2.431	123790.	4.575.	1.232.	1.151

Gente de remo.

En las Galeaças.	1.200.
En las Galeras.	888.
	2.088.

De mas de la dicha poluora se lleuã de respecto para si se ofreciere alguna bateria 600. q̃s. **600.**

5.175.

POr manera que ay en la dicha armada, segun parece por este sumario, ciento y treynta nauios, que tienen cincuenta y siete mil ochocientas y sessenta y ocho toneladas, y diezinueue mil dozientos y nouenta y cinco soldados de Infanteria, y ocho mil y cincuenta y dos hombres de mar, que todos hazen, veyntisiete mil trezientas y setenta y cinco personas, y dos mil y ochenta y ocho remeros, y dos mil y quatrocientas y treynta y vna pieças de artilleria, las mil quatrocientas y nouenta y siete de bronze, de todas suertes en que ay muchos cañones, y medios cañones, culebrinas, y medias culebrinas, y cañones pedreros, y las nouecientas y treynta y quatro restantes de hierro colado de todos calibos, y ciento y veyntitres mil ciento y nouenta balas para ellas, y cinco mil ciento y setenta y cinco quintales de poluora, y mil y dozientos y treynta y ocho de plomo, y mil ciento y cincuenta y vn quintales de cuerda: y los generos de los nauios son en esta manera.

A 9

Although the list of ships in *La Felicissima Armada* was published in May, Lord Burghley did not receive this copy, captured from a Spanish ship, until two months later. English spies in Lisbon, however, sent details before the Armada sailed

With us go faith, justice and truth, the benediction of the Pope, who holds the place of God on earth, the sympathies of all good people, the prayers of all the Catholic Church; we have them all on our side. God is stronger than the devil, truth stronger than error, the Catholic faith stronger than heresy, the saints and angels of Heaven stronger than all the power of hell, the indomitable spirit and sturdy arm of the Spaniard stronger than the drooping hearts and lax and frozen bodies of the English . . . Courage! steadfastness! and Spanish bravery! for with these the victory is ours, and we have naught to fear.

7

By the end of May all Europe knew that the King of Spain's fleet had sailed from Lisbon and practically everyone assumed that it was bound for England. But if that were so, it should have arrived by early June. Perhaps it was really bound for the Indies after all, or perhaps for Scotland.

Those who supplied the merchants and international bankers with the information on which their livelihood depended could usually be relied upon for both speed and accuracy. There was therefore every reason to believe the report received in London at the beginning of June by Sir Horatio Palavicino, Queen Elizabeth's financial adviser and international banker. According to his information, the Spanish fleet had been in such a state of unreadiness when it left Lisbon that it was inconceivable that an attempt would be made on England this year. Probably Spain would wait for the French situation to clear before contemplating an invasion.

Much the same information came from Sir Edward Stafford in Paris, derived from the French ambassador in Madrid, who thought the Armada was bound for America. On the other hand, Stafford reported that Don Bernardin de Mendoza had publicly announced that the fleet had sailed and was bound for England; he 'had been to all the churches of Paris to have it prayed for the good success'. A few days later Stafford wrote:

> The Spanish ambassador does nothing but trot up and down from church to church to pray for the good success of this army, and assureth that before October, his master will cause mass to be publicly said in St Paul's; and I tell them . . . that if he come there himself, it is ten to one that he shall be hanged at Tyburn afore that time.

Even Don Bernardin de Mendoza, as he went from church to church to attend secret meetings of the Holy League, was becoming anxious about the lack of progress of the Armada and told King Philip that everyone was surprised at its failure to appear.

The Armada's troubles had in fact begun as soon as it moved out of the mouth of the River Tagus into the open sea, after having already waited for three weeks for the storms which battered the coast of Portugal to abate. The calm, sunny day on which it eventually sailed on 19 May proved to be the exception. Soon a strong northerly wind arose which blew the hulks carrying the soldiers due south; the remaining ships had to follow. It was two weeks, and nearly June, before the fleet fought its way back to the mouth of the Tagus. But this time the Armada continued north on its course towards England. The Duke of Medina Sidonia ordered that the ships, if separated, should meet just south of the Scilly Isles.

The ships were indeed separated and continually battered by adverse winds. Furthermore the casks of provisions proved to be made of green wood and were liable to burst or leak. The food was rotten, the wine turned to vinegar, and the crews and soldiers grew sick. The Duke of Medina Sidonia decided to put into Corunna to make the necessary repairs, replenish supplies, and find reinforcements. Part of the Armada reached the Scillies, the red cross of Burgundy on their sails, where it was briefly glimpsed by an English merchant vessel before being ordered to turn back. As the last stragglers from the scattered fleet found their way into Corunna, the Duke was able to assess the full extent of the damage. The hopelessly sick were put ashore and replacements from the local population pressed into service.

On 14 June the Duke sat down to write an unhappy but courageous letter to the King of Spain. He pointed out that some of his ships were missing and itemized the damage suffered by the rest. His crews and soldiers had been reduced by sickness, the food and water was spoiling, and some of his ships were scarcely seaworthy. As a result, his fighting strength was a great deal less than when he had left Lisbon and barely sufficient for the success of the Enterprise. Since the Duke of Parma had also reported that the strength of his forces was depleted by half, while England and her allies had had more time to prepare their defences, would it not be better to put off the expedition to another year and to conclude a temporary truce with the English?

The King replied almost by return from the Escorial, on 21 June: 'Make all ready with speed so that at the latest you may sail on the 1st of next month without fail and without further delay, leaving somewhat earlier rather than delay in order to take everything with you.' He appreciated that his Admiral had written out of zeal and loyalty rather than faintheartedness, and attached a memorandum outlining the principal reasons for his decision.

The expedition, he explained, had already cost a great deal of time and money. There could be no better time than the present for the invasion of England, when her allies were in disarray. France was locked in internal feuds, the Huguenots and German Protestants were a negligible force, while the King of Denmark, England's most potent ally, was dead. Since the execution of his mother, the King of Scots was more likely to join forces with the invader than to help England.

But perhaps the argument that most motivated the King was the question of prestige.

> If the Armada were now to remain in Corunna, this would be construed as proof of our weakness, and, far from enhancing our prestige at the treaty negotiations (if indeed we were working to conclude a treaty), would provide the enemy with an opportunity to rise to greater heights of insolence.

When he had first seen the Duke of Medina Sidonia's printed summary of *La Felicissima Armada*, King Philip had been appalled at this breach of security. But later

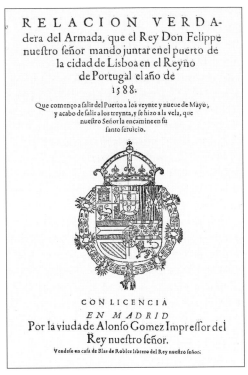

The Duke of Medina Sidonia had the list of ships, men, munitions, etc., in 'The Most Happy Fleet' printed in Lisbon for the information of his captains and his king. But an updated version was later published in Madrid, with the sanction of King Philip, copies of which were sent to all his dominions as well as to Rome and Paris. There seems to have been an embargo on publication of translations until the Armada approached the shores of England

he seems to have changed his mind and taken steps to see that the proof of Spain's strength should be published throughout Europe. He licensed the King's Printer in Madrid, Alonso Gomez, to print the list, slightly updated, under the title *Relacion Verdadera del Armada, que el Rey Don Felippe nuestro señor mando juntar en el puerto de la ciudad de Lisbon en el Reyno de Portugal el ano de 1588* (A True Relation of the Fleet, which the King our lord has ordered to be assembled in the port of the city of Lisbon in the Kingdom of Portugal in the year of 1588).

Probably before the end of June copies of the *Relacion Verdadera*, printed in Madrid, were on their way to all the provinces of the Spanish Empire, to be published in translation in Naples, Milan, Cologne and Ghent, and even in Rome and Paris. Publication was to be delayed until as near as possible the time of invasion, when the papal bull deposing Queen Elizabeth would come into effect, and when the Pope was due to pay the first instalment of his promised million ducats. The long and detailed lists of ships and officers, almost all from Spanish provinces, the soldiers, artillerymen, munitions and equipment would make an impressive display of the might of Spain and the massive investment in the Enterprise by the King. Not only would England's allies be discouraged from interference, but after England was conquered all Europe would know that it had been gained for Christendom by Spanish arms and with Spanish money. That would be important when it came to choosing an English monarch and appointing new English bishops.

8

The two other publications to be issued at the moment of invasion were also in the hands of the printer. After receiving, at the beginning of May, and checking Cardinal Allen's *Admonition to the Nobility and People of England and Ireland* and *Declaration of the Sentence and Deposition of Elizabeth*, the Duke of Parma put them in the hands of an Antwerp printer under conditions of strict secrecy.

The printer, however, had a Protestant assistant who realized the import of what was being produced. Page by page, he smuggled copies out of the bindery and arranged for them to be conveyed secretly across the lines into the rebel State of Holland. The theft was discovered and the assistant put in prison, but somehow he bribed his way out and fled with his family to the sanctuary of the church in Antwerp, eventually escaping to Holland. By that time a copy of the *Admonition* was on its way to England, sent by Henry Killigrew, Queen Elizabeth's representative on the Council of the States, to his brother-in-law Lord Burghley.

CHAPTER FIVE

A ROARING HELLISH BULL

Awake each English wight,
  both high and low awake:
Fear not the froward boasting brags,
  that foreign foes do make,
Conspiring you to spoil,
  for sticking to the troth:
And for reforming vile abuse,
  of such as lived in sloth.

Anon.: *An Exhortation to all English Subjects*

1

Lord Henry Seymour, left to patrol the Narrow Seas in foul weather, with fourteen ships of war plus the usual complement of pinnaces and supply vessels, arrived off the coast of Flanders at Gravelines on 2 June, which was Trinity Sunday. He had decided to make his own contribution to the peace negotiations.

The peace commissioners had been happy to leave the drab surroundings of Ostend and arrive in Bourbourg on 24 May. Three days later they held a formal meeting with the Spanish commission to exchange credentials. This only left the terms of a cessation of arms before the treaty negotiations proper could begin. The next afternoon the English commissioners bluntly taxed the Spaniards with their intentions. They instanced the dealings of the Spanish ambassador in Paris with the Earl of Westmorland and other dissident English Catholics. They knew of the voyage of the Earl of Morton and Colonel Sempill to Scotland. They had heard of the departure, nine days before, of the King of Spain's navy from Lisbon to attempt something against Scotland or England. In consequence, the Queen had put her sea and land forces in readiness and wished to know whom she could trust, for if invasion were intended she must direct her actions accordingly.

The Spanish commissioners must have been startled that the English were so well informed. Richardot went off to see the Duke of Parma and returned four days later with fresh instructions. He proposed that the commissioners proceed directly to the peace treaty without settling the cessation of arms. The English commissioners were not satisfied. They pointed out that if the Spaniards had agreed to a cessation of arms in the first place the treaty would have been settled by now. 'Now they had lingered five times twenty days and nothing done at all.' The Earl of Derby added: 'As touching their invasion of England, they should find it hot coming thither, for it was never so ready and what we spoke thereof was only to show their unreasonableness.'

A little later that day one of the Spanish secretaries came in, looking rather frightened. He said there were thirty English ships of war off Gravelines, and two men had landed in a boat who had asked to see the English commissioners. The messengers brought letters from Lord Henry Seymour, asking if he could be of any assistance. The commissioners 'desired him to show himself towards Dunkirk to cause them better to know themselves and also to give comfort to Ostend and them of Holland and Zealand which lie before the mouth of the haven of Sluys'.

The next day Lord Henry Seymour 'did ride the whole day before Gravelines with 32 ships of Her Majesty's navy, which brought a marvellous great terror before this coast'. In the afternoon the Spanish commissioners rode down to the shore to see the sight. That evening the ships began firing salvoes of blanks, whose roar could be heard all the way down the coast to the Spanish-held ports of Dunkirk and Sluys, blockaded by the Dutch fleet of shallow draught vessels.

Despite this demonstration of naval support, the commissioners were becoming nervous about their position. On 4 June, while Richardot was away on another conference with the Duke of Parma, Dr Dale wrote to Walsingham: 'If we should linger here until there be broken heads on the sea or some other great accident in what case there should be, God knoweth; for I can trust Champigny and Richardot no further than I can see them.' If the Queen wished, he added hopefully, there was a good excuse for breaking off the negotiations; the Spaniards had refused to agree to any of the requests regarding the cessation of arms.

But the Queen was not ready to do so. There had been a dramatic turn of events in France. Sir Edward Stafford had sent Richard Hakluyt with a despatch to London intimating that King Henry was at last prepared to use force against the Holy League and was moving his court from Chartres to Rouen, which controlled the approach to Paris. Sir Robert Leighton was on his way to Rouen with another offer of English troops.

2

On 12 June Lord Burghley received from Henry Killigrew a copy of Cardinal Allen's *Admonition to the Nobility and People of England*, printed in Antwerp under the instructions of the Duke of Parma. He was appalled at its contents.

It confirmed, if confirmation were required, that the fleet which had sailed from Lisbon and the Duke of Parma's military preparations in Flanders were both directed against England and, what was more, had the blessing of the Pope. There was an organized plan to draw Catholics in England to assist the invader against the Queen. Pope Pius V's bull of excommunication and deposition of Queen Elizabeth was to be put into execution, and all Catholics released from their oaths of allegiance and indeed abjured to take up arms to assist the invader, on pain of excommunication.

Burghley's first thought was to take steps to suppress the book and to prepare an answer. Forwarding it to Walsingham, he suggested that it should be made a treasonable offence to possess the book or fail to destroy it without bringing it to the notice of a Privy Councillor. By 15 June Walsingham had drafted the Queen's instructions to her Lords Lieutenant of counties, warning them that the King of

AN ADMONITION
TO THE NOBILITY
AND PEOPLE OF ENG-
LAND AND IRELAND CON-
CERNINGE THE PRESENT VVARRES
made for the execution of his Ho-
lines Sentence, by the highe
and mightie Kinge Ca-
tholike of Spaine.

By the CARDINAL *of Englande.*

Aº. M. D. LXXXVIII.

Cardinal Allen's *Admonition* was intended to be distributed only after the Spanish invasion, but copies were leaked from the printing house. The remainder were eventually burned on the orders of the governor of Antwerp

Spain's fleet was on the seas and that an invasion of England was contemplated. They were ordered to put their forces in readiness and to provide, if possible, double the number of fully equipped mounted troops previously demanded.

Particular care was to be taken to prevent the spread of rumours:

> And because in such doubtful times it falleth out commonly that divers false rumours and reports are given forth and spread abroad, which do distract the minds of the people and breed confusion, it is thought very requisite a care should be had thereof, and that the authors of such rumours and tales should be diligently found out from time to time and severally and speedily punished.

A watch was to be kept on 'vagrant and idle persons, that go about the country'. But for once the Privy Council was prepared to relieve the burden carried by the hard-pressed justices of the peace. Provost marshals with special powers of arrest were to be appointed to assist them.

Sir Thomas Egerton, the Solicitor General, was given the task of drafting a proclamation against Cardinal Allen's *Admonition* on the lines suggested by Lord Burghley. England was, in effect, to be placed under martial law as a protection against the invasion, not of armed men, but of seditious literature.

Curiously, the next batch of instructions to the peace commissioners in Bourbourg contained no mention of the *Admonition* and no hint that the negotiations were about to be broken off. But they were to suggest that the Queen's patience was not inexhaustible:

> They should take occasion to say that the world finds it very strange that she should continue the treaty, seeing the great preparations for invasion, and that she only does so to show the world her reluctance to omit any occasion of peace, though she has small cause to think it will come to pass.

The commissioners were to be allowed to make substantial concessions. The demand for religious toleration in Holland and Zealand could be limited to a period of two years after the provinces were returned to Spain, after which it would become a matter for the States General. If the Dutch did not like these terms, the Queen was prepared to abandon them to their own defence. The commissioners were permitted to proceed immediately to the terms of the treaty itself without insisting on the cessation of arms first.

Nor was there any leak about the receipt of Cardinal Allen's *Admonition* to the Court, who were chiefly preoccupied with the French situation. Sir Robert Leighton had returned to London from his mission to Rouen with nothing accomplished. Once again there had been a polite refusal of the offer of armed support and a lot of brave talk from the French king. Once again there was no action. Philip Gawdy wrote to his father on 18 June after meeting Sir Robert at Court: 'No likelihood but that we are like to have wars as well with France as Spain, and jointly together. It is expected there should be open wars proclaimed upon the coming home of the commissioners, which is now somewhat fresh in speech, and their return very shortly expected.'

3

In Plymouth, Lord Howard of Effingham and Sir Francis Drake impatiently awaited a wind that would carry their ships to Spain before a countermanding order arrived from the Queen. On 23 June the captain of an English merchantman, which had been carrying salt to France, reported sighting nine Spanish ships between the Scillies and Ushant, 'all great ships, and, as I might judge, the least of them from 200 tons to five and 800 tons. Their sails were all crossed over with a red cross.'

As he prepared his fleet to sail out to meet them, Howard wrote to the Queen: 'For the love of Jesus Christ, madam, awake thoroughly and see the villainous treasons round about you, against your Majesty and your realm, and draw your forces round about you, like a mighty prince, to defend you.'

His warning was superfluous. Lord Burghley had just received from Henry Killigrew the second of Cardinal Allen's pamphlets which were being printed in Antwerp. This was the broadside *Declaration of the Sentence and Deposition of Elizabeth, the usurper and pretensed Queen of England*. Forwarding it to Walsingham at Court, he called it 'a roaring hellish bull'. Burghley knew quite enough about papal bulls to have appreciated that it was nothing of the sort. It was written in English rather than Latin, in the third person rather than the first, and it bore no date. Indeed Burghley described it, correctly, as 'but a summary of Cardinal Allen's book'. But this was no time for such niceties. The document certainly implied that it had the Pope's authority to put Pius V's bull of excommunication and deposition into execution, and that the Duke of Parma's army was to be the papal instrument. Nor did it contain any proviso that it was to take effect only if Spanish troops landed on English soil.

Within a week, new and much stronger instructions were prepared by Lord Burghley for the peace commissioners in Bourbourg and approved by the Queen. The

The beginning of Cardinal Allen's *Declaration of the Sentence and deposition of Elizabeth*, misrepresented in England as a papal bull

commissioners were to make it plain that the Queen knew that she had not been dealt with sincerely. Only her desire for peace had moved her to leave nothing undone.

But now having discovered that this treaty is entertained only to abuse us, and understanding that the preparations in Spain and the Low Countries are against us, and for furtherance of these points there is a vile book of Dr Allen and a bull of the Pope, to stir up our subjects against us, the Duke of Parma being expressly named to be the executioner of these enterprises, we cannot think it honourable to continue longer the treaty with them.

The commissioners were to send one of their number – Dr Valentine Dale was suggested – to take up the matter with the Duke himself and to demand a plain answer. If the charge were admitted, the commissioners were to return home immediately. If denied, they were to demand the punishment of the printer, the burning of the books, and a public declaration of the Duke's disapproval.

Dr Dale was duly sent on the mission, the purpose of which was concealed from Sir James Croft and Dr Rogers, whose Spanish sympathies had by now made their loyalty suspect. He saw the Duke of Parma on the morning of 8 July. After the customary exchange of courtesies, Dr Dale first referred to a misunderstanding that had arisen at their last meeting over the cautionary towns. The Queen had sent her assurances that the towns would be restored to the King of Spain in the event of a peace treaty.

Dr Dale paused. The Duke asked if that was all he had come about. Dr Dale replied that the Queen looked for some assurance on another point.

'There was a book printed at Antwerp,' he continued, 'and set forth by a fugitive of England which calleth himself a Cardinal.'

At this point the Duke began to listen with close attention.

'This book', said Dr Dale, 'is an admonition to all the nobility and people of England and Ireland, touching the execution of the sentence of the Pope against the Queen, my sovereign and mistress: the which the King Catholic [of Spain] hath embraced (as this Cardinal writeth) and hath appointed your Altesse for the chief of the enterprise.

'There is also a bull set forth by this Pope Sixtus V, whereby the Pope doth pronounce a sentence to declare my said sovereign and mistress illegitimate and an usurper, with other matter too odious for any prince or gentleman to name or hear, and not to be tolerated. In which bull, the Pope saith that he hath dealt with the King Catholic to employ all the means that he hath to the deprivation and deposition of my said sovereign and mistress, and doth charge her Majesty's subjects to assist the army appointed by the King Catholic for that purpose under the conduct of your Altesse.'

Her Majesty's subjects could not endure this, Dr Dale concluded, nor treat for peace in such circumstances. He was instructed to ask the Duke to deal plainly and tell her Majesty the truth.

Parma, while he collected his thoughts, began by thanking the Queen for her trust in his sincere dealing. As for Allen's book, 'he had never read it, nor seen it, nor did he take heed to it.' He could not stop men writing or printing what they wished.

Dr Dale noticed that Parma had not referred to the 'bull'. He pointed out that if war broke out on the Pope's instigation, the Queen would have to revoke her peace commission. He trusted, therefore, that the Duke would provide safe conduct for the commissioners.

'Yea, God forbid else', answered the Duke. He neither knew or cared nothing about a bull. He took his orders from his master the King, whom he had been pressing to conclude peace so as to put an end to the devastation in his provinces. But England, being closer, he felt had more need of peace than Spain.

Surprisingly, Dr Dale took issue. He began to justify the Queen's intervention in the Netherlands wars and her conduct of them. It was an extraordinary argument to take place between a civil servant and a prince of the blood. When Parma found himself disputing with Dale whether England could be conquered in one battle, he decided that it was time to close the meeting. He told him that if he had any other points to make he should put them in writing. The audience was at an end.

Dr Dale was relieved to escape with a whole skin after such a 'tickle' business. Before he left Bruges he checked with Andrea de Loo, the Venetian merchant who had first set the peace negotiations in train. De Loo assured him that the Duke had stated 'on his honour' that he had no knowledge of the Pope's bull or Allen's book.

4

Meanwhile the Queen's diplomats in other countries were doing their best to salvage England's alliances.

Denmark was in good hands. Dr Daniel Rogers, the able Latin Secretary of the Privy Council, was off to Denmark and was soon expressing condolences to the Queen Mother on her bereavement and addressing the Council of Regents for the eleven-year-old heir in his fluent German (he had been born and brought up in Wittenberg). The Netherland states of Holland and Zealand were of no account; they had no one but England to turn to. But they expressed their disapproval of the peace negotiations by refusing to join Lord Seymour's fleet patrolling the Narrow Seas.

In France, things had been going from bad to worse. 'All the cunning in the world', wrote Richard Hakluyt to Lord Burghley from Paris, 'hath been used to bring the king to yield' to the demands that he abandon his alliance with England. The Spanish ambassador, Don Bernardin de Mendoza, had printed and circulated his speech to the King at Chartres, declaring that the alliance was at an end and that war was to be declared on heretics. The King was unable to resist the combined pressure of the Holy League, the Spanish ambassador and the papal nuncio. He signed an edict rejecting the claim of Henry of Navarre to the throne, which was to be made irreversible by a meeting of the Estates General in September. It looked as if all the French channel ports would be open havens for the Spanish fleet when it came.

The time was thought ripe or desperate enough to send William Ashley with the status of a fully fledged ambassador to the King of Scotland. 'I have sent you this gentleman', wrote the Queen in the letter he took with him, 'as well to declare my good agreement to send some finishers of our league.'

The young king had made no secret of the price he wished to exact for an alliance with England: acknowledgement of his claim as heir to the throne, an English dukedom, about £25,000 in cash, and a contingent of English horse and foot. But these demands had been made through unofficial channels, during the period of estrangement, about which the Queen could profess ignorance:

And for that you speak oft of satisfaction, I have much urged, as now again I do, to know what thereby is meant, since I both mind, and also do, whatsoever may honourably be required of such as I profess myself; and therefore I require you therein to answer me.

When Ashley arrived in Edinburgh, he found that the king was occupied in suppressing an uprising of Scottish Catholic nobles, under the instigation of the Earl of Morton and Colonel Sempill. He delivered the Queen's letter but was unable to gain an audience until 24 July, by which time Morton's rebellion had been contained.

5

The proclamation against seditious books was sealed by the Queen at Greenwich on 1 July and copies printed by the Queen's printer were soon being circulated all over England and read at market crosses.

The first draft had been specifically directed against Cardinal Allen's *Admonition*, 'which although but a blast or puff from a beggarly scholar and traitor, was intended as a traitorous trumpet to wake up all robbers and Catholics in England against their sovereign'. But at some stage it appears to have dawned on the Privy Council that Allen's book and broadside had not yet been distributed in England and that there was little purpose in publicizing a book they were intending to suppress. In its final form, therefore, the proclamation contained no reference to the *Admonition* and described the *Declaration* or 'bull' only in general terms that did not reveal its purpose. It followed the usual form of a proclamation.

First, a preamble explained the circumstances in which it was issued: 'many Jesuits and seminary priests and other persons of like quality have by direction of the pope been of late years sent into the realm . . . [to spread] sundry false, slanderous, and seditious rumours and reports tending wholly to move the people's hearts to discontentment and offence.' The Queen had now received 'certain intelligence that Sixtus V, now Pope of Rome, hath of late published and set forth a most malicious and detestable bull or libel against her majesty, and against her most gracious and peaceable government, and against all her loving, dutiful, and faithful subjects'. No doubt her subjects would 'continue in humble fear and service to Almighty God, in their loyal and dutiful obedience to her Majesty', who would in turn protect them.

'Nevertheless,' began the second part ominously, 'lest any of her people should be seduced or their simplicity abused', the Queen's instructions were that no one was to bring any of 'the said bulls, . . . libels, books, pamphlets or writings' into the country or to offer or circulate them. Anyone coming across such a publication was to put it in the hands of his nearest Privy Councillor or the Lieutenant or Deputy Lieutenant of his county. Any person found offering it was to be apprehended, if possible, or reported to a justice of the peace.

Finally came the penalties: offenders were to be proceeded against under martial law (which carried the death penalty) and their goods and chattels confiscated and sold, half the proceeds being offered as a reward to the informer, the other half to the Crown. Officers who failed to carry out their duties, which included searching for bulls and pamphlets, were to be brought before the Privy Council for summary justice. But so long as the Queen's loving subjects delivered the bulls, libels or pamphlets as directed, none of them would be 'molested, troubled, or impeached for any offence'.

Sir Thomas Egerton, the Solicitor General, had the predilection common among legal draftsmen for trying to fit everything into one sentence. Hence even when declaimed at market crosses the proclamation cannot have been instantly intelligible to all who heard it. But it was compulsory reading for those who mattered, and the gist of it was soon being disseminated in other forms. For example William Averell probably preached a sermon in London before he added an exhortation to a pamphlet which was already in the press:

I have penned this pamphlet (most loving and natural countrymen) not with suspicion, much less knowledge of any discord among you . . . but for because I see, and you all do generally hear, what seeds of sedition are here daily sown amongst us, and to be more daily expected, as sent over here by pelting Priests from that pedlar the Pope, that continually unleadeth his pack to make some sale with us of his Popish trash, whereby to increase his mart, as he hath lately done with his bulls, brought hither by some of Balaam's calves, with other Libels most slanderous to our state, dangerous to our peace, and infamous for their untruth. . . .

These counterfeit sheep, these papistical Jesuits . . . are dispensed by the Pope to wear sundry habits, you cannot know them by their Priestly garments, for sometimes they jet [show off] in Lion's skins, but you may descry them by their ass's ears, peeping out from under their hoods . . . They will give you Popish books, and poisoned Pamphlets, but at first make squeamish and dainty to lend them, praising them for their goodness, godliness, and learning, when within them there is nothing but mischief, popery, and error.

6

Both members of the Jesuit mission were in London at the beginning of July. In his letter to General Aquaviva, written on 11 July, Robert Southwell interpreted the Queen's proclamation as a new phase in the persecution of Catholics, rather than anything connected with the rumoured invasion.

'Now at long last the Serpent's Eggs are hatched,' he wrote, 'and a poison is gushing that looks likely to be the ruin of many.' To Southwell, the state of martial law meant that an informer only had to plant a book in a gentleman's house to have him condemned instantly and to claim half his goods as a reward. His letter ended: 'This looks like the last stage before the expected end; and it puts us, as some fear and others hope, very close to martyrdom.'

The letter written the same day by his Superior, Henry Garnet, was in complete contrast. It was largely concerned with the problem exercising the minds of extreme puritans and the Church established of the validity of the ceremony of baptism. He told a story of 'the daughter of a heretic' who took her child to be baptized by a puritan minister who refused to make the sign of the cross, even though it was laid down in 'the Queen's sacrosanct injunctions' and the Book of Common Prayer. The mother insisted: 'Even if you do omit that ceremony, I at least wish to see it done.'

Garnet did, however, admit that there had been a falling away of sympathizers to the Catholic cause. Many of them, members of families of the old nobility, were torn by a choice between loyalty to their country and supporting the efforts of a foreign enemy to restore their faith by force. At the same time, stronger measures against Catholics discouraged any remaining waverers.

Early in July Sir Thomas Tresham and fifteen other leading recusants were removed from house arrest to confinement in the former bishop of Ely's palace at Wisbech in Cambridgeshire. They protested, and expressed their willingness to fight for their country, asking Lord North, the Lord Lieutenant of the county, to intercede on their behalf. But the Privy Council would not take the risk. English Catholics, though they were unaware of it, had been placed in a hopelessly ambiguous position by Cardinal Allen's *Declaration*. While on one day they could protest their loyalty to Queen and country in all sincerity, on another they might be bound, on pain of excommunication, to assist the invader.

The Privy Council sought the advice of the Solicitor General and the Recorder of London on the legal problem: if a Catholic refused to give a straight answer to the question whether he would take the Queen's part or the Pope's, in the event of an invasion authorized by the Pope, could he be convicted of treason? The two law officers gave their reply on 20 July. To obtain conviction for treason the prosecution had to prove *acts* of treason. Refusal to answer the question, even if it were an indication of treacherous intent, was not in itself sufficient grounds for conviction under the statute of Edward III. The prosecution would have to rely on the statute of 1585 against priests from abroad and persons reconciled to Rome. The later statute, passed by a Protestant Parliament after Pope Gregory's modification of the Bull of 1570, rather smacked of persecution for religion, though it carried the same penalty.

Shortly after writing his letter to Aquaviva, Henry Garnet left London for a tour of the Midlands and his native Derbyshire. It was there, only two weeks later, that he witnessed the execution of three priests, the first since the Queen had put her peace negotiations in train over a year before. Garnet thought it was a result of a change of heart on the part of the Earl of Shrewsbury.

7

The Trinity law term ended on 7 July. The justices of the peace had not been called in time to attend the customary assembly in the Star Chamber, but the justices of assize were there along with the leaders of the judiciary and the usual 'gentlemen of sort and quality'. On this occasion, after the speech by Sir Christopher Hatton, the Lord Chancellor, they were addressed by Lord Burghley.

Burghley first discussed William Allen's book. He referred to Allen as a 'base companion' whom one would not have expected to have been chosen a cardinal of the

Roman Catholic Church. He did not mention the attack on the Queen, but was scornful of the 'Luciferian authority' with which Allen claimed to have been appointed to set the crown of England on the head of whomever the Pope and the King of Spain might choose.

Next Burghley turned to the threat of invasion. He boasted that the Queen's navy was stronger than that of any sovereign before her, and that with God's grace she would win. Although his fellow privy councillors were eager for battle, he himself doubted that the Spanish fleet would risk an engagement. Referring, perhaps, to Lord Henry Seymour's demonstration off the Flemish coast at Gravelines, he claimed that the Queen's fleet in the Narrow Seas had challenged the Duke of Parma to come out and fight, but Parma's soldiers had refused to follow him.

Burghley must have been aware of the widespread resentment of the peace negotiations among those present. Blandly he declared that on three separate occasions the Duke of Parma had written to the Queen asking her to negotiate peace terms. The Queen had at first been wary, 'but being further pressed, her highness, knowing that peace was the gift of God, was very loth that the world should imagine that she had refused any honourable means to come to the same.' She had sent her commissioners to negotiate reasonable and honourable terms, but the conditions Parma had offered were 'so injurious to her dignity' that they were unacceptable.

Lord Burghley concluded 'with a great exhortation that every man should provide to serve his Queen and his country, men of peace with looking to the peace, men of arms with addressing themselves to arms'.

Three days later, Archbishop Whitgift sent out a letter to all the bishops in their dioceses:

Salutem in Christo. Considering the dangerousness of the time, I think it very convenient that you cause public prayers to be had in every parish within your diocese, according to letters heretofore [in March] written unto you: foreseeing, that no order of fasting, or other exercise to be used, than such as you shall prescribe according to the laws and orders of the Church established. I have caused a book, upon the like occasions penned, to be newly printed with some additions: which you may have for your diocese, if you send for the same. And so wishing you to be careful herein, I commit your Lordship to the Almighty.
    Lambeth, the 10th of July, 1588.
        Your loving brother in Christ,
        Jo. Cant.

The newly printed book was *A form of Prayer, necessary for the present time and state*, printed by the 'Deputies of Christopher Barker', the Queen's printer. It contained prayers against rebellion, in favour of 'the clergy, nobility, Judges, magistrates, people and commonalty', and for God's protection against invasion.

And forasmuch as thy cause is now in hand, we beseech thee to direct and go before our Armies both by sea and land, bless and prosper them and grant unto them, O Lord, so good and honourable success and victories, as thou didst to

Abraham and his company against the four mighty kings, to Joshua against the five kings and against Amalech, to David against the strong and mighty Goliath, and as thou usest to do to thy children when they please thee . . . O Lord, give good and prosperous success to all those that fight thy battle against the enemies of thy Gospel, show some token continually for our good, that they which hate us may see it and be confounded. And that we thy little and despised flock may say with good King David, Blessed are the people whose God is the Lord Jehovah, and blessed are the folk that he hath chosen to be his inheritance. . . .

In the preface, curates and pastors were enjoined to exhort their parishioners to come to church, not only on Sundays and holy days, but also on Wednesdays and Fridays, with 'so many of their families as may be spared from their necessary business'. They were given the following recommendations for the First Lesson:

Exodus 14 [How the Lord delivered Israel out of the hands of the Egyptians], Exodus 17 begin at the 8 verse [How Joshua smote the Amalekites with the aid of Moses and the Lord], Joshua 10 until the 28 verse [Joshua against the five kings of the Amorites], Judges 7 [Defeat of the host of Midian by Gideon and three hundred men], 1 Samuel 17 [David and Goliath], 2 Kings 7 [How the Lord put the Syrians to flight with a noise of chariots and horses], 2 Kings 19 [Exhortations of Isaiah and King Hezekiah], 2 Chron. 20 unto the verse 30 [King Jehosaphat smiting the Ammonites and Moabites].

Church administration took time, and even someone as close to Lambeth as the Archdeacon of St Albans did not receive his instructions through the Bishop of London until 20 July. He was to instruct his parish priests 'to have a special care with the churchwardens that they cause their parishioners to come to Church of every family some, for the Ministers do complain that they are many times at Church to say prayers, and not one present to hear them.' Those ministers who were licensed to preach were 'to make some exhortation every week at the time of those prayers' but were expressly forbidden to preach more than one sermon on any one day. The Bishop sent copies of the book with his letter to the Archdeacon, to be distributed to the parishes, the money collected for them to be paid to Christopher Barker's deputy, 'Master Bishop the printer in Paul's Churchyard'.

William Averell's *Exhortation* shows the sort of sermon a licensed preacher was expected to deliver:

She is your true and natural Queen, bred, born, and brought up amongst you, and as she has naturally loved you even from the beginning of her reign, so do you most naturally, like English men, defend her, fight for her, and not only guard her with danger of your lives, but also aid her with your lands and livings, and as God has blessed you by her means with gold and silver . . . open your purses and bestow largely upon her now in time of war, by whom you have filled your coffers richly in time of peace . . .

Pugnate pro patria, fight for your country, your dearest country, wherein you have been bred, born, nourished, and brought up, toward which you ought to be as inwardly affected, as you are naturally moved to your mothers. It is your native soil, and therefore most sweet; for what may be dearer or sweeter than your Country?

8

When Lord Burghley had received, on 12 June, the copy of Cardinal Allen's *Admonition to the Nobility and People of England and Ireland*, he had considered the need for a reply. Two months later he was to write such a book himself, but now there was hardly time to prepare, print and distribute it. Fortunately there was something suitable in manuscript ready to hand which, moreover, dealt with most of the points raised in Allen's *Admonition* without revealing that such a book existed.

Eighteen months before in the Netherlands, Sir William Stanley, an English Catholic entrusted by the Earl of Leicester with the defence of the city of Deventer, had opened the gates and surrendered his entire force, mostly Irish mercenaries, to the Duke of Parma. On the same day, Rowland York, another English Catholic, surrendered a fort and garrison overlooking Zutphen. The episode shocked both the English and their Dutch allies and confirmed the suspicions of those who considered Catholics inherently disloyal and untrustworthy. Six months or so later, a pamphlet printed in Antwerp began to be smuggled into England.

This was the reply by Dr Allen (not yet a Cardinal) to a letter from an English Catholic gentleman involved in the incident. Allen's reply applauded the justice and correctness of their action and commended Sir William Stanley for following the example of his forebear, who had deserted another tyrant, Richard III, at the battle of Bosworth Field. Allen's pamphlet dealt briefly, and therefore the more effectively, with matters such as the requirement of Catholics to oppose an excommunicated and deposed monarch, the authority of the Pope to depose unjust kings, and the duty of all Catholics not to support an unjust war.

Although a Dutch reply to Allen's pamphlet was translated and printed in England, an English reply was written but for some reason not printed. It was circulating in manuscript at Court and in London during the winter of 1587–8, when the Jesuit Robert Southwell described it as 'a vapid production, quite alien to a Christian sense of justice: the work of some atheist or indifferent courtier who is playing at theology and mistaking military precedents for moral principles'.

It was very probably this manuscript which the Privy Council placed in the hands of Francis Coldock, one of the wardens of the Stationers Company, at the beginning of July, with authority for it to be printed. It was called *A brief discovery of Dr Allen's Seditious Drifts* and the author was indicated only by the initials G.D.

The first thirty-six pages were mainly devoted to the thesis that Stanley and York owed their first duty to the Earl of Leicester, who had entrusted them with their commands, rather than to a foreign authority or to a moral principle. Then G.D. declared roundly that Allen's purpose was not

> to satisfy the consciences of Sir William Stanley and his complices [but] wholly
> to prepare the minds of the Romish Recusants . . . for the furtherance and

THE COPIE
OF A LETTER
VVRITTEN BY M. DOC-
TOR ALLEN: CONCERNING
THE YEELDING VP, OF THE CITIE
of Dauentrie, vnto his Catholike
Maieftie, by

Sir VVilliam Stanley Knight.

VVherin is fhewved both hovve lavvful, honorable, and neceffarie
that action vvas: and alfo that al others, efpeciallie thofe of the
Englifh Nation, that detayne anie tovvnes, or other places, in the
lovve countries, from the King Catholike, are bound, vpon paine
of damnation, to do the like.

Before VVhich is alfo prefixed a gentlemans letter,
that gaue occafion, of this difcourfe.

Matth. 22.
Reddite ergo quæ funt Cæfaris, Cæfari:
Render therfore the things that are Cæfars, to Cæfar:

Imprinted at Antuarpe, by Ioachim
Trognæfius, Anno 1587.

A
BRIEFE DISCO-
VERIE OF DOCTOR AL-
lens feditious drifts, contrived in a Pamphlet
written by him, Concerning the yeelding vp of
the towne of Deuenter, *(in Ouerriffel) vnto*
the king of Spain, by Sir VVil-
liam Stanley.

The contentes whereof are particularly fet downe
in the page following.

Reuelation Cap. 17. ver. 3.
And I fawe a woman fit vpon a skarlet-coloured beaft, full of
names of blafphemy, which had feuen heades, and ten hornes.
and Ver. 9. The feuen heads are feuen mountaines, whereon
the woman fitteth.
Matth. Chap. 15. Ver. 6.
Thus haue ye made the commandement of God of no authoritie
by your traditions. *and Chap. 23. Ver. 13.* Woe therefore be
vnto you Scribes and Pharifees, Hypocrites, becaufe ye fhut vp
the kingdome of heauen before men, for ye your felues goe not
in, neither fuffer ye them that would enter, to come in.
Matth. Chap. 7. Ver. 15.
Beware of falfe prophets, which come to you in fheepes clo-
thing, but inwardly they are rauening woolues.

LONDON
Imprinted by I. W. for Francis Coldock,
1588.

A Brief Discovery of Dr Allen's seditious drifts (right) was ostensibly published as a reply to a pamphlet (left) printed in Antwerp in 1587, but was really intended to counter Cardinal Allen's *Admonition* should copies succeed in circulating

assistance of seditious practices that may be moved and attempted against her Majesty . . . and especially of the most injurious invasion, long since conspired, and complotted, and now presently provided to be put in execution against her Majesty and her Realm, by the King of Spain, the Pope, and their Adherents.

He attacked Allen's arguments for the Pope's authority to depose princes and ended with 'an Exhortation to true obedience of her Majesty', in which he gave practical reasons why English Catholics should not put their trust in foreign invaders:

Small favour or courtesy (God wot) is an Englishman to hope for at a Spaniard's hand, be he never so Catholic. The Spanish soldier, where he is lord, never useth to ask (or to hear) whose wife this is? whose daughter, whose sister, whose house, or goods these are? A Catholic's wife, daughter, house and goods are as sweet to him, as another man's. And what pleasure would this be to an English man, whatsoever his religion be, to see his wife forced, his sisters ravished, his daughters deflowered, his house sacked, his goods pilled and spoiled by a stranger before his face? yea, and his own throat cut, if he but offer to make defence? . . . What availeth him then the name of a Catholic, if it please the lion in his ravening mood to take the hare for an ass, because he hath long ears? To whom shall his headless body complain for redress?

Even without a lengthy 'encouragement to all true subjects', which may have been added at the last moment, *A Brief Discovery of Dr Allen's seditious drifts* was an apposite reply to Cardinal Allen's *Admonition* should copies ever succeed in circulating. The Privy Council evidently thought so, for they sent a letter to all the Lords Lieutenant commending the pamphlet, 'which treatise coming now forth in the dead time of the year, is as yet scarcely known at all . . . We finding this treatise very convenient for the use of the Common subject, who is easiest to be abused by the cunning and lewd allurement of the adversary, and most necessary for the present time and occasions, have therefore thought good to give notice thereof unto your Lordship.'

Their lordships were further instructed to recommend the pamphlet to their deputies, justices of the peace, and mayors and officers of corporate towns, with 'present care and consideration as a thing especially recommended unto you by us'. 'Present', in Elizabethan English, meant 'immediate', and the letter was an order. It cannot have been long before justices, mayors and local commanders were thumbing through the book in search of suitable passages to be read to the common subject at quarter sessions, meetings and musters. Perhaps their choice fell on the following:

Let us therefore all of us (seeing the quarrel is general and common to us all, for the defence of true Religion, our Prince, and our Country,) let us all prepare ourselves cheerfully to the encounter; let us not respect the cry of wife, or child, let us respect their defence: let us pluck up our hearts, take up our arms, and march hardily to meet with our enemy; let us fight with him, let us die upon him, yea, let us seek him, if he seek not us.*

The book of 128 pages was placed in the hands of the printer (John Wolfe, beadle of the Stationers Company), printed, bound and distributed in less than a fortnight, for on 16 July a Spanish agent referred to its publication, describing it as 'very impertinent and ridiculous'.

---

* I have been unable to find anyone who could be identified by the initials G.D. There are some slender clues: 'I am far from the profession of divinity' (p. 9) and a reference to Allen's claim that two out of three Englishmen were Catholics in their hearts (p. 80), which occurred in the *Modest Defence of the English Catholics* but not in the letter defending Sir William Stanley. G.D. also refers to Allen's pamphlet as 'a treatise of eighty pages' although it was much shorter, while the *Admonition* was exactly that length. G.D. was therefore privileged to read banned Catholic books. A possible candidate is John Stubbe, a puritan lawyer who had his right hand cut off in 1579 for writing a pamphlet against Queen Elizabeth's projected marriage with the Duke of Alençon. He was later employed by the government in writing an answer to Allen's *Modest Defence* which was never published. Puritans were frequently employed in writing answers to Catholic propaganda, helping their rehabilitation if convicted of a crime. Another possible author is William ('Gulielmus') Davison, the puritan secretary of the Privy Council who was in the Tower for his part in authorizing the execution of Mary Queen of Scots, but this is no more than a wild guess.

A ballad seller

9

While *A brief discovery of Dr Allen's Seditious Drifts* was in the press, John Wolfe entered in the Stationers Register 'A Ballad of Encouragement to English soldiers valiantly to behave themselves in defence of true religion and their country'.

Ballads were the popular press, composed to inform or entertain the great mass of the population who could not read or write. They were printed on broadside sheets of paper, usually illustrated by a crude woodcut, and normally gave the name of a popular tune to which they were to be sung. Ballad singers purchased them from the printers in St Paul's Churchyard, hawked them at streetcorners and alehouses and carried them throughout the country to be sung at fairs and markets. The broadsheets were often posted on the walls by hospitable innkeepers or passed from hand to hand. But most people learned them by rote, helped by the tune and rhyme scheme. The more popular the ballad, the less printed copies are likely to survive.

Ballad writers were unlikely to be contentious; they could be whipped through the streets to the pillory if they were. Their subject matter varied from the sensational to the sententious: 'The most cruel and tyrannous murder committed by a mother-in-law upon a child of seven years of age, in Westminster this year' or 'A pleasant dialogue between plain Truth and blind Ignorance.'

During the first half of 1588 there had been only two ballads even remotely connected with military matters. One of them, now lost, was 'A new ballad, briefly showing the hard hap of a prentice of London, being a soldier'. The other was 'A pleasant song made by a soldier, whose bringing up had been dainty, and partly by those affections of his unbridled youth is now beaten with his own rod; and therefore termeth this his Repentance, or the Fall of Folly'. It ended:

> Let no good soldier be dismayed,
> To fight in field with courage bold,
> Yet mark the words that I have said:
> Trust not to friends when thou art old.

Neither was calculated to encourage recruitment.

But on 29 June less than a week after Lord Burghley had received Cardinal Allen's *Declaration*, Henry Kirkham, one of the wardens of the Stationers Company, entered in the register 'A Ditty of Encouragement to English men to be bold to fight in Defence of prince and country', shortly followed by John Wolfe's entry. But the first such ballad to survive, probably because it was printed as a pamphlet rather than the usual broadside, was 'An Exhortation to all English Subjects'. It came from the press of the Welsh printer, Richard Jones, who specialized in ballads (in 1580 he had published 'A new northern ditty of my lady Greensleeves').

> What should us daunt one jot,
>   or make us be dismayed?
> Let never threats of foreign foes
>   make English men afraid . . .
>
> I trust as of one realm,
>   even so they shall us see,
> Of one allegiance, of one heart
>   and firm fidelity . . .

Our foes like friends will feign
  to come for our souls' health,
But God doth know their foul pretence:
  they shoot but at our wealth,
With loss of life to all,
  let each himself assure,
The protestant and papist both
  like torment shall endure.

Almost as soon as all these efforts to stir up the country had been set in train, it seemed that they were no longer necessary. On 9 July Walsingham wrote to Sir Edward Norris:

> For the navy of Spain we have lately received advertisements that by reason of their great wants, as well of mariners as of necessary provisions, but especially through the infection fallen among their men, they are forced to return and have dispersed themselves.

That same day, the northerly wind arose which the Lord Admiral and Sir Francis Drake had been awaiting for so many weeks. Their combined fleet of over ninety ships set sail from Plymouth to attack the Spaniards in their home waters. Three days later they were back in port again. Just as they were approaching the Spanish coast near Corunna, the wind had shifted to the south and forced them to return. They had seen no sign of the Armada and came to the conclusion that the expedition had been called off. To save expense, they began to discharge some of their ships from the Queen's service.

By this time the despatch had reached the Privy Council describing Dr Dale's last meeting with the Duke of Parma. After a discussion on 15 July they agreed that the Duke had evaded the main questions and wished to charge him even more strongly with complicity in the enterprise. Burghley and Walsingham both hoped that the Queen would at last accept the inevitability of war. But three days later Walsingham had to inform Burghley that the Queen 'had resolved that the treaty should be continued as a thing proceeding from the commissioners themselves' and that no further charges be laid against the Duke 'lest it might breed a present breach before things be put in readiness for defence'. It was the first occasion the Queen had ever suggested that the peace negotiations be used for gaining time.

Lord Burghley was almost wishing the Spaniards would come, for the burden of maintaining the navy, ever since March, on top of normal expenses, was proving a strain on the Treasury. The Admiralty was calling for £13,000 to meet past debts and current needs. The Ordnance department required £8,000 for equipment for the musters. To tide things over until the next instalment of the parliamentary subsidy of £50,000, due in November, he was seeking a loan from the Merchant Adventurers Company. 'A man could wish, if peace cannot be had, that the enemy would no longer delay but prove (as I trust) his evil fortune.'

Furthermore there were still complaints coming in about payment of ship money and the cost of equipping the musters, all of which had increased local taxation fourfold in some towns. Burghley recognized that local taxes were spread unfairly. 'If these demandings for musters, powder and weapons were not demanded of the poor in towns, the matter were of less moment, for the rich may well bear greater. I see a general murmur of people, and malcontented people will increase it to the comfort of the enemy.'

CHAPTER SIX

THEY COME UNTO OUR COAST

In happy hour, our foes we did descry,
And under sail with gallant wind as they came passing by.
    Which sudden tidings to Plymouth being brought,
Full soon our Lord high Admiral for to pursue them sought.
    And to his train courageously he said:
'Now, for the Lord and our good Queen, to fight be not afraid.
    Regard our cause, and play your parts like men:
The Lord no doubt will prosper us in all our actions then.'

Thomas Deloney: *The Great Galleazzo*

1

The invasion warning system had now become very sophisticated. On all the sea approaches to England were posted the small, fast ships usually called pinnaces, to give advance warning if enemy ships were sighted. The pinnaces might be fishing smacks, privately owned merchant vessels, or the scouting and communications ships attached to one of the fleets. Merchant ships and coastal boats were also expected to keep a look-out.

A ship at sea, on seeing the enemy, was to come in sight of the coast, strike a sail twice, fire a cannon, and then repeat the sequence. At night the signal was two lights, one above the other, to 'shoot a piece' and then continue firing. A look-out was also kept from prominent points along the coast, where beacons were maintained and watched twenty-four hours a day from March to October. The beacons were no longer a crude system of signalling a general alarm. At strategic points, key beacons were maintained in groups of three. According to which beacons were lit, the musters were called to assemble at a particular part of the coast or warned simply to hold themselves in readiness. Edmund Spenser, at this time in Ireland, showed himself familiar with the system when in *The Faerie Queene* he described a dragon's eyes blazing

As two broad Beacons, set in open fields,
Send forth their flames far off to every shire,
And warning give, that enemies conspire,
With fire and sword the region to invade;

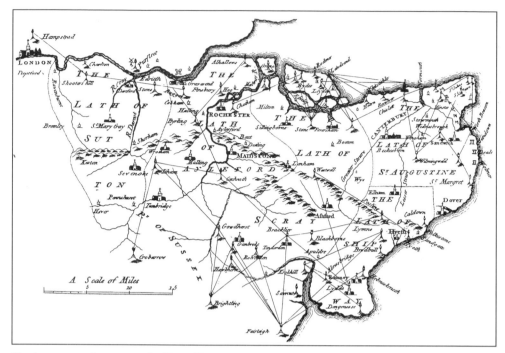

The beacon warning system in Kent. The purpose was to summon the inland musters, not to convey news of threatened invasion

According to which region was being summoned to arms, minor beacons relayed the message across country. Normally they would be placed on hills, but in low-lying country 'cresset lights' could be lit in an iron basket at the top of a church tower. Two men were constantly on watch at each beacon site, but were not permitted to fire a beacon without the authority of a justice of the peace, who had first to verify the authenticity of the alarm.

Mobilization did not depend wholly on the beacon warning. Lords Lieutenant were responsible for maintaining a post service in their county, employing both horsemen and runners according to the nature of the terrain. With fresh horses available along the post route, a more elaborate message could be transmitted almost as fast as a beacon signal. A Court official, Thomas Randolph, Master of the Posts, was responsible for coordinating the post system and for sending orders from the Privy Council to the Lords Lieutenant.

The Spanish Armada was first spotted on Thursday 18 July by an English merchant ship on its way to Bridgwater in Somerset, 'twenty-five leagues to the west of the headland of France holding course towards England'. Probably ignorant of the elaborate signalling arrangements, the ship did not stop to strike a sail or fire a piece, but maintained its course to Bridgwater, where it arrived the following Saturday. On Sunday morning, Sir John Popham, the Attorney General, who was in Wellington on his way to Ireland, heard the news and sent a message to Lord Burghley by post horse: 'Haste Haste I say – haste post haste – haste.'

But in the meantime Captain Thomas Fleming had sighted the Armada on Friday 19 July and made straight for Plymouth. He was commander of the *Golden Hind*, one of the screen of pinnaces patrolling the western approaches for the Lord Admiral's fleet. He arrived in Plymouth late on the same day. Doubtless the captains and commanders may have been whiling away the time playing bowls or other common pastimes, though no one mentioned it until nearly thirty years later. The Lord Admiral's own account suggests that they were taken completely by surprise and lost no time in getting their ships out to sea. There was a strong south-westerly breeze blowing into Plymouth Sound, the tide was coming in, and all the Queen's ships were penned in harbour. The conditions were ideal for a Spanish attack by fireships.

The next twenty-four hours were spent manhandling the ships out of the harbour and beating out to sea against the wind. At dawn on Saturday the Armada was spotted by the look-out at Falmouth Castle. Justices of the peace were roused from their beds and beacons lit along the coast of England as the Armada, in a half-moon formation, began its slow journey up the Channel. By the afternoon it had arrived near Plymouth, just in time to see through the drizzle the last of the English ships working out of the Sound. The remainder, dangerously downwind of the Spanish fleet, had struck their sails to render themselves inconspicuous.

By the following morning, which was Sunday, Howard and Drake had worked their way round against the wind to the rear of the Armada, a feat of seamanship that amazed the Spaniards. But before they attacked, the Lord Admiral had to give his defiance, just as knights in the days of chivalry signalled their intention of giving battle. He sent out his pinnace, the *Disdain*, to fire an ineffective broadside at what he thought was the Spanish admiral's flagship. His Vice-Admiral, Sir Francis Drake, probably followed his usual practice of praying to the Lord of hosts for his support in the forthcoming engagement.

After these preliminaries, the combined English fleet moved into the attack. One of the first things they noticed was that the Armada carried a far greater number of guns than they had been led to expect. They were obliged to keep a safe distance and therefore did little damage.

2

Late in the evening of Sunday 21 July Sir Francis Drake sent a fast pinnace along the coast to Dover to warn Lord Henry Seymour, commanding the eastern fleet; it arrived the following Tuesday, having averaged at least five knots. Richard Hawkins, Mayor of Plymouth (and John Hawkins' brother), sent a messenger to Court by post horse. By Sunday, Sir John Popham's messenger was also on his way. The beacon signals were not intended to carry news but to summon the musters, hence they were only lit when their particular section of the coast was threatened.

As the Armada approached Portland, on Monday 22 July, the Portland beacon was lit and the Earl of Sussex sent another messenger by post horse. This messenger must have ridden for twenty-four hours without a break, for he arrived at Court, which had moved from Greenwich to Richmond, the following morning. He was the first to bring the news.

The Privy Council was instantly summoned and a flurry of messages, mostly prepared in advance, began to go out. The nobility were reminded of their duty to send lances and light horse for the defence of the Queen's person within three days. The nobles included some of known Catholic sympathies, though the names of two of these have been struck out of the Council's minutes, perhaps being regarded as unreliable. One Catholic nobleman who was not on the list was Viscount Montague, who had heard of the Portsdown beacon being fired as the Armada approached the Isle of Wight that Tuesday and was already writing to the Privy Council for instructions about putting his horse and foot at the disposal of the Queen. With some embarrassment, next day the Privy Council asked this loyal Catholic to send his forces to Court in the charge of his son, in view of his age and infirmity.

Lords Lieutenant were instructed to send their mounted troops to Brentwood in Essex by 27 July and their trained foot-soldiers to London or Stratford-of-the-Bow by 6 August. The Lord Mayor of London was to send a thousand of the trained bands to Gravesend by 26 July. A thousand veteran shot were ordered to return from the Netherlands.

Not the least important act of the Privy Council that first Tuesday was to send a letter to the Archbishop of Canterbury, 'praying his Lordship to give orders to all the Bishops and pastors in all the dioceses . . . to move their auditories and parishioners to join in public prayers to Almighty God, the giver of victories, to assist us against the malice of our enemies'.

A *form of Prayer, necessary for the present time and state* was already being slowly distributed through the Church hierarchy. The Queen and her government preferred prayers to sermons as a means of instructing the common sort. Members of the congregation were not required to stay for the sermon after the service. Moreover, although prayers were addressed to Almighty God, they claimed the attention of the congregation as much as a sermon or homily and, being shorter, were easier to fit to the occasion.

Oliver Pigge, one of John Field's 'apostles', circulated his own prayers and meditations in manuscript among his puritan colleagues.

> The superiors in the commonwealth, in the church, and in the house, have not done their duty to their inferiors. The inferiors likewise have been marvellous undutiful to their prince . . . The land hath abounded with murders, slaughters, quarrels, fightings and contentions, with incests, adulteries, whoredoms, drunkenness, excessive pride in apparel: filthy stage plays have been suffered in our chiefest city, and upon the Sabbath.

Preachers who were carried away by their theme might almost make their congregation believe that England deserved to be conquered, as well as their betters criticized; it is not surprising that the authorities were less than keen on sermons.

Probably most prayers composed at the time were circulated in manuscript, but one has survived which was printed on a broadsheet, implying a wider distribution:

> Be favourable and gracious O Lord to this thy English Sion, behold in the bowels of thy mercy our Navy on Sea, guard, guide, protect and defend the right

honourable the Lord high Admiral of England, the Vice-Admiral, with all honourable and worshipful personages, Captains, Masters, Officers, Sailors, and Soldiers now employed, whether on the Western or South Seas, . . . let not furious storms, winds, or tempests hurt them, nor surging Seas harm them, let not Papists amaze them, nor foreign enemies fear them [make them afraid]: but thou Lord of hosts encourage their hearts, enable their hands, indue them with valour, grant them safely to return with glorious victory . . . Also O Lord we thy Servants humbly beseech thee, to bless and prosper not only our Sea causes, but also our land service, her Majesty's most honourable General, Marshal, Captains, Officers, and English soldiers whatsoever, strengthen them with courage and manliness, that they may suppress the slights of Antichrist, with all the force and power of foreign enemies, and papistical practices, that dare presume to attempt any harm or hurt to her royal Majesty, their honours, her English people, or to this noble Realm of England: so shall we sing forth the songs of glory in our great congregations unto thee, and declare to our posterity these things among the wonders that thou hast done of old.

The sentiments of prayers that gradually began to be heard in every church in England were soon echoed in the popular broadside ballads:

> O Noble England
> fall down upon thy knee
>   And praise thy God with thankful heart
> which still maintaineth thee.
>   The foreign forces
> that seek thy utter spoil
>   Shall then through his especial grace
> be brought to shameful foil.
>   With mighty power
> they come unto our coast:
>   To overrun our country quite,
> they make their brags and boast.
>   In strength of men
> they set their only stay:
>   But we upon the Lord our God
> will put our trust alway.

3

For the first time in that year of storms, a soft westerly breeze blew up the English Channel. The weather could not have been better for the Armada as it made its unhurried way towards the rendezvous with the Duke of Parma. As the beacons carried the warning of its approach along the coast and inland, the musters and the trained bands of the maritime counties were summoned to man the strong points. As soon as the Armada passed by, they returned to their farms and workshops and hung up their pikes, bows, muskets and armour. On paper, they made up 27,500 foot and 2,300 horse, but probably never more than a few thousand were under arms at one time.

Inland, that last week in July, the roads of southern England began to fill with little straggling bands, bearing a motley collection of weapons and armour, making their way on foot (it could hardly be called marching) towards the camp which her Majesty's most honourable General, the Earl of Leicester, was setting up at Tilbury in Essex. By 24 July he had marked out the site, on the hill at West Tilbury overlooking the Thames estuary, and some musters were beginning to arrive. But Leicester was already in difficulties. His two deputies, Sir John Norris and Sir Roger Williams, both of whom had served, and quarrelled with him in the Netherlands campaigns, were at Dover and seemed reluctant to come and do their share of the work. To make matters worse, the young noblemen and courtiers on whom Leicester had relied for leadership had come to realize that the sea was where the action and the glory were, and had rushed off to the coast to join any ship that would take them.

The thirty-year-old Earl of Cumberland and Robert Carey, Lord Hunsdon's son, rode to Portsmouth, where they borrowed a pinnace and sailed out to find the English fleet. After cruising around for a day, during which they were nearly caught up with some ships of the Armada, they eventually found the Lord Admiral's flagship, the *Ark Royal*. But it was already overcrowded, so they joined Sir Thomas Fenner in the *Elizabeth Bonaventure* and stayed with him for the rest of the fighting.

The Earl of Cumberland, whose main interests were gambling, womanizing, and the sea, was probably a useful asset, but the same could hardly be said for the Queen's Genoese banker, Sir Horatio Palavicino, who was fifty years old but fired with patriotism for his adopted country. At least he had the grace to write a letter of apology to Walsingham:

Right Honourable:
If I err, I beseech your Honour to pardon me and to be as a mean that her Majesty and the rest of the Lords may likewise pardon me – especially my very good Lord, the Earl of Leicester, to whom I was a suitor to serve aland under his charge. But the greatness of my zeal . . . doth constrain me, with an honourable company, to depart as this night toward Portsmouth, where I hope to be present in the battle, and thereby a partaker in the victory or to win an honourable death, thus to testify to the whole world my fidelity to her Majesty. Especially do I commend my affairs to your Honour, and pray God to give you every happiness. From the Court, the 24th day of July 1588.
    Your Honour's most assured friend to command
      Horatio Palavicino.

Other courtiers and noblemen, particularly those with horsemen, were joining the army being assembled by Lord Hunsdon, the Lord Chamberlain, around the Queen's person at Richmond. But her Captain of the Guard, Sir Walter Raleigh, slipped off to join the navy. The total number of the army guarding the Queen, some of whom should have been at Tilbury, may have reached four thousand.

So slow were the musters in arriving at Tilbury that Leicester himself rode off to Chelmsford to hasten four thousand men of Essex. The diary of Richard Rogers of Wethersfield gives a brief glimpse of the effect of the summons on his quiet community:

[One] day, when our neighbours were gone to training 3 mile hence, on a sudden there was proclaimed amongst them, when all were not yet together, that they must with speed depart to the seacoast more than 20 miles off, so that few returned from the first place, but went on to rights, never seeing wife nor taking order about their goods and business, which sudden thing flayted [frightened] many, and yet we know not the end of their going. Whereupon we consented to fast, 40 of us, with good grace. . . .

When the men of Essex arrived at Tilbury, they brought, complained Leicester, 'not so much as one meal's provision of victual with them' and 'there was not a barrel of beer nor loaf of bread for them.' It was enough to have discouraged them, after twenty miles march, but they 'said they would abide more hunger than this to serve her Majesty and their country'. Leicester found he had to do everything himself, chasing up the victuallers and being 'cook, cater and hunt'. The thousand trained men from London were asked to turn back if they did not have rations with them, but fortunately they had.

It seems to have been through the grapevine rather than official channels that the first news reached Tilbury camp of the activities of the English fleet, 'of the taking of the Admiral or Vice-Admiral of the Spanish fleet and the capture of the great galleass, and one great ship sunk'. Church-bells were rung and bonfires lit that night in the streets of London.

The news was fairly accurate. One Spanish ship had been blown up through the explosion of a powder magazine. Another had damaged her bowsprit in collision with another Spanish ship and been left behind by the Armada. The following morning her captain, Don Pedro de Valdez, found himself being hailed by none other than Sir Francis Drake, and surrendered without a shot being fired. It was certainly true, as the ballad said:

> Strong was she stuffed
>   with Cannons great and small,
> And other instruments of war,
>   which we obtained all,
> A certain sign
>   of good success we trust,
> That God will overthrow the rest,
>   as he hath done the first.

Don Pedro de Valdez, who indeed turned out to be a Vice-Admiral of the Armada, was kept on board Drake's ship, the *Revenge* – for the ransom, everyone assumed. About forty of the more important prisoners were taken to Portsmouth and from there sent up to Kingston in Surrey, not far from the Court at Richmond. In charge of the party was Captain Thomas Cely, who had done service for the Queen in Spain, including a spell in a Spanish prison, and so would be useful in interrogation. The remaining prisoners were kept on their ship, to live on their own rotting provisions, as it was towed to Dartmouth by Captain Thomas Fleming in the *Golden Hind*.

There had been several engagements in the Channel that week, with tremendous expenditure of powder and shot, but little serious damage done on either side. The last battle was fought on Thursday 25 July, off the Isle of Wight, where it was feared the Spaniards might land. The Spanish Armada had been equipped for a six month campaign. After less than a week's fighting, they had exhausted most of their powder and the lighter weight cannon-balls on which they depended for defence. One observer on the Duke of Medina Sidonia's flagship, seeing the English firing their cannon to such little effect, thought it a ruse to draw the Spaniards' fire and to exhaust their ammunition.

The English were doing nothing of the sort. They were easily able to outmanoeuvre the Spanish ships but had to keep clear of their short range, heavy guns. Consequently the missiles from their own cannon and culverins had insufficient power to penetrate the stout oak hulls. But the English had the advantage of being able to send into port from time to time and take on fresh supplies. Nearly 90,000 lb of powder were despatched to the ports in three days that week.

Still in the strong defensive crescent formation that it had maintained throughout, and without having lost a single ship through enemy action, the Armada reached the coast of France near Calais on the afternoon of Saturday 27 July. Smartly and in perfect order the Spanish ships dropped anchor. The English fleet hove to and anchored just over a cannon-shot away.

4

That Saturday, as the Armada lay within sight of the cliffs of Dover, all England prayed for deliverance. By this time, no one was in any doubt about the Spaniards' intentions.

> Our pleasant country,
>   so fruitful and so fair:
> They do intend by deadly war
>   to make both poor and bare.
> Our towns and cities
>   to rack and sack likewise:
> To kill and murder man and wife.
>   as malice does arise.
> And to deflower
>   our virgins in our sight:
> And in the cradle cruelly
>   the tender babe to smite.
> God's holy truth,
>   they mean for to cast down:
> And to deprive our noble Queen,
>   both of her life and crown.

Some such stories may have been picked up by a French sailor in an English port who then sailed on to Brill in the Netherlands. By that time some corroborative detail had been added. He claimed that while sailing south-west of 'Plainmue' (Plymouth) he had sighted the Spanish fleet, travelled with them for two days, and witnessed the first action with the English fleet. There were some sixty thousand sailors and soldiers aboard the Armada, he said, and over a thousand monks and priests. He had heard from the Spanish captains that they meant to carry off the English women to Spain and that the King's commission instructed them to massacre everyone they met in England, even the children.

Meanwhile in London the Lord Mayor issued orders for the citizens to be summoned to church, 'by toll of bell or otherwise', both in the morning and afternoon, that humble and hearty prayers might be offered to Almighty God 'by preaching and otherwise'. Indeed all over England, where the news had penetrated, people were flocking to church. As Petruccio Ubaldini, the Florentine refugee in London, remarked: 'nothing makes us run to God more than the fear of impending danger.' At Morning Prayer, that Saturday when the Armada lay at Calais, Psalm 121 was prescribed in the Book of Common Prayer to be spoken or sung in every parish church and cathedral:

I will lift up mine eyes unto the hills, from whence cometh my help.
My help cometh even from the Lord, who hath made heaven and earth.
He will not suffer thy foot to be moved, and he that keepeth thee will not sleep.
Behold, he that keepeth Israel shall neither slumber nor sleep.
The Lord himself is thy keeper, the Lord is thy defence upon thy right hand.

In Richmond, where the Court was preparing to move to London, Anthony Marten, one of the gentlemen who served the Queen at table, composed some special prayers which were used in the Queen's Chapel.

Now is the time, O Lord, now is the time, that by a glorious victory in thine own cause, thy Son, Christ Jesus, and his holy word, shall be magnified in all the world. For lo, thine enemies have sworn to lay waste thy sanctuary, and that thy servant Elizabeth, her people, and kingdom, shall be rooted out, and no one remembered more upon the earth. And now that we have long and earnestly sought unto them for peace, they are most proudly come forth by land and sea against us: in such wise, that if thy mighty Providence had not foreseen their dissembled malice, we had suddenly perished, and come to a fearful end. Wherefore make frustrate their devices, and fight thou with Israel, against all the host of the Assyrians . . . Destroy their armies, confound their forces, terrify their captains. Scatter, break, and sink into the sea their huge and strong vessels, and as it was with Pharaoh on the Red Sea, so let it be with them that seek the death of thy servants. We trust not in the multitude of horsemen, nor in the power of our own arms, but in the justice of our cause, and in the help, mercy, and assistance of thy heavenly power.

5

The Queen and the Court moved from Richmond to her palace of St James on Sunday 28 July. St James, in the middle of a deer park just outside London, was more a hunting lodge than a palace, but it was not far from White Hall and the grounds provided space for the army that her Chamberlain, Lord Hunsdon, was gathering to protect her. It was also a symbolic gesture to the citizens of London that in the hour of danger the Queen was residing near her capital and her people.

London was being prepared for siege. Every householder had to provide himself with a leathern bucket for fire-fighting. The main streets were barred with strong chains held up by stout wooden posts, which could be opened and closed to control the crowds of soldiers, apprentices and vagabonds as well as more sober citizens. All the principal crossroads were guarded day and night. Two aldermen were commissioned to keep a close eye on the prices charged by brewers, bakers and butchers, and to see that all soldiers arriving in the city were properly looked after.

A close watch was kept on foreigners within the city, whatever their country of origin or religious persuasion. Petruccio Ubaldini, a loyal Protestant who had lived nearly forty years in England, though without learning to speak English, was aggrieved by the treatment of foreigners. Even those from France and the Low Countries 'received insulting words from the apprentices and lower classes'. It is easier, he said, 'to find flocks of white crows than one Englishman (and let him believe what he will about religion) who loves a foreigner, either as a master or companion in his own house, even if a benefactor'.

While feeling was so high, it is understandable that the Privy Council ordered the Lord Mayor to convey the Spanish prisoners from Kingston to Bridewell prison under cover of night. Two Englishmen among the prisoners received less considerate treatment; they were brought before the Privy Council, questioned, and summarily hanged.

There was no news from the fleet. The Lord Mayor issued instructions on 29 July to each of the aldermen to see that the citizens of their wards refrained from crediting news of vessels at sea 'for the avoiding of some dislike that may come thereof'. All over the country, a watch was being kept for vagabonds and strangers who might spread 'false, idle and mutinous reports'.

While the Queen and the Privy Council were awaiting news from the fleet at St James, a searching examination was being prepared of the Lord Admiral's conduct of the battle. Richard Drake, Sir Francis's brother, was sent to Dover on 31 July with a 'memorial . . . to the Lord Admiral for such things as her Majesty doth desire to be informed of'.

She wanted a good account, for example, of the amount of powder and shot he had expended, and how much he had received. She was surprised that Don Pedro de Valdez and other valuable prisoners had been allowed to stay aboard Drake's ship and wanted them sent promptly to England. She also required an explanation of her Lord Admiral's handling of the fighting. 'What causes are there why the Spanish navy hath not been boarded by the Queen's ships? And though some of the ships of Spain may be thought too huge to be boarded by the English, yet some of the Queen's ships are thought very able to have boarded divers of the meaner ships of the Spanish navy.'

There had been murmuring in some quarters about the Lord Admiral's behaviour ever since that first day off Plymouth, when he had broken off the engagement just as it seemed that the English were getting the upper hand. Returning from a visit to Dover, the young Earl of Essex and Sir Thomas Gorge were entertained by the Countess of Lincoln at Horsely on 28 July. During their exchange of gossip they told her that 'there is much grief conceived in the court that my Lord Admiral hath suffered them to pass on so far without fight, and that he prevented not the opportunity they have now gotten of refreshing their men.'

Very likely Gill of Brightempson (Brighton) said something similar. But he was reported by his Lord Lieutenant to the Privy Council, who had him committed to gaol in irons for 'having uttered slanderous [words] against the Lord Admiral'.

Had the Lord Admiral perhaps been fooled by the Spanish strategy? 'Some Englishmen, and Spaniards also that are taken, do say the intent of the Spanish navy is to draw the English navy from the coast of Flanders; that the sea being clear, the Duke of Parma might come out with his force to invade the realm, and namely come to London.'

But while Richard Drake was on his way with the Queen's memorial to the Lord Admiral, news began to trickle in of what had happened since that Sunday night when the two fleets lay at anchor off Calais, less than two miles apart.

CHAPTER SEVEN

ADVERTISEMENTS FROM DIVERS PLACES

What printed Books were sent about
  as filled their desire:
How England was by Spaniards won,
  and London set on fire.
Be these the men that are so mild,
  whom some so holy call?
The Lord defend our noble Queen
  and Country from them all.

Thomas Deloney: *Ballad of the Whips*

1

Since the beginning of July, when King Henry III of France had been forced to capitulate to the Holy League and sign the Edict of Union, Don Bernardin de Mendoza, the Spanish ambassador in Paris, had been eagerly awaiting the arrival of the Armada. It no longer seemed important that the King had not been deposed. It was enough that he was powerless to resist the Holy League's demands.

King Henry had complained through his ambassador in Madrid about Mendoza's interference in French domestic affairs, but King Philip had replied offhandedly that his ambassador's activities were only motivated by zeal for religion. At the same time he had sent Mendoza a copy of the correspondence and a further 150,000 escudos to help secure the Channel ports for the Armada.

The Duke of Aumale had still not succeeded in capturing the fortified centre of Boulogne, which he had been besieging since April. But Mendoza felt he had secured a promise from King Henry at Chartres that all his ports would be open to Spanish shipping for shelter and provisions, although he had lingering doubts about the King's sincerity.

As soon as he heard of the Armada's departure from Corunna he published, through a French printer, a translation into French of the *Relacion Verdadera* of the fleet that had been assembled in Lisbon. Publication had been delayed for nearly two months, but Mendoza had the satisfaction of adding to the original title, which had not revealed the Armada's destination, '*contre l'armée anglaise*'.

As it happened, King Henry had failed to send any instructions to the governors of his ports about Spanish shipping. It was unfortunate, therefore, for the Armada to

LE VRAY

DISCOVRS

DE L'ARMEE, QVE LE ROY CATHOLIQVE DOM

Philippe a faict assembler au port de la ville de
Lisbone, au Royaume de Portugal, en l'an
1588. contre l'armee Angloise.

Laquelle commença de sortir dudit Port, le 29. May, &
acheua le 30. & se meit à voile. Nostre Seigneur
l'achemine à son sainct seruice.

Traduit d'Espaignol en François.

A PARIS,
Chez Guillaume Chaudiere, ruë S. Iacques, à l'en-
seigne du Temps, & de l'Homme sauuage.
M. D. LXXXVIII.

Auec Permission.

The French translation of the *Relacion Verdadera*, published in Paris under the auspices of the Spanish
ambassador, Don Bernardin de Mendoza. Another edition was printed in Rouen

arrive on 27 July at Calais, whose royalist governor, Girault de Mauleon, Seigneur de Gourdan, felt obliged to maintain a policy of strict neutrality. When the Duke of Medina Sidonia's messenger arrived on shore with a request for victuals, powder and shot, M. Gourdan agreed to allow food and water to be supplied, but not munitions. Within minutes, boats were plying back and forth between the Calais shore and the Spanish ships, which after a month at sea were in dire need of fresh provisions. The price of eggs in Calais rose to sixpence each.

On the following Sunday morning, M. Gourdan sent a boat to the Admiral's flagship with a placatory gift of fruit and other refreshment. He warned the Duke, quite unnecessarily, that his fleet was anchored in an exposed and dangerous position, but firmly refused to allow him to enter Calais harbour. The Duke of Medina Sidonia, in the meantime, was anxiously awaiting a reply to messages sent along the coast to Dunkirk, where the Duke of Parma was supposed to be. His four galleys had vanished somewhere off the Scilly Isles, so that he urgently required the protection of shallow draft fighting ships until the invasion army was ready to embark.

<h1 style="text-align:center">2</h1>

In Paris, Don Bernardin de Mendoza had received no official word either from the Duke of Medina Sidonia or from the Duke of Parma about the arrival of the Armada, but had to rely on his own sources of information. After a number of false reports that the Armada had landed in Scotland, about 27 July his merchant informant in Rouen, Issoard Capello, sent a message that a fishing-boat had seen two hundred sail off Dartmouth. A day or so later, confirmation of a sort came in an eyewitness account by a Breton captain in Havre de Grace of a great sea battle off the Isle of Wight the previous Tuesday, 23 July. The Spaniards had got the best of it, sinking fifteen English ships, including the Lord Admiral's flagship. Three more English ships had been dismasted and captured, while another had been set on fire.

Another Breton sailor had been captured by the English and actually served for a time on Drake's ship, but he had later managed to escape. He had seen a Spanish galleon attack Drake's flagship, cut down her masts with the first broadside, and sink her with the second. Drake himself had escaped in a boat under cover of the thick smoke. The surviving English ships had fled to the Narrow Seas between Dover and Calais where the rest of the English fleet was lying.

The news was substantiated by letters from Dieppe, where the sound of gunfire had been heard. A packet-boat had arrived bearing reports of a battle in which sixteen ships had been sunk and three captured, including the Lord Admiral's flagship, while Drake and the remainder of the English fleet had fled.

Within two days, Mendoza had a pamphlet printed in Paris and Rouen proclaiming the good news. He did not, of course, reveal his own connection. The pamphlet purported to be the copy of a letter from Pierre Le Goux, a merchant of Dieppe, who also recommended his readers to purchase a copy of a previous pamphlet, *Le vrai discours* of the fleet that the King of Spain had ordered to be assembled in Lisbon. But Mendoza personally informed other members of the diplomatic corps in Paris of the victory and sent off four couriers by different routes with despatches to the King of Spain. Soon he was on his way to Chartres to deliver the news to King Henry III and to demand a mass of thanksgiving to be sung in Notre-Dame. Before he left Paris, he prepared a victory bonfire in the courtyard of the Spanish embassy to be lit on his return.

Count Morosini, the papal nuncio in Paris, lost no time in sending the good news to Rome. 'All good Catholics and friends of the common good are full of joy and happiness', he wrote. The Venetian ambassador was more cautious, and first checked with the English ambassador. Sir Edward Stafford told him that his own information from Rouen was that the Spanish and English fleets were close together, but had not yet engaged. He, too, had had accounts from fishermen in Dieppe, but they had said that it was the Spanish ships which had been 'spoiled and sunk'.

Sir Edward Stafford, isolated in a hostile Paris dominated by the Holy League, was no better informed by his own people than was Mendoza. Writing to Walsingham on 1 August, enclosing a copy of Mendoza's victory pamphlet, he asked for immediate and frequent news of what was happening, 'because it is greatly looked for at my hands, and importeth both her Majesty's service and the state of things here to be truly advised, and to have the means with truth to break off his artificious bruits'. He was certain that any news he put out would be believed, 'for I have not used them to tell lies, and in very truth I have not the face to do it.'

Mendoza's reports he discounted completely as coming from a Breton captain 'that saw things afar off and ran away for fear, and thinking to get some reward at the Spanish ambassador's hand, as he hath, came and made this fair tale'. He ended: 'I beseech your honour that I may have as often and as true news as I can.'

Richard Hakluyt, who had just returned to Paris, wrote in the same vein to Sir Thomas Heneage in London. 'It is very necessary that if we have any good news it should be printed in French and the copies sent over with speed, whereof I beseech you to advertise Mr Secretary.'

On his arrival at Chartres, the Spanish ambassador demanded that the King should order services of thanksgiving for the Spanish victory throughout France and return to Paris as earnest of his support for the Catholic cause. The King heard him courteously, but when he had finished informed him of a letter he had received from M. Gourdan, the governor of Calais, which related that the Spanish navy had arrived at the port pursued by a strong English fleet. During Sunday night, the Spaniards had been dislodged from their anchorage by fire-ships and on the following day chased north by the English. One Spanish galleass had been run aground at the entrance to Calais harbour.

Remarking coolly that their reports appeared to differ, the Spanish ambassador withdrew. On his return to Paris he found a number of Italian sailors from the stranded galleass awaiting him at the embassy. Leaving his bonfire unlit, he wrote to King Philip that his earlier reports had perhaps been too optimistic, but promised further news.

Sir Edward Stafford was still impatiently awaiting word from London. 'For the honour of God, sir, spare not letters nor charge,' he wrote desperately to Walsingham on 5 August, 'for it is looked for and upon it depends the success of things here.'

The news was in fact already on its way. Two days later an English courier arrived from the Privy Council in London with a 'Journal of all that passed between the two armies of Spain and England from July 18th to August 1st, 1588, according to advertisements from divers places'. Before the day was out, Stafford had a copy translated into French in the hands of Count Morosini, the papal nuncio, who forwarded it to the Pope with the warning that it came from English sources. A reconstruction of the original English despatch can be made from the French versions and the naval despatches on which it was based:

Friday 19 July 1588
The Army of Spain was discovered about the isles of Scilly.

Saturday 20
The Lord Admiral of England came in sight of them about three of the clock in the afternoon.

Sunday 21
The Lord Admiral recovered the wind of them about nine o'clock in the morning and they gave them fight, which continued until one in the afternoon. In this fight there was a ship of theirs spoiled and the men forced to abandon her.

Monday 22
The greatest galleon in the whole fleet was taken, and Don Pedro de Valdez with 450 men.

The navy of Spain drew nigh to Portland.

Tuesday 23
The Earl of Sussex, the Queen's lieutenant in this county, advertised their arrival at Portland unto the Court.

Wednesday 24
The Earl of Sussex wrote news of the capture of the aforesaid ships to the Court.

Thursday 25
Sir Tristram Gorge was sent by the Lord Admiral with a particular report of the battle.

Swanson the messenger arrived about eight o'clock, bearing letters from the Lord Admiral about the same.

Sunday 28
The Lord Steward of England [Leicester] sent advertisement from Dover that the navy of Spain was over against Dover between Calais and Gravelines.

The same evening fire works were sent out, causing their ships to slip their anchors and make away.

Monday 29
The Lord Admiral advertised that he engaged them in battle and drove aground a galleass before Calais, which was taken by an armed long boat of the Lord Admiral and pillaged: but the galleass hath been detained by M. de Gourdan, governor of Calais.

The captain of the said galleass was named Hugo de Moncada, one of the greatest personages in the fleet, who was killed with a musket shot, and his Lieutenant was brought prisoner into the fleet of England with several other men of rank.

Thursday 1 August

There arrived a messenger with letters from Sir [Francis] Drake of 30 July, by which he advertised that they continued to chase the army of Spain, which is now forced so far to leeward, that he is assured that the Duke of Parma and the Duke of Sidonia will not meet together this year.

They are chased a long way to the North, almost as far as Newcastle, and have sore need of fresh water and other necessaries.

The same day came news that they are driven yet further towards Scotland, and that the English follow them and every day take some of their ships.

The Lord Seymour who had joined the Lord Admiral hath returned before Dunkirk with 14 English ships and 90 from Holland and Zealand.

Her Majesty hath caused two camps to be put in hand, one in Essex of 25,000 men, under the command of the Lord Steward, the other about her person of 30,000 foot and 3,000 horse, under the charge of Lord Hunsdon her Lord Chamberlain. The footsoldiers are for the most part men of valour, well armed, and very eager for battle, and into the said armies, both on sea and on land, the English Catholics come to offer themselves and beg that they may be received, furnishing everything necessary for both horse and foot at their own charge: and it is a thing to remark, that (as Her Majesty is ever assured of the loyalty of her subjects) they are all now shown more devoted in her service than could be hoped for, and there is not so much as one Catholic who did other than offer to venture his life and his goods to serve her.

Besides passing copies around his diplomatic colleagues, Sir Edward Stafford was determined 'to have the revenge of the Spanish ambassador, who set out lies and made them be cried so lively about the town', by publishing the Journal in print. The bald narrative was factual and convincing, and reads as if it had been hurriedly compiled by a Privy Council clerk from the file of naval despatches.

The final paragraph, containing some pardonable exaggerations of the strength of the English defences and of the loyalty of English Catholics, betrays the hand of Lord Burghley, who had in 1587 ordered all Catholics to surrender their arms.

Stafford, however, copied Mendoza's technique, and provided a preamble, 'A Letter from a Flemish merchant, a good Catholic, Apostolic and Roman, sent to a Spanish gentleman, Don Diego de Mandragon'. Apologizing for the delay in sending news from London, 'this country being surrounded by a ditch which may not be crossed without leave', the Flemish merchant regretted that he bwas too late to warn Don Mandragon about those false reports, so lightly published in France, which were now being mocked by the Lutherans in England. Not a single English ship had been lost, while the Spanish fleet was in flight, 'chased by our mortal enemies, who are never likely to give up until they have sent them on a pilgrimage to St Nicholas [Archangel] in Muscovy'. He wished Don Mandragon the blessings of all the saints in heaven, with whom at that moment was the soul of his friend Don Hugo de Moncada, the general of the galleasses, but not that of Don Pedro de Valdez, whose capture had served the triumph of the Lutherans.

COPIE D'VNE

LETTRE ENVOYEE
DE DIEPPE, SVR LA REN-
contre des armees d'Efpaigne &
d'Angleterre , & de la victoire
obtenue par les Efpagnols.

A PARIS,
Chez Guillaume Chaudiere, ruë S. Iaques, à l'en-
feigne du Temps, & de l'Homme fauuage.
M. D. LXXXVIII.
Auec permiſſion.

DISCOVRS

VERITABLES,

DE CE QVI S'EST
paſſé entre les deux armees de Mer
d'Angleterre & d'Efpaigne, depuis
le vendredy 29ᵉ. de Iuillet 1588 , iuf-
ques à l'onziefme du mois d'Aouft
de la mefme annee.

M. D. LXXXVIII.

The anonymous reply (right) by Sir Edward Stafford, the English ambassador in Paris, to Don Bernardin de Mendoza's published claim (left) of a Spanish victory. The dates are New Style

In a postscript he described the misery of Spanish prisoners brought in carts to Bridewell prison in London and put to forced labour. 'Please God that we did not first set this example in Spain, by sending their men to the galleys, to the Inquisition, and by letting them starve miserably to death in prison.'

Stafford bragged to Walsingham that he had arranged the printing personally (400 copies for 5 crowns) 'because I would have it covertly to touch home their impudency, yet I am not willing to have it known here other than to be a thing done by chance by somebody that had heard my news.'

Nobody was fooled. Mendoza saw the pamphlet as he paid another visit to Chartres, this time to ask the King to return the galleass and guns held by the governor of Calais. According to Stafford, the King laughed and was ready to wager that the pamphlet was the English ambassador's doing. According to Mendoza, the English bearer was driven angrily from Court.

3

Wild and contradictory tales continued to reach Paris of the fate of the Spanish and English fleets. From the Netherlands came a story of a great battle in the North Sea in which Drake had sunk fifteen Spanish ships. From Calais came a report of battered ships dumping mules and baggage into the sea. On 10 August Stafford told Walsingham of another Spanish galleon brought by the Dutch to Flushing and of a rumour, which he did not dare yet believe, of ten thousand Spaniards killed and most of their ships perished or taken.

Opinion in Paris, he thought, was swinging towards an English victory, 'for now they be here carried away with the falseness of the Spaniards' news and with the freshness of our good success, which they believe, they will as long as that humour lasteth make news run every day our side.'

Mendoza, on the other hand, wrote the same day to King Philip: 'The English ambassador here had some fancy news printed, stating that the English had been victorious, but the people would not allow it to be sold, as they say it is all lies.' He enclosed a despatch from one of his agents in England giving much more palatable news: On 3 August fifteen English ships had returned to port, from whom it was heard that the *San Martin*, the Duke of Medina Sidonia's flagship, had grappled with Drake's flagship and captured him, along with other English nobles and a further fifteen ships, besides doing damage to other ships. The Duke and the Armada had made their way to Scotland, whence they would return as soon as the wind was favourable. From this the King would see, remarked Mendoza complacently, that the Breton sailors were not telling lies about the fifteen English ships lost off the Isle of Wight.

Another of Mendoza's informants, who had left England on 2 August, said that the English had suffered heavy losses and that Drake had been wounded in the legs by a cannon-ball. Yet another report from London confirmed that Spanish prisoners had been paraded through the streets in carts in order to raise the morale of the terrified population. The Queen had retired to St James's Palace, where she was surrounded by a guard of 4,000 foot and 1,000 horse for her personal safety.

It was a good bundle of news, if not entirely consistent, and the Spanish ambassador felt his honour vindicated. When he had finished his despatch, he lit his bonfire in the courtyard of the embassy.

4

Mendoza's first despatch about the Spanish victory arrived at the Escorial on 8 August. That same day, King Philip wrote to his admiral, the Duke of Medina Sidonia, hoping that he would be able to follow up his victory. A few days later came the warning that the news was unreliable. The following week the King received Mendoza's second batch of despatches with the news of Drake's capture, but prudently decided to await further confirmation.

At last, on 26 August, a despatch arrived from the Armada itself, or at least from one of the Spaniards who had gone ashore at Calais. It gave a detailed report of the fighting in the English Channel and appeared to give adequate confirmation of the Armada's victory in the North Sea. Together with a summary of Mendoza's despatch about Drake's capture it was published as a broadside to be read out and posted in churches throughout Spain.

Relation of that which hath passed till this Day, the Twenty-sixth of August, 1588, till Three of the Clock in the Afternoon, known by the Relations and Advice come to his Majesty from the happy Fleet, whereof is General the Duke of Medina, in the Conquest of England.

That, upon the twentieth of July, without seeing any sail of the enemies in the sea, he came to the channel, six leagues from Plymouth, where understanding the enemies were, he gathered together and set in order all the fleet; and sailing, the twenty-second of July there was discovered some sails of the enemies, the which, the twenty-third day were numbered to be 60 sail, of which the Duke took the wind, and passed without any fight, although he presented the same to them. Howbeit, they began to shoot at the rearward, but the Duke, in the galleon San Martin, set the prow of his ship against the biggest of the enemies, the which, being succoured by twenty others, fled away. Of this fight and first encounter, there was sunk three galleasses and four mighty galleons of the Queen's; there was burnt of ours (by negligence of a gunner) the Admiral [flagship] of Oquendo, and the enemies took the chief ship of Don Pedro Valdez, which being entangled with some others under his charge, was left without tackle, and so near the enemies that she could not be succoured by others.

With this, our fleet seeing that the enemy, in every point, did fly from giving battle, they sailed with some calm weather, and the enemies after them, shooting always at the rearward, until the twenty-eighth, that our fleet anchored in the road of St John, betwixt Calais and Boulogne, nine miles from Dunkirk; and the enemies did the like, the nearest they could to England.

The night being approached, the enemies got up their anchors to get the wind, and not to suffer our ships to go out of the road to sea, because they had trimmed 8 ships of fire, which (with the current of the water) should have put themselves amongst our ships, to have burnt them. But my Lord the Duke, foreseeing the danger, prevented them, with commandment that the ships that were nearest should cut their cables and to take up the others with a readiness uncredible; and with this the enemies' pretence was hindered, . . . and with such good fortune, that if he had not done it, our army would have been in evil case; for in the very place which we left, there was shot off by them, out of those fiery ships, such fires and other engines, that were sufficient to burn the sea, much more ships, which are made of wood and pitch.

In this departure, the captain of the galleasses had a great mischance; for, getting up her anchor, a cable fell foul of her helm, that she could not follow the rest, which caused one of her sides to lie so high that her ordnance could not play; and so 25 pinnaces came and battered her; and withal this, if the mariners, soldiers, and rowers that were in her had not cast themselves into the sea, it is holden for certain that Don Hugo de Moncada had defended her, as he did until she came into Calais, where, at the entrance thereof, he was killed of two caliver shot. . . .

At this time, the Duke had a very frank wind, and the like had the Queen's fleet, and so they both passed by the sight of Dunkirk, insomuch as they on land knew the galleon San Martin and others, that went fighting with the English army: and in this order they went till the second of August.

Afterwards they write, That there came into Calais a ship which saith that the second day they did see the two fleets together in sight. Another, which came afterwards, said he had seen some ships spoiled and torn, and that amongst them, some of the crews had been saved in boats: which argueth that they were ships of the enemies', for that our men had no place to save themselves, nor there were none of them arrived into Flanders, which was their place of return.

Out of England was advice given, That on the third [of August] arrived fifteen of the Queen's ships and they said that the galleon San Martin, wherein my Lord the Duke is (whom God preserve) had encountered with Drake, and had grappled his ship, and captived his person, and other noble English men, and taken other fifteen ships, besides others that were distressed; and the Duke, with his fleet, followed his way to Scotland, because the wind was not come about.

With these news, his Majesty resteth very much contented, and caused them to be sent to the Empress, by the hands of Francisco Idiaquez, his secretary of estate.

One of Walsingham's informants later wrote how the news was received in Spain:

A month after the fleet did depart from the coast there came news from Don Bernardino that the Spaniards had gotten the victory, and it was my fortune to be at the reading of the letters in San Sebastian; and as they did read, some said of me, 'See how the dog looks at the news,' which was that the Lord Admiral and Sir Francis Drake was taken, with the loss of many of her Majesty's ships, that Plymouth was theirs, with the Wight, Hampton, and Portsmouth, and that they thought in a few days to be in London. The town made great feasts all that day, running through the streets on horseback, with rich apparel and vizards on their faces, crying with loud voices 'That great dog Francis Drake is prisoner, with chains and fetters' and at night the town was made full of bonfires, crying and shouting, with other their dances accustomed, reviling at her Majesty with villainous words; and when they could not do any more, with stones they brake down all the windows of my house.

But even while Spain was celebrating, King Philip received a disturbing despatch from the Duke of Parma: that he had arrived before dawn at Dunkirk on 29 July to find that the Armada had departed, pursued by the English, and that he could do nothing further until it returned.

5

In the rest of Catholic Europe, the pattern of news was much the same.

In Venice, on 17 August, the Doge and Senate, in consideration of the Spanish victory, decided by 186 votes to 1, with one abstention, to instruct all their ambassadors in Spanish provinces to convey their congratulations to the King of Spain. In Prague, on 20 August, the Spanish ambassador ordered a *Te Deum* to be sung in St Wenceslaus Cathedral; but a contradictory report of a Spanish defeat arrived from Antwerp almost immediately afterwards.

When the news of the victory arrived in Rome, Count Olivarez lost no time in seeking audience with the Pope. He demanded a special mass of thanksgiving in St Peter's and victory services in all the Roman churches. Cardinal Allen should be given his authority as papal legate and despatched immediately to the Netherlands to avoid any delay in his joining the Duke of Parma, who must by now be in England. The first instalment of the million gold ducats was now due.

The Pope replied that he was quite prepared to meet these demands if the news were correct, but pointed out that it came from only one source; he preferred to wait for independent confirmation. On 24 August the Pope remarked to the Venetian ambassador how providential it was that the Turks were occupied in the Persian war while the Armada of Spain was in English waters. 'The Queen of England' he said, 'has no need of the Turk to help her. Have you heard how Drake and his fleet have offered battle to the Armada? With what courage! Do you think he showed any fear? He is a great captain.' But he did add that he was intending to send 500,000 ducats to the King of Spain within fifteen days if the news of the successful invasion was confirmed.

As the days went by, more and more conflicting reports arrived in Rome, but no confirmation of a Spanish victory that would satisfy the Pope. Count Olivarez remained hopeful that the Armada was revictualling in Scotland and would soon return for the invasion of England. But on one of the Pasquil statues in Rome, someone put up a satirical notice:

1,000 YEARS' INDULGENCE

will be granted by the Pontiff out of his supreme authority to whomsoever gives him certain information of the whereabouts of the Spanish Armada.

Whither is it gone? Taken up into heaven or thrust down into hell? Suspended in air or floating somewhere on the sea?

CHAPTER EIGHT

A FAMOUS VICTORY

Her Royal ships to sea she sent,
    to guard the coast on every side:
And seeing how her foes were bent,
    her realm full well she did provide
With many thousands so prepared
    as like was never erst declared
Of horsemen and of footmen plenty,
    whose good hearts full well is seen
In the safeguard of their country
    and the service of our Queen.
        Thomas Deloney: *The Queen's visiting of the Camp at Tilsbury*

1

It is time to return to the events of Sunday 28 July when the English fleet lay at anchor off Calais, just over a cannon-shot from the Spanish Armada. The Spanish fleet was drawn up with the larger, fighting ships on the seaward side, protecting the hulks and smaller ships nearer the shore. 'Huge castles' they must have seemed to the courtiers who had joined the Queen's ships and who were later to recount their adventures.

Lord Henry Seymour with the eastern squadron, impatient with conflicting orders from London, had now joined Howard and Drake with the western fleet. Other small craft had joined at various stages during the journey up the Channel, including fourteen Huguenot ships from La Rochelle. The Dutch fleet was conspicuously absent, despite messages calling them to come out. Nevertheless, there were now nearly two hundred sail on the English side. The English could see boats plying between the Spanish fleet and Calais and readily assumed that the perfidious French, far from upholding the alliance, were aiding their enemies with supplies of ammunition and victuals.

Fire-ships, already prepared in Dover for just this contingency, were sent for, but before they arrived the English commanders decided that time, tide and the wind could not wait for them. Eight old ships were nominated to 'volunteer' and hurriedly stuffed with pitch and tinder. Either through haste or by intention, the guns were left on board, some of them loaded. Shortly after midnight they were towed towards the Spanish fleet, set on fire, and left to drift with the wind on the incoming tide. The Duke of Medina Sidonia was prepared for them. Spanish pinnaces were quickly sent out to intercept the blazing fire-ships and towed two of them out of harm's way.

Suddenly, the guns left on one of the remaining fire-ships exploded. A signal shot was fired from the Spanish admiral's flagship and the sounds of frenzied activity came across the water.

Next morning, the English saw the eight burned-out hulks of their fire-ships on the Calais shore. Not a single Spanish galleon had been set on fire, though one huge galleass had been run aground, just below the governor's castle at the entrance to Calais harbour. The rest of the Armada had escaped clean away and was resuming its defensive, crescent formation a little further along the coast. Drake's sharp eyes noticed that the Spaniards had cut the cables of their anchors in their haste.

Drake and Seymour quickly moved in with their own squadrons to engage the Spanish fleet before it could reorganize. But the Lord Admiral sent a longboat, soon joined by other small craft, and waited while a boarding party attacked the stranded galleass. No doubt he had heard of the criticism at Court of his failure to board and capture a Spanish ship.

The galleass lay on its side, its useless guns pointing to the sky. As the English swarmed aboard, the crew put up a stout resistance until their captain, Don Hugo de Moncada, was killed by a musket shot in the face. Some of the galley slaves and crew escaped ashore, while the remainder surrendered, leaving the English to pillage their ship. The English had started to remove the guns when M. Gourdan, watching the scene from his castle just above, decided that it was time to intervene. The galleass was on French soil and therefore not a legitimate English prize. He fired some warning shots on the ship until the English withdrew in disgust. It was at this point

The storming of the grounded galleass outside Calais harbour, as depicted in a tapestry later commissioned by the Lord Admiral

that Lord Howard and his flagship the *Ark Royal* at last left the sideshow and joined the rest of his fleet, who by now were heavily engaged with the Spaniards off the coast at Gravelines.

But the boarding of the galleass far outshone any previous exploits when the news reached England. This was real fighting, with Englishman and Spaniard face to face with cold steel. The story became a little garbled – the Spaniards supposedly putting up a flag of truce and then treacherously firing on the boarding party,

> Which when our men,
> perceived so to be,
> Like Lions fierce they forward went
> to quite this injury.
> And boarding them,
> with strong and mighty hand,
> They killed the men until their Ark
> did sink in Calais sand.

Those who took part in the sea battle off Gravelines were almost equally confused about what was happening. But its outcome had been decided when M. Gourdan refused to provide the Spanish Armada with munitions or shelter. For the first time, the English ships moved in close enough to do real damage with their broadsides. Only once did they attempt to board, without success. The Spaniards more frequently, but with equally little success, tried to grapple, their standard means of attack. But they were short of powder and unprepared for the English hit and run tactics. Much of their 123,790 cannon-balls lay useless. Many ships could only reply with smallshot.

One sinking Spanish galleon drifted ashore between Nieuport and Ostend; pinnaces from Spanish-held Nieuport rescued the crew before the Zealanders arrived to tow the ship to Flushing. Another galleon ran aground between Ostend and Sluys; after a two hour battle, it was captured by the Dutch, who butchered or threw overboard all the crew except the ransomworthy captain, Don Pimentel. At sunset, the *Maria Juan* sank from the effects of gunfire with 275 men still on board. These were the only Spanish ships certainly seen to be lost, a total of only six since Plymouth. The Armada was still a formidable force.

Late that night, Howard wrote to Walsingham:

Ever since [Calais] we have chased them in fight until this evening late, and distressed them much; but their fleet consisteth of mighty ships and great strength; yet we doubt not by God's good assistance, to oppress them. I will not write unto her Majesty before more be done. Their force is wonderful great and strong; and yet we pluck their feathers by little and little. I pray to God that the forces on land be strong enough to answer so present a force. There is not one Flushinger nor Hollander at the seas.

On the following morning, the English found the Armada, back in its defensive formation, being driven slowly by a north-westerly wind towards the sandbanks of

Zealand. The English, having powder and shot for less than two hours' fighting, kept their distance. Many of the Spanish fighting ships had no shot at all and no anchors; their crews and commanders could only pray.

Their prayers were answered. The wind suddenly shifted from north-west to south-west, just enough for them to escape to the open waters of the North Sea. The English commanders hurriedly wrote their despatches and prepared to follow the Armada north.

Sir Francis Drake, putting ashore his prize prisoner, Don Pedro de Valdez, wrote with his usual confidence, but with not a hint that the opportunity for a decisive victory had passed:

> There was never anything pleased me better than seeing the enemy flying with a southerly wind to the northwards. God grant you have a good eye to the Duke of Parma; for with the grace of God, if we live, I doubt it not but ere long so to handle the matter with the Duke of Sidonia as he shall wish himself at St Mary Port among his orange trees.

Sir John Hawkins (who had been knighted by the Lord Admiral between battles in the Channel) calmly assessed the outcome of the future battle:

> Our ships, God be thanked, have received little hurt, and are . . . of such advantage that . . . sufficiently provided of shot and powder, we shall be able, with God's favour, to weary them out of the sea and confound them. Yet, as I gather certainly, there are amongst them 50 forcible and invincible ships, . . . 30 hulks, and 30 other small ships whereof little account is to be made.

2

It was two days later, on Thursday 1 August, before London knew that the Spanish fleet had been driven from the Narrow Seas and was being chased north by the Lord Admiral and Sir Francis Drake. Their last message came in a letter which Drake sent to Walsingham by pinnace from just east of Great Yarmouth:

> God has given us so good a day in forcing the enemy so far to leeward as I hope in God the Prince of Parma and the Duke of Sidonia shall not shake hands this few days; and whensoever they shall meet, I believe neither of them will greatly rejoice of this day's service. The town of Calais has seen some part thereof, whose Mayor [M. Gourdan] her Majesty is beholden unto.

Lord Henry Seymour, to his intense disgust, was left behind with four Queen's ships and some coastal and fishing-boats to guard the Narrow Seas in case the Duke of Parma should venture forth from Sluys and Dunkirk. Convinced that Howard and Drake were trying to steal all the glory, he sent a furious letter to the Queen signed 'your Majesty's most bounden and faithful fisherman'. The Privy Council had to advise him that the Lord Admiral's order for him to stay behind was at the Queen's express command.

The Privy Council's more pressing concern was to prevent a Spanish landing in the north of England, where Catholic sympathy was suspected to be widespread. Moreover the King of Scots was still an unknown quantity. Reinforcements from the Midlands were sent to the Earl of Huntingdon, the Lord President of the North. Supplies of powder and shot were hurried to Newcastle for the English fleet to pick up. Word was sent to King James VI that the northern armies were ready to come to his aid to repulse the Spaniards; he was left to guess what they would do if he neglected to keep the Spaniards from landing.

The Queen, meanwhile, had her own priorities. She wrote to M. Gourdan, the governor of Calais, demanding the return of the galleass bought with English blood, or at the very least the guns. The English navy had had little success so far in bringing her prizes and plunder to meet her mounting expenses.

London continued to be prepared for a state of siege, an invasion by the Duke of Parma being still thought imminent. Householders were forbidden to leave the city, on the Queen's orders, in case their services were required. To entertain the population, the new batch of Spanish prisoners, including Vice-Admiral Don Pedro de Valdez, were brought openly through the streets in carts on their way to prison. Prisoners 'of quality' were lodged in merchants' houses, while any citizen of London with a friend, relative or servant in Spanish hands was invited to apply for a Spanish prisoner who could be exchanged or ransomed.

There were bonfires, dancing, ringing of handbells, firing of guns and processions to celebrate the victory at sea. Soldiers continued to pass through London on the way to the camp at Tilbury. The trained bands practised arms drill at their musters. A contemporary play suggests that such activity was not without an eye to the enemy:

> Myself will muster upon Mile-End Green,
> As though we saw, and fear'd not to be seen;
> Which will their spies in such a wonder set,
> To see us reck so little such a foe,
> Whom all the world admires, save only we.

Life in the country was quieter, but not without anxiety. Richard Rogers wrote in his diary for 4 August:

> And it shameth me that I should be trifling out my time thus, while the troubles are so great as we are every day and hour fearing them coming upon us . . . Oh the cheerfulness and courage in teaching that which I have been able, and now I feel little ability to stir up either our selves or the soldiers, to whom I would go if I felt meet to do them good.

Despite the fears of her people and to the dismay of her military advisers, the Queen had already decided that the emergency was over and that the drain on her financial resources must be stopped. On 3 August calling up further musters in southern England was halted, while on 5 August the Earl of Leicester was ordered to send home a third of the foot-soldiers at Tilbury, as soon as he thought fit.

Leicester was in no hurry to discharge any of his soldiers, despite the expense to the Queen. For the Queen had finally accepted his invitation to visit his camp, to the great alarm of her Privy Council, who did their best to dissuade her. Sir Francis Walsingham determined to go along and keep an eye on things while she was at Tilbury, and meanwhile sent a messenger with a note to the Earl of Leicester:

> My very good Lord, the trustiness of this gentleman maketh me the shorter. How we like of the Queen's repair to the camp, he will tell you, and what doubts are made of misadventure that may fall out. I have let him understand what I hear. . . .
> From the Lord admiral we hear nothing. The last messenger that came from thence doth assure me that the Duke of Sidonia hath but 86 sail left. I mean to steal to the camp when Her Majesty shall be there. And so in the mean time I most humbly take my leave.
> At the Court, the 6th August, 1588.
> Your Lordship's to command, Ffr. Walsingham

3

The following Thursday the weather was cold and stormy, as it seemed to have been for the whole of the past summer. Nevertheless the Queen rode with her Court from St James's Palace to the covered quay at White Hall known as the Privy Bridge. As she embarked in the royal barge, the bells of St Margaret's, Westminster, rang out and were answered by those of Lambeth across the river.

The churches of London joined in with their bells as the procession of barges made its way down river to London Bridge. There was no excuse for any Londoner not to know that his Queen was on her way to visit her camp at Tilbury. The crowds watching from the banks, the bridge, or the boats of the Thames watermen heard the trumpets sounding and the drums drubbing as the oars of the royal bargemen clove the water in unison. Representatives of the popular press were there to cover her visit (both referring to the camp at Tilsbury):

> On Thursday the eight of August last
> Her Majesty by water passed
> When storms of wind did blow so fast
>   Would fear some folk in England;   [frighten]
> And at her fort she went on land
> That near to Tilsbury strong doth stand
> Where all things furnished there she fand
>   For the safe defence of England.

To the roar of cannon fired in salute, she landed at Tilbury fort, opposite Gravesend, where a bridge of boats was being constructed so that the army could move quickly from Essex to Kent. She was greeted by a mounted escort and provided with a horse to take her up the causeway that led to the camp at West Tilbury, two miles away.

All the way her Grace was riding,
   on each side stood armed men,
With Muskets, Pikes and good Caleevers
   for her Grace's safeguard then.

She was accompanied by her Lord General, the Earl of Leicester, and her Lord Marshal, Sir John Norris, each with a standard bearer displaying a tattered ensign which had seen service in Flanders. As the procession approached the camp, the soldiers lining the route began to fall on their knees, according to custom in the presence of the Sovereign,

   desiring God to save her Grace:
For joy whereof her eyes was filled,
   that the water down distilled.
'Lord bless you all, my friends,' she said,
   'but do not kneel so much to me.'
And then sent warning to the rest
   they should not let such reverence be.

So every man stood up for a good sight of the Queen as she rode through the camp, wearing a tall head-dress of nodding plumes.

One of the first people to greet her in the camp was the Earl of Cumberland with news from the fleet. Together with Robert Carey, he had taken a fast pinnace to Harwich and then ridden by post horse to Tilbury. His news was not encouraging. Finding that they had scarcely enough powder and shot for an hour's fighting, the English fleet had followed the Armada at a safe distance as far north as the Firth of Forth. The Spaniards had then sheered off to the north-east, towards Denmark or Norway. The English had been driven south by sudden storms which gave them no opportunity to take on food or water in Scotland. The fleet was now scattered in various ports, in dire need of repairs, and the crews were suffering from cold and hunger. Only Lord Seymour's ships remained between England and the Duke of Parma, for the Dutch had been driven to shelter by the same storms.

After all his difficulties of the past two weeks, the Earl of Leicester could at least claim that his camp was now in good order. Although some of his soldiers from neighbouring areas had been sent home, there were still nearly ten thousand men in the camp, with a further thousand or two horse:

   Of tents and cabins thousands three,
   Some built with boughs and many a tree,
   And many of canvas she might see
      In Tilsbury camp in England.

   Each captain had his colours brave
   Set over his tent in wind to wave;

> With them their officers there they have
>   To serve the Queen of England.
> The other lodgings had their sign
> For soldiers where to sup and dine,
> And for to sleep, with orders fine
>   In Tilsbury camp in England.
> And victualling booths in plenty were,
> Where they sold meat, bread, cheese, and beer;
> One should have been hang'd for selling too dear
>   In Tilsbury camp in England.

The last was no idle threat. The Queen had issued a proclamation the previous day fixing maximum prices 'of grain, victuals, horse meat, lodgings and other things' to any of her soldiers within twenty miles of Court. A few examples:

a full quart of good single ale or beer	½d.
a pound of best fresh butter	3d.
a pound of good Essex or Suffolk cheese	1½d.
Seven best eggs in market	2d.
8 lb of best beef	12d.
a couple of best chickens or rabbits	8d.

A soldier's pay was 8d. a day, out of which he had to find his keep. An adequate dinner or supper of 'good wheaten bread and drink, beef, mutton or veal boiled, and pig, beef, mutton, veal or lamb roasted' would cost him up to 3d. Lodging for the night, with a feather bed, would cost him a penny, but hay and litter for his horse, if he had one, would be 3d. for a day and a night, or 3½d. at an inn. The main grumble was not so much prices as lack of pay. The money was distributed to the captains, but some of them were slow to pass it on to their men.

The Queen's lodging for the night had been arranged for her at the house of a country gentleman (one of the influential local Rich family) some three miles from the camp. Most of her Court who travelled with her presumably found accommodation in the camp itself. Those who accompanied the Queen on progress were used to living in tents.

Next morning there was an early start to preparations for the Queen's formal review of her army:

> The captains early did prepare
> To have their battle set out fair
> Against her Highness' coming there,
>   To Tilsbury camp in England.
> And long before her Highness came,
> Each point was ordered so in frame
>   Of a royal camp in England.

When all was ready, the Queen arrived in full state to be greeted by the Earl of Leicester 'with his guard of yeoman tall'. A sergeant bearing the mace led the procession, followed by nine trumpeters in scarlet coats, a herald bearing the arms of England embroidered in gold on blue and crimson velvet, two sergeants on horseback in velvet coats with gold chains and bearing gold maces, and then the Earl of Leicester and Sir John Norris, riding side by side, carrying their plumed hats in their hands in the presence of the Queen. The onlookers can rarely have seen such important personages bareheaded, and the ballad writer thought it worthy of note.

> Then came the Queen on prancing steed,
>   attired like an Angel bright:
> And eight brave footmen at her feet,
>   whose Jerkins were most rich in sight.
> Her Ladies likewise, of great honour,
> Most sumptuously did wait upon her,
> With pearls and diamonds brave adorned,
>   and in costly cales of gold.   [cowls]
> Her Guard in scarlet then rid after,
>   with bows and arrows stout and bold.

The proceedings began with a mock battle in which each unit was able to demonstrate its prowess in manoeuvre and with pike, lance, musket, caliver, longbow or arquebus. Then there was a march past of all the troops.

> How they came marching all together,
> Like a wood in winter's weather:
> With the strokes of drummers sounding
>   and with trampling horses than   [then]
> The earth and air did sound like thunder
>   to the ears of every man.

At the end of the review, as the army 'stood still, and drummers left their drubbing sound', the Queen did something entirely unexpected.

> Her Ladies she did leave behind her
> And her Guard which still did mind her:
> The Lord general and Lord marshal
>   did conduct her to each place.

With this tiny escort, the Queen rode among the throng of pikemen, bowmen, lancers and musketeers.

> And many a Captain kissed her hand,
> As she passed forth through every band,

> And left her train far off to stand
> From the martial men of England.

For two hours she rode through her army, visiting every quarter of the camp. It was then that she delivered her most famous speech, perhaps many times:

> My loving people, we have been persuaded by some that are careful of our safety, to take heed how we commit our self to armed multitudes for fear of Treachery; but I assure you, I do not desire to live to distrust my faithful and loving people. Let Tyrants fear, I have always so behaved my self, that under God I have placed my chiefest strength, and safeguard in the loyal hearts and good will of my subjects. And therefore I am come amongst you as you see, at this time, not for my recreation, and disport, but being resolved in the midst, and heat of the battle to live, or die amongst you all, to lay down for my God, and for my kingdom, and for my people, my Honour, and my blood even in the Dust. I know that I have the body, but of a weak and feeble woman, but I have the heart and Stomach of a King, and of a King of England too, and think foul scorn that Parma or Spain, or any Prince of Europe should dare invade the borders of my Realm, to which rather than any dishonour shall grow by me, I my self will take up arms, I my self will be your General, Judge, and Rewarder of every one of your virtues in the field. I know already for your forwardness, you have deserved rewards and crowns, and we do assure you in the word of a Prince, they shall be duly paid you. In the mean time my Lieutenant General shall be in my stead, than whom never Prince commanded a more Noble or worthy subject, not doubting but by your obedience to my General, by your Concord in the Camp, and your valour in the field, we shall shortly have a famous victory over those enemies of my God, of my Kingdom, and of my People.

One ballad writer's version perhaps indicates what was most remarked at the time, the promises about pay:

> What princely words her grace declared,
> What gracious thanks in every ward,
> To every soldier, none she spared
>   That served anywhere for England.
> With princely promise none should lack
> Meat and drink or cloth for back,
> Gold or silver should not slack
>   To her martial men of England.
> Then might she see the hats to fly,
> And every soldier shouted high,
> 'For our good Queen we'll fight or die
>   On any foe to England.'

Allowing for the constraints of his medium, the other ballad writer, Thomas Deloney, seems to have been a reasonably accurate reporter:

> And then bespake our noble Queen,
>   my loving friends and countrymen:
> I hope this day the worst is seen,
>   that in our wars ye shall sustain.
> But if our enemies do assail you,
>   never let your stomachs fail you.
> For in the midst of all your troupe
>   we our selves will be in place:
> To be your joy, your guide and comfort,
>   even before your enemy's face.

At noon the Queen returned to her Lord General's tent for dinner. A number of fresh despatches from the fleet awaited her, but there was little fresh news. The commanders unanimously blamed lack of powder and shot for their failure to defeat the Armada decisively but had no idea where it had gone or when it would return. Drake thought to Denmark and urged the Queen to send someone there — superfluously, for Thomas Bodley had been despatched to Denmark the previous week.

More agreeable news was that the peace commissioners had arrived back in Dover, having been given safe conduct by the chivalrous Duke of Parma. They knew nothing about the Duke's immediate plans. But the thousand veteran shot, summoned from the Netherlands two weeks before, had arrived in Margate, and their commander, Sir Thomas Morgan, warned that the Duke of Parma had gathered an army of 50,000 foot and 5,000 horse and was expected to come out for the invasion on the next spring tide, when the Armada would return to protect their crossing.

This gave the Queen 'a conceit,' Walsingham wrote to Burghley, 'that in honour she could not return, in case there was any likelihood that the enemy would attempt anything. Thus your Lordship seeth that this place breeds courage.' Nevertheless, the Queen was prevailed upon to return to St James. The Lord Admiral and Lord General were both to attend a Privy Council meeting the following Sunday to discuss demobilization. Clearly the Queen did not take the danger from Parma very seriously.

Before she left, she handed Leicester a copy of her speech to her soldiers with instructions that it should be read again to the army the following day; the instructions were carried out by one of Leicester's chaplains, Dr Leonel Sharpe, to whom we owe the preservation of her speech.

The Queen embarked in the royal barge at Tilbury fort in the early evening, as the tide was turning to help her passage upriver.

> And when that she was safely set
>   within her Barge, and passed away,
> Her farewell then the trumpets sounded,
>   and the cannons fast did play.

She did not return to St James that night, but stopped at Erith, where lodging had been arranged. She travelled the following morning overland to Greenwich, then to

Lambeth, where she was ferried across the river to Westminster on her way to St James. But the two ballad writers must have returned to London immediately, for their ballads were both entered in the Stationers Register the following day.

Another visitor to Tilbury was Richard Rogers of Wethersfield, who had finally stirred himself from his lethargy to go and preach to the soldiers. He wrote in his diary of 13 August:

> If any thing may be fit to stir up to the continual and earnest meditation of a godly life, this may: that we are now in peril of goods, liberty, life, by our enemies the Spaniards, and at home papists in multitudes ready to come upon us unawares. For my part I am so readily persuaded that God will visit us some way, that if he should not by some universal calamity sweep us away, I protest that I should be in a most woeful case if I should not recover myself better than here of late.

He then went on to describe a visit he had made to a military camp. But alas! the corner of the page has been torn away, and only a few tantalizing scraps of words, like 'her Majesty', remain to indicate the time and place of his visit.

4

Lord Burghley visited the camp at Tilbury the week after the Queen. He had been unable to come at the same time because he had been busy raising the 'rewards and crowns' for the troops by levying forced loans on the London livery companies.

The Earl of Leicester put on a good show for him, which he felt made a good impression. Dr Leonel Sharpe, the chaplain, recalling the occasion thirty years later, confused it with the Queen's visit of the week before, but he is unlikely to have invented the part he was called upon to play.

He remembered how 'the old treasurer Burghley came thither, and delivered to the Earl of Leicester the examination of Don Pedro [de Valdez], who was taken and brought in by Sir Francis Drake, which examination the Earl of Leicester delivered unto me, to publish to the army in my next sermon.'

Don Pedro, being asked the intentions of the Spaniards, was said to have replied: 'What, but to subdue your nation and root it out.'

What did they mean to do with the Catholics? 'We meant to send them (good men) directly to heaven, as all you that are heretics to hell.'

And what was the purpose of the whips of cord and wire, of which great quantities had been found in their ships? 'What? we meant to whip you heretics to death, that have assisted my master's rebels, and done such dishonour to our Catholic king and people.'

But what would they have done with the young children? 'They which were above seven years old should have gone the way their fathers went; the rest should have lived, branded in the forehead with the letter *L*, for *Lutheran*, to perpetual bondage.'

The official record of the interrogation of Don Pedro de Valdez shows him to have been the soul of discretion, who knew nothing of the King of Spain's intentions; he was only a soldier obeying orders. But Burghley's more imaginative version gave new life to a rumour which had already spread from England to the Netherlands three weeks before. Leonel Sharpe was not the only preacher to take it up, as Petruccio Ubaldini recorded:

As in those days news was spread (and perhaps not by chance in London, for preachers in several churches discussed the matter extensively), which served to incite even further the feelings of the English people. These preachers, in public sermons, stated that the Spaniards were carrying a large number of women of every kind, and together with this report was spread the rumour that in the Spanish ships there were many instruments of torture with which to afflict the English people. These things being easily believed, the whole of the lowest and most credulous part of the people were moved to a mortal and dangerous hatred against all foreigners living there.

The Duke of Medina Sidonia's orders to the Armada had in fact expressly forbidden women to be taken on board in such a holy enterprise. Such an unusual deprivation in fleets at the time seems to have given rise to sailors' comment. The result was a fanciful story that a number of patriotic Spanish women had chartered a ship to follow their menfolk in the Armada, but the ship had been wrecked in France. The story sounds French. A later rationalization explained that the Armada was carrying three or four thousand wetnurses to suckle the infants remaining after the English men and women between seven and seventy had been rooted out.

Such stories, as Ubaldini himself realized, were not necessarily taken seriously but helped to relieve anxiety, and 'must be classified as a piece of pleasant entertainment or rather vain boasting of the enemy, used only among the lower soldiers as a joke without much thought'.

The cargoes of whips and halters, consistent with stories of Spanish atrocities in the Indies and at the sack of Antwerp, became a popular theme not only in England but also in the Netherlands, where Dutch printers were bringing out new editions of the *True Relation* of the fleet assembled in Lisbon, adding instruments of torture to the lists of pikes and arquebusses. In London, Thomas Deloney elaborated on the theme in a ballad published late in August:

> One sort of whips they had for men,
>   so smarting fierce and fell:
> As like could never be devis'd
>   by any devil in hell.
> The strings whereof with wiry knots,
>   like rowels they did frame,   [spurs]
> That every stroke might tear the flesh
>   they laid on with the same.
> And pluck the spreading sinews from
>   the hardened bloody bone,
> To prick and pierce each tender vein,
>   within the body known.

¶A new Ballet of the straunge and most cruell Whippes

which the Spanyards had prepared to whippe and torment English men and women:

which were found and taken at the ouerthrow of certaine of the Spanish Shippes
in Iuly last past. 1588. To the tune of the valiant Soldiour.

K. D. 7.

Whippes for the women.

Whippes for the men.

AL you that list to looke and see
what profite comes from Spayne,
And what the Pope and Spanyards both,
prepared for our gayne.
Then turne your eyes and bend your eares,
and you shall heare and see,
What courteous minds, what gentle harts
they beare to thee and mee.

They say they seeke for Englands good,
and wish the people well:
They say they are such holie men,
all other they excell:
They bragge that they are Catholikes,
and Christes only Spouse:
And what so ere they take in hand,
the holie Pope allowes.

These holie men, these sacred Saints,
and these that thinke no ill:
See how they sought against all right,
to murder, spoyle and kill.
Our noble Queene and Countrie first,
they did prepare to spoyle:
To ruinate our liues and lands,
with trouble and turmoyle.

And not content by fire and sword
to take our right away:
But to torment most cruelly
our bodies night and day.
Although they ment with murdring hands
our guiltlesse bloud to spill:
Before our deathes they did deuise
to whip vs first their fill.

And for that purpose had preparde
of whips such wondrous store,
So straungely made, that sure the like
was neuer seene before.

For neuer was there Horse nor Mule,
nor dogge of currish kinde,
That euer had such whips deuisde
by any sauadge minde.

One sorte of whips they had for men,
so smarting fierce and fell:
As like could neuer be deuisde
by any deuill in hell.
The strings whereof with wyerie knots,
like towels they did frame,
That euery stroke might teare the flesh
they layd on with the same.

And pluckt the spreading sinewes from
the hardned bloudie bone,
To pricke and pearce each tender veine,
within the bodie knowne.
And not to leaue one crooked ribbe,
on any side vnseene:
Nor yet to leaue a lumpe of flesh
the head and foote betweene.

And for our seelie women eke,
their hearts with griefe to clogge,
They made such whips wherewith no man
would seeme to strike a dogge:
So strengthned eke with brasen tagges,
and filde so rough, and thin
That they would force at euery lash
the bloud abroad to spinne.

Although their bodies sweet and fayre,
their spoyle they ment to make:
And on them first their filthie lust
and pleasure for to take.
Yet afterward such sower sauce
they should be sure to finde,
That they shoulde curse each springing
that cometh of their kinde. (braunch

O Ladies fayre what spite were this,
your gentle hearts to kill:
To see these deuilish tyrants thus
your childrens bloud to spill.
What griefe vnto the husband deere,
his louing wife to see
Tormented so before his face
with extreame villanie.

And thinke you not that they which had
such dogged mindes to make
Such instruments of tyrannie,
had not like hearts to take
The greatest vengeance that they might
vpon vs euery one?
Yes, yes, be sure, for godlie feare
and mercie they haue none.

Euen as in India once they did
against those people there,
With cruell Curres in shamefull sorte
the men both rent and teare:

And set the Ladies great with childe
vpright against a tree,
And shoot the through with pearcing darts,
such would their practise bee.

Did not the Romans in this land,
sometime like practise vse,
Against the Brittaines bolde in heart,
and wonderously abuse
The valiant king whom they had caught
before his Queene and wife,
And with most extreame tyrannie
dispatcht him of his life?

The good Queene Voadicia,
and eke her daughters three:
Did they not first abuse them all
by lust and lecherie:
And after stript them naked all,
and whipt them in such sorte:
That it would grieue each Christian heart
to heare that iust reporte.

And if these ruffling mates of Rome
did Princes thus torment:
Thinke you the Romish Spanyards now
would not shewe their desent.
How did they late in Rome reioyce,
in Italie and Spayne:
What ringing and what Bonfires,
what Masses sung amaine.

What printed Bookes were sent about,
as filled their desire:
How England was by Spanyards wonne,
and London set on fire.
Be these the men that are so milde,
whom some so holie call:
The Lord defend our noble Queene,
and Countrie from them all.

FINIS. T.D.

Imprinted at London by Thomas Orwin and Thomas Gubbin, and are to be solde in Paternoster-row, ouer against the blacke Rauen. 1588.

And for our seely women eke,
   their hearts with grief to clog,
They made such whips wherewith no man
   would seem to strike a dog:
So strengthened eke with brazen tags,
   and fil'd so rough and thin,
That they would force at every lash
   the blood abroad to spin.

Although their bodies sweet and fair
   their spoil they meant to make:
And on them first their filthy lust
   and pleasure for to take.

One of Mendoza's more reliable informants in London who enclosed two ballads with his despatch, which were duly forwarded to the Escorial in Spain, commented: 'This is the reason these people are so enraged with the Spaniards. Their anger would certainly be justified if the above and similar things were true.'

5

While her subjects entertained each other in these various ways, the Queen and her Privy Council were grappling with the cost of maintaining the armed forces. Lord Burghley had managed to raise £29,000 from the livery companies, but it was costing over £13,000 a month to maintain the navy while the armies at Tilbury and in Kent cost nearly £5,500 a week.

The Lord Admiral's hands were full with another problem. His crews were falling victim to a mysterious disease which spread rapidly through the fleet. When the sailors sought shelter on shore, the people shut their doors to them, fearing plague. The captains blamed it on bad beer, which may not have been far from the truth, for England had not generally adopted the Dutch practice of preserving beer with hops, and it soon turned sour, causing dysentery.

Most of the sailors had been continuously at sea for a month. Some of the ships in Plymouth had only been provisioned for two days. When taking on supplies from shore, priority had been given for powder and shot. Then after their return to port the crews had been confined to their ships, perhaps for reasons of security, perhaps to refit them, or perhaps to prevent desertions. The combination of exposure, hunger and confinement is sufficient to explain a sickness that does not seem to have affected their captains, and not so much Lord Henry Seymour's squadron. Howard wrote of men sickening one day and dying the next. Replacements had to be found for as much as two-thirds of the crews. In the meantime there was hardly a ship which could put to sea should the Armada return. Yet not a hint of this disaster seems to have reached the ears of Mendoza's agents in England. Security at the ports was very strict.

Nevertheless, both the Lord Admiral and the Earl of Leicester felt that the navy and army should be kept in a state of readiness. The Queen and Lord Burghley thought that the question of cost was paramount. Moreover there was the problem of the harvest, which though late through the unseasonable weather, required the temporary soldiers to return to their fields if England were not to starve during the winter. These two factors were decisive. The navy was to be gradually run down by releasing the merchant ships from service. Tilbury camp was to be reduced from 16,500 men to 6,000.

Nothing had been heard from the Armada for three weeks and it was assumed to be sailing around Scotland on its way back to Spain. It was decided that there had been a famous victory after all. On Tuesday 20 August the members of the Privy Council, though not the Queen, rode in state to St Paul's Cathedral. There, in the presence of the Lord Mayor and aldermen of the city of London and of all the London companies in their best livery, they heard a sermon preached at Paul's Cross by the Dean, Dr Nowell, 'and every man praised God for our delivery from the Spaniards and driving them out of the narrow seas.'

CHAPTER NINE

THE TRUE FRUITS OF
PEACE AND WAR

Therefore good worthy Drake,
  serve thou thy sovereign Queen,
And make the Spanish foe to quake,
  and English force be seen
For help and aid thou shall not want
  thy virtuous queen is bent,
Money and victuals is not scant,
  and men will not repent.
If thou wilt follow victory,
  as first thou didst begin:
All Protestants will pray for thee,
  and for our gracious Queen.

David Gwynn: *Certain English verses presented to*
the Queen's most excellent Majesty in the park of
St James, on Sunday the 18th of August 1588

1

While the Armada was going about the north of Scotland, at least the Privy Council felt no cause to worry about the conduct of the King of Scots. William Ashley had not had an easy time, however, since he arrived in Edinburgh as English ambassador. At his first audience, on 24 July, King James had made it plain that he expected more than fair promises from the Queen of England and had even hinted that he could do better by accepting Spanish offers. When the news of the Armada's arrival in the English Channel reached Edinburgh, after ten days on 29 July, Ashley felt bound 'to make such offers as follow to satisfy his Majesty for the time and to qualify the minds of the nobility to keep all in quiet whilst her Majesty and her council resolve what is to be done'. His offers in fact amounted to all the King's demands: an English duchy with appropriate revenues, a pension of £5,000 a year, a royal guard of fifty gentlemen maintained at the Queen's expense, and a company of a hundred foot and a hundred horse maintained at the border, also at her expense. He was able to avoid making any promises about the succession.

On 1 August, a day before the Armada arrived off the Scottish coast, the King wrote to Queen Elizabeth:

Madame and dearest sister,

In times of straits true friends are best tried . . . and so this time must move me to utter my zeal to the religion, and how near a kinsman and neighbour I find myself to you and your country. For this effect then I have sent you this present, hereby to offer unto you my forces, my person, and all that I may command, to be employed against yon strangers in whatsomever façon, and by whatsomever mean, as may best serve for the defence of your country.

On 5 August he ordered Scotland to repel invasion in a proclamation read at market crosses throughout the country.

After the Armada had departed, Sir Francis Walsingham sent a letter sternly reproving Ashley for having exceeded his authority in the promises he had made. But this was probably intended as something to show the King to explain Ashley's impending recall. A week later, after his recall was confirmed, Walsingham informed Ashley that the Queen had forgiven him, recognizing that he had acted only from excessive zeal. In the meantime a replacement was on his way in the person of Sir Robert Sidney, younger brother of Sir Philip and a nephew of the Earl of Leicester.

An early illustration of the fighting in the Channel, by a Dutch engraver

The Queen prepared the ground carefully in the letter which the new young ambassador took with him:

> To my very good brother the king of Scots,
> Now may appear, dear brother, how malice conjoined with might strivest to make a shameful end to a villainous beginning, for, by God's singular favour, having their fleet well beaten in our narrow seas, and pressing, with all violence, to achieve some watering place, to continue their pretended invasion, the winds have carried them to your coasts, where I doubt not that they shall receive small succour and less welcome, unless those [Catholic] lords, that, so traitors like, would belie their own prince, and promise another king relief in your name, to be suffered to live at liberty, to dishonour you, peril you, and advance some other (which God forbid you suffer them leave to do). Therefore I send you this gentleman, a rare young man and a wise, to declare unto you my full opinion in this great cause . . . You may assure yourself that, for my part, I doubt no whit that all this tyrannical proud and brainsick attempt will be the beginning, though not the end, of the ruin of that king, that, most unkindly, even in the midst of treating peace, begins this wrongful war.

The Queen well knew that King James's hopes of succession to the throne of England weighed more heavily than pensions, dukedoms, or armed retainers. She hinted gently: 'if by leaving them [the Spaniards] unhelped, you may increase the English hearts unto you, you shall not do the worst deed for your behalf.'

2

On 22 August, two days after the Lords of the Council had ridden to St Paul's to thank God for England's deliverance, a letter arrived from Scotland stating that the Armada had revictualled in a Scottish harbour and was on its way south again. Either it was going to join the Duke of Parma or else to force its way through the Narrow Seas back to Spain. 'The Queen and her Council', wrote Lord Burghley, 'were not a little perplexed what to do, but, in the end, order was given to stay the disarming of her Navy, and so the whole Navy was very speedily made ready again.' But this was in a propaganda pamphlet intended for foreign consumption. The truth was very different.

'Sir, God knoweth what we shall do if we have no men', wrote the Lord Admiral to Walsingham on receiving the news. 'Many of our ships are so weakly manned that they have not mariners to weigh their anchors.'

More men were pressed into service from neighbouring counties, but sickness had taken such a toll that the navy was still in no fit state to put to sea. The Privy Council ordered the Lords Lieutenant of counties to send back the musters to Tilbury, but on second thoughts the order was cancelled. Two fast pinnaces were sent north to discover more specific information about the Armada. Meanwhile the musters were allowed to go home to the harvest.

One reason why the Privy Council felt more secure was that they had at last realized that the Duke of Parma's army was securely blockaded in Dunkirk and Sluys by the Dutch fleet. The Dutch consul in London had warned his government on 12 August that the English were under the impression that they had had to beat the Spaniards singlehanded, with no assistance from their allies. This drew an indignant letter to the Queen from the States of Zeland at Middelburg:

> We understand that in place of attributing to us and our fleet a part of the victory, our ill-wishers do unjustly blame us for that our ships should have been withdrawn, as unwilling to assist your Majesty's; although it is apparent that the defeat of the said armada of Spain doth consist chiefly and entirely in this, that the said prince [of Parma] remaining where he still is, was unable to succour and strengthen it with his forces.

Shortly afterwards, Admiral Justin of Nassau turned up off Dover with his entire fleet of forty vessels to demonstrate the extent of his contribution to the victory. While the English remained reluctant to share the glory, they were happy to acknowledge the benefit. On 1 September the Privy Council, having 'received advertisement that the Spanish fleet lieth still on the furthest part of the coast of Scotland and that they intend to return into the Narrow seas', asked the Dutch to continue their fleet at sea.

Another Dutch engraving of the battle with the Armada published about fourteen years later, but probably based on an earlier design

Meanwhile, despite an 'excellent song of the breaking up of the camp', printed by John Wolfe, demobilization from Tilbury was not going smoothly. The captains who had led their men a month before to glory and the Court were showing less enthusiasm to lead them home again.

One reason was pay. The Queen and her Lord Treasurer had done their best to honour the promises she had made at Tilbury. But as Lord Burghley was to declare later, there were 'some few Captains of some Shires of England that did a little begin to imitate [captains abroad] in defrauding their soldiers of their pay, at such time as the camp was at Tilbury'. As a result, some of the soldiers sold their arms, the property of their county for the most part, to provide themselves with food and shelter on their homeward journey. The Queen issued an indignant proclamation on Sunday 25 August that some soldiers had 'most falsely and slanderously given out that they were compelled to make sale of [their armours and weapons] for that they received no pay, which is most untruly reported'. But on the same day the Privy Council ordered Lords Lieutenant to 'examine certain matters of abuse complained of in the captains for not paying the soldiers having received their full pay here'.

The 'godly and profitable sermon' preached at Paul's Cross, that same Sunday, dealt with 'the true fruits of Peace and War, as also the rare virtues of Godly wise Captains, etc.'.

Unlike the navy and the soldiers at Tilbury, the bands of horse and foot gathered to provide the army about the Queen's person were equipped, armed, and paid by the nobility and gentry who supplied them. There was therefore not the same urgency to disband them. A series of reviews of these troops was arranged in the grounds of St James's Palace in which the leading noblemen of the realm vied with each other as to who could mount the best display. The people of London flocked to see them.

One of the first displays was put on by the old Lord Montague, the loyal Catholic who had offered his services to the Queen even before the Privy Council had heard of the Armada's arrival. He came with his son and grandson to demonstrate his family's loyalty. On 19 August Sir Christopher Hatton, the Lord Chancellor, displayed a company of a hundred men-at-arms, dressed in his red and yellow livery. Lord Burghley and the Earl of Leicester presented their forces the following day.

But the last and best, most people thought, was the review staged by the Earl of Essex, Master of the Queen's Horse, and already a Knight of the Garter at the age of twenty. This was on 26 August, when the Queen and the Earl of Leicester watched from a window in the palace a company of sixty musketeers, sixty mounted harquebusiers, and two hundred lancers, dressed in the Dudley colours of orange and white embroidered with silver. The Earl of Essex and the Earl of Cumberland, both renowned for their horsemanship, jousted in the open field, and were then joined by other gentlemen-at-arms in a mock cavalry engagement. The two young earls fought a mock battle on foot with sword and buckler, which the Queen pretended she was too anxious to watch. Finally the horsemen were divided into two squadrons and ran several times against each other, lowering their swords as they approached, while the musketeers and harquebusiers fired off a simultaneous volley.

3

A grimmer spectacle for the people of London was also in preparation.

On the eve of the Armada's arrival, the Privy Council had been investigating the legal position of Catholics in the light of Cardinal Allen's *Declaration of the Sentence and Deposition of Elizabeth*. The Solicitor General had advised that they could only be convicted for treason under the 1352 Act of Edward III if they could be proved to have committed treasonable acts. Otherwise, the Act of 1585 must apply, directed mainly at Catholics who had entered the country from seminaries overseas and those helping them.

On 11 August the Privy Council appointed a commission to examine priests and recusants in London prisons. The members included Sir Owen Hopton, Lieutenant of the Tower, Richard Topcliffe (then at the outset of his sadistic career), Richard Young the Middlesex justice, and the young lawyer, Francis Bacon. By 20 August they had a list of some forty prisoners, mainly from the south-eastern counties. Their first task was

> especially to enquire which of them are Jesuits or Priests, and have either not departed out of the Realm or have returned hither again contrary to the statutes made in that behalf, and [to] propound such questions as were heretofore made to others, and are in a printed book wherewith some of them are acquainted, and such other questions as they shall think meet touching their allegiance to her Majesty and their country etc.

The printed book must have been Lord Burghley's anonymous pamphlet, *The Execution of Justice in England*, which did contain advice on how to distinguish political traitors from professed religious martyrs:

> Examine further, how these vagrant, disguised, unarmed spies have answered, when they are taken and demanded, what they thought of the bull of Pope Pius Quintus, which was published to deprive the queen's majesty, and to warrant her subjects to disobey her: whether they thought that all subjects ought to obey the same bull, and so to rebel? Secondly, whether they thought her majesty to be the lawful queen of the realm, notwithstanding the said bull, or any other bull of the Pope? Thirdly, whether the Pope might give licence, as he did to the Earls of Northumberland and Westmorland, and other her majesty's subjects, to rebel, as they did? . . . Fourthly, whether the Pope may discharge the subjects of her majesty, or of any other princes christened, of their oaths of obedience? . . . Lastly, what were to be done if the Pope, or any other assigned by him, would invade the realm of England; and what part they would take, or what part any faithful subject of her majesty's ought to take?

The last question, generally known as 'the bloody question' through its consequences, had taken on a new significance since the Privy Council had received Cardinal Allen's *Declaration* that the Spanish invasion was authorized by the Pope, who had ordered all Catholics to take the invaders' part, on pain of excommunication. The prisoners knew nothing about this new papal 'bull', any more than the examiners knew that the Pope's injunction was conditional on a Spanish landing.

The Jesuit Robert Southwell described the prisoners' bewilderment in one of his letters to General Aquaviva:

> They are dragged in gangs to the courthouses, and there examined not only as to their past deeds, but about their future conduct, what forsooth they would be disposed to do under such and such circumstances. If they refuse to answer, the refusal is set down as a clear proof of a rebellious will and of treason; if they answer that they will do nothing contrary to their just and bounden duty to Queen and country, they falsely accuse them of hypocrisy and insincerity. In a word, whatever answer they give, it never satisfies the minds of these judges unless it is the one that imperils the prisoner's life.

Sixteen Catholics were brought to trial at the Old Bailey on 25 August, which, being a Sunday, allowed for a large public attendance. The Bench, presided over by the Lord Mayor of London, included Recorder Fleetwood, Bishop Aylmer of London, and several justices; the total may even have outnumbered the jury of twelve.

The first to be tried were six seminary priests, including Richard Leigh, who had been caught not long before among a number of Catholics who had celebrated mass in the Tower of London with the recusant Earl of Arundel. There were allegations that they had prayed for the success of the Armada.

The six priests relied for their defence on the dispensation given in the bull of Gregory XIII and declared their allegiance to the Queen. They were asked whether, in the event of an invasion sanctioned by the Pope, they would take the Queen's part or the Pope's, but their answers did not satisfy the court or jury. They were quickly condemned, as priests who had entered the realm from abroad, contrary to the statute of 1585. The sentence did not differ from the penalty under the statute of Edward III:

> That you shall be had from hence to the place whence you came, there to remain until the day of execution; and from thence you shall be drawn upon a hurdle through the open streets to the place of execution, there to be hanged and cut down alive, and your body shall be opened, your heart and bowels plucked out, and your privy members cut off and thrown into the fire before your eyes; then your head shall be stricken off from your body, and your body shall be divided into four quarters, to be disposed of at the Queen's pleasure. And God have mercy on your soul!

When it came to the ten lay prisoners, the trial seems to have run into difficulties. According to Southwell, who may have been present in disguise as a spectator, 'such paltry evidence was relied upon that, after sentence was passed, the judges themselves vigorously protested, and there were open expressions of regret at the unworthy proceedings.' In a letter written a few weeks later, Henry Garnet said that Recorder Fleetwood had carried his protest to the Queen herself.

These comments are substantiated, by implication, in the authorized pamphlet published shortly afterwards, *A brief Treatise Discovering in substance the offences, and ungodly practices of the late 14 Traitors*. It is unusually non-committal about the trial, merely stating that the prisoners were 'severally arraigned, indicted and found guilty and condemned . . . with much more circumstances than is here needful to be set down'.

Southwell related that at one point the young priest, Richard Leigh, probably defending one of the lay prisoners, challenged Bishop Aylmer to a disputation. The bishop replied pompously that Leigh was behaving like Alexander's dog, who disdained even to growl at a bear or vulgar animal, but would bark at an elephant. 'I am that elephant, and thou the puppy. What right hast thou to dispute with me, who surpass even your Dr Allen in extent of reading and depth of knowledge.' Everybody laughed, no doubt for different reasons.

The lay prisoners were offered a pardon 'if they became conformable to her Majesty's laws'. Two of them, John Valentine and William Pere, accepted and agreed to recant. Of the remainder who refused, four were condemned to the full sentence of treason and four simply to be hanged. They were 'pinioned and their hands bound' before being taken in carts back to Newgate prison 'in such sort that all the people might easily see them'.

The authorized pamphlet was at pains to show 'how these sorts of Traitors in general have sought the deprivation of her Majesty from her Crown', how they intended 'to murder, massacre, spoil, and put down the chiefest props and pillars of this land', and how they had complotted with foreign power 'to procure invasion, set up some foreign usurping Potentate, and . . . bring in a new kind of religion, stuffed full of blasphemy, idolatry, hypocrisy, and such other trash mixed with the dregs and relics of old Antichrist'. The priests in particular had moved from house to house to persuade the Queen's subjects to take up arms against her 'when any insurrection was, . . . and as it had been seen at the late coming of the Spaniards to invade this Realm, had not the same been very providently and carefully foreseen and prevented by the queen's most excellent majesty and her wise and honourable Council.' Nevertheless the Queen had decided, on the day after the trial, that none of those convicted should be drawn or quartered, 'but with great mercy and compassion towards them did mitigate the same, only commanding that they should be hanged in sundry places near London'.

On the morning of 28 August William Gunter, one of the seminary priests, was the first to enter the cart at Newgate. He remained silent, but Henry Webley, who followed him, declared to the crowd that he had committed no offence against the Queen but was dying for his conscience; he had been convicted for sheltering priests. According to the pamphlet, when William Deane, the second priest, came out 'mumbling to himself in Latin' the people cried 'down with him into the cart.' According to Southwell, Deane tried to speak to the crowd, but his mouth was stopped with a gag.

One of Mendoza's agents also described the scene at Newgate:

> I saw them being taken in a cart to be executed, followed by an enormous crowd of people, who were exhibiting every sign of rejoicing. A gentlewoman present

said some words expressive of pity for the death of the poor creatures, and one of the two sheriffs who were going to hang them at once ordered two serjeants to arrest the lady and take her to prison. I have not heard what happened to her afterwards.

By a curious coincidence, Robert Southwell seems to have witnessed the same incident:

> A certain woman, of no mean station, when she saw the priests passing by, unable from grief to check her tears and words, begged them on their knees to pray to God for her. At this she was arrested and on this sole charge cast into prison.

A seventeenth-century depiction of a hanging. The executioner led the victim up the ladder to be 'turned off'

The three prisoners were taken through the crowds in the cart to Mile End, on the southern outskirts of London, where Deane and Webley were hanged. William Gunter was then taken east of the city to Holywell fields, 'near to the Theatre or Playhouse'. The sheriff called on him to ask God's pardon and acknowledge his offences. 'He answered that he would ask pardon of God, but not of her Majesty, saying that he had never offended her, and so he was hanged on a new Gibbet prepared for him.'

The sheriffs and officers then returned with the cart to Newgate to collect three more prisoners, two of them to be hanged in Lincoln's Inn fields on the north side of London and the third at Clerkenwell in the south. Finally they returned to Newgate for the last two prisoners, one of whom, Thomas Felton, was the son of the John Felton who had published the bull of Pope Pius V on the gates of the Bishop of London's palace eighteen years before. These two were tied astride horses, which were whipped up to take them to their executions in Brentford and Hounslow in Middlesex.

The last six executions did not take place until two days later, on 30 August at Tyburn, three miles from London on the Oxford road. Among those hanged were a woman, Margaret Ward, and the only remaining priest, Richard Leigh, who was left to the last. The executions were not described in *A Brief Treatise*, which was probably already in the press, or even on sale, at the time.

4

Early in September the two pinnaces returned from their search for the Armada in Scottish waters. They reported sighting a number of Spanish ships making their way round the north coast, some of them 'in very evil case'. The Privy Council could now feel secure that no further attack need be expected this year at least. The remainder of the land and sea forces were promptly disbanded. By 4 September only 34 ships and 1,453 seamen remained on the Queen's charge, compared with 197 ships and 15,925 men at the beginning of August.

On 8 September the members of the Privy Council once again rode to St Paul's for a thanksgiving service. This time, the Lord Admiral and other naval commanders had been induced to lend the banners they had captured from Spanish ships. The eight banners were hung on the lower battlements of the cathedral, within sight of the preacher and large congregation at Paul's Cross. One streamer, 'wherein was an image of our Lady, with her son in her arms . . . was held in a man's hand over the pulpit'.

The following day, the banners were taken first to the Market Cross in Cheapside and then to the south end of London Bridge, where they were displayed along with the blackened heads of traitors on the ends of pikes, in full view of the crowds assembling for Lady Fair in Southwark.

Services of thanksgiving were soon being held in parish churches throughout the realm. Archbishop Whitgift had arranged for the printing and distribution of *A Psalm and Collect of thanksgiving, not unmeet for the present time: to be said in Churches*. The Collect, as usual, was part prayer, part homily:

> We cannot but confess, O Lord God, that the late terrible intended invasion of most cruel enemies, was sent from thee, to the punishment of our sins, of our pride, our covetousness, our excess in meats and drinks, our security, our ingratitude, and our unthankfulness towards thee, for so long peace . . . And indeed our guilty consciences looked for (even at that time) the execution of thy terrible justice upon us, so by us deserved. But thou O Lord God, who knowest all things, [knew] that our enemies came not of justice to punish us for our sins . . . but that they came with most cruel intent and purpose to destroy us, our cities, towns, country, and people, and utterly to root out the memory of our nation from off the earth for ever: and withal, wholly to suppress thy holy word, and blessed gospel of thy dear son our Saviour Jesus Christ, which they (being drowned in idolatries and superstitions) do hate most deadly.

In Norwich on 22 September, 'the day of giving God thanks for the overthrow of the Spaniard', guns were fired all day from dawn to dusk. In the village of Reyfham (Reepham?) in the same county, Robert Humston preached a sermon which was later printed with a dedication to his bishop. His text may have been Habbakuk 3:3 ('God cometh from Teman and mount Paran, his glory covereth the heavens, and the earth is full of his praise.') but his inspiration was surely the special Collect for the day:

> The Lord of hosts menaced of late to stretch the line of Samaria over the Realm of England, and to sound our Cities and measure our families with the plummet of the house of Ahab, and not leave one to make water against a wall. While the danger was fresh, we were suddenly daunted, and began to curse the days spent

in vanity and wickedness, which had brought the day of destruction so near on our heads. Wherein our enemies came against us as fierce as the wolves in the evening, or as the Eagles greedy of their prey, with purpose, had not the Lord in mercy prevented them, to have taken away and trampled under feet the glorious Gospel of Christ, and to have erected superstition and idolatry in all our land, to have bereft us of our most lawful and loving Sovereign, the Lord's annointed Queen, and to have turned our inheritance to heathenish strangers, to have invaded our country with Edom's alarm, and turned our floods of peace into channels of blood, to have murdered the honourable councillor and grave Judge, the reverend Bishop and venerable magistrate, the wealthy Citizen and painful craftsman, the aged matron and chaste virgin, the infant in the cradle and the cripple at the gate, without remorse or respect of sere degree or age. And for execution of these so heavy judgements, the Lord threateneth us with a people and Nation idolatrous and uncircumcised as the Philistines, extremely cruel and tyrannous as the Scythians, achieving their exploits not so much by courage of their own, as by corrupting th'adverse Captains, a thing whereof we have had too late experience, of whom I trust I may speak a truth without scandal.

The treachery of Sir William Stanley and Rowland York had taken place twenty months before, but even in Norfolk the memory had been kept alive.

What sounded like a sermon also formed the introduction to *A true Discourse of the Army which the King of Spain caused to be assembled in the Haven of Lisbon, in the Kingdom of Portugal, in the year 1588 against England*, which was now at last published in September, translated from Mendoza's French edition, a month or more after editions had been appearing all over the Continent.

The Spaniards, it declared, wicked and ungodly as they were, had neglected the Almighty and trusted in their own might, 'relying on themselves and their own power to glory and boast thereof unto the world'. They had not produced an English version of the discourse, but 'published it to all beside ourselves, in Italian, Spanish, Dutch, and French, and yet to them thereby to discourage us', telling us that he had 'thus many huge ships, so many thousands of armed men, such multitudes of munition as no man could deliver us out of his hand'.

The purpose of now publishing it in the English tongue was not, 'as theirs was, to daunt or discourage the fearful multitude, but to propound unto the world their folly in boasting thus vainly, and then to encourage ourselves to go forward in that hope and confidence we have in the Lord.'

The introduction ended with an account of the fire-ships at Calais and the battle off Gravelines, and demonstrates how news was transmitted through sermons:

For the Lord hath caused the forces of the Spaniards, this their great Armado, to be daunted, and greatly endangered by his great wisdom, putting into the minds of our Captains and soldiers, to provide six or seven of the worst of the ships they had at sea, with such necessaries as should serve best to set them on fire withal, which they sent amongst the Spaniards, thereby to remove and

A true Discourse of the Armie

which the King of Spaine caused to bee assembled in the Hauen of Lisbon, in the Kingdome of Portugall, in the yeare 1588. against England. The which began to go out of the said Hauen, on the 29. and 30. of May.

Translated out of French into English, by Daniel Archdeacon.

Whereunto is added the verses that were printed in the first page of the Dutch copy printed at Colen, with answeres to them, and to Don Bernardin de Mendozza.

2. King. 19. ver. 28. Because thou ragest against me, and thy tumult is come vp to mine eares, I will put mine hooke in thy nostrels; and my bridle in thy lippes, and will bring thee backe againe the same way thou camest.

Imprinted at London by Iohn Wolfe. 1588.

The English version of the *Relacion Verdadera*, not published until the Armada was no longer a threat

scatter them, yea even when they thought themselves most sure, and likeliest to receive more succour, and as they lay fast at Anchor near Calais. Wherefore they arose and sought every man to help himself, hewing and slipping their cables, and leaving their anchors behind them. Yea and some he hath caused to run aground upon one shore, and some upon another, and some sunk, and other some taken with divers of their men, some of them of great name, with their ensigns, banners, streamers, and gitterns, whereof divers were hanged about the battlements and cross of Paul's, on the 8 September 1588 and on the 9 at London bridge, thereby to comfort his English Elizabeth, and all her faithful subjects.

A True Discourse of the Army was printed by John Wolfe, who may have been establishing a special relationship with the Privy Council as a publisher of semi-official pamphlets. Perhaps a sheet which he added at the end reveals the learned clerks of the Privy Council at play.

A certain Michael Eizinger of Cologne had produced translations into High and Low German of the *Relacion Verdadera* which were printed in Nuremberg just about the time the battle of Gravelines was being fought. At the end of the translation Eizinger added a message to the people of England from the people of Cologne in the form of a two-line Latin verse or distich:

> Ad Angliam et eius asseclas Europae
> *Tu, quae Romanas volui spernere leges,*
> *Hispano disces subdere colla iugo.*

> To England and her hangers-on of Europe
> Thou, who hast wished to spurn the Roman laws,
> Shalt learn to bend thy neck to a Spanish yoke.

The temptation of Latin scholars to compose replies to the Cologne distich was irresistible, and John Wolfe printed a selection of them at the end of the long catalogues of Spanish ships, men, stores and provisions.

> Ad Hispanum et eius asseclas
> *Tu qui Christigenum voluisti perdere gentem,*
> *Supremo disces subdere colla Deo.*

> To Spain and her hangers-on
> Thou which of Christians wouldst root out the race
> Shalt learn to feel of God the high disgrace.

> *Hoccine Romanas leges, Hispane, tueri?*
> *Hoc est Nostra tuo subdere colla iugo?*
> *Vix prius armatas Anglorum cernere classes,*
> *Absque mora turpi quam terga fugae.*

> Is this the Romish lore to hold,
> and yield our necks to Spanish yoke?
> Not erst to see our English Fleet,
> but fly amain and strike no stroke?

For a particularly lively one directed at that favourite target of the Privy Council, Don Bernardin de Mendoza, see the heading of Chapter Ten.

5

> And neither are they so chased from you, that you are to expect them no more. For though the Lord hath done this time very great things for you, and hath covered them with shame and dishonour that sought your life: though the dragon be driven into his den, yet is his sting and poison still in force: . . . though some of their ships and men be sunk in the sea, yet the sinews of their commonwealth remain. Neither will they ever come to any peace and atonement with you, till ye have plucked those sinews in sunder.

So said Anthony Marten, the Queen's server, introducing in September the prayers he had composed when the Armada lay in the Narrow Seas. The mood of the Court, which reflected the mood of the Queen, was not content to rest on victory. As soon as the Armada returned to Spain it would begin to prepare another attack on England. Queen Elizabeth, who had spent the first half of 1588 trying to negotiate a peace, was now the most active proponent of counter-attack.

In mid-August, Lord Henry Seymour had suggested that the Duke of Parma might be the subject of Spanish recriminations for his failure to join forces with the Armada. This led the Queen to revive an old plan to make a separate peace with Parma which would allow him to continue as governor of an independent Netherlands. Feelers were put out through her banker, Sir Horatio Palavicino, and Sir Edward Stafford in Paris.

The suggestion was rebuffed by Parma, though he was indeed being accused of cowardice by Spaniards in the Netherlands. His answer was to issue an individual challenge to any man who doubted his courage. For a day he waited, rapier in hand, in the *Grand Place* of Dunkirk, but no one came to take up his challenge.

Sir Francis Drake and the other naval commanders remained at Court during August and were able to revive the proposals for an attack on Spain and Portugal which had been discussed earlier in the year. The project which the Queen most favoured was an attack on the Spanish treasure fleet, due back from the Indies towards the end of August or early in September. But her Lord Admiral found that the English fleet could not be brought into dry dock for refitting until the next spring tide and would be unable to sail before mid-September, when it would be too late.

Another enterprise, strongly favoured by Sir Francis Drake and Sir John Norris, was to send a large fleet to Corunna and Lisbon, before the Armada had time to return and refit. Drake and Norris should be in charge of the expedition and the Dutch should also be involved. Sir John Norris had a plan drawn up by 22 September. But as before, the project threatened to founder on the problem of finance. It was agreed that the cost and any eventual proceeds should be shared between the Queen, the Dutch, and individual subscribers; in effect, the war was to be financed by a joint stock company. Preparations had scarcely begun before news came from the Netherlands that the Duke of Parma was laying siege to Bergen-op-Zoom, a key fortress in the Brabant. The Dutch thought that it could not be defended and were prepared to withdraw. But the town had an English garrison and moreover was one of the 'cautionary towns' held by the Queen as security for her loans to the Netherlands.

The Queen's reaction was swift and decisive. The Portugal expedition was abandoned for the time being. Sir John Norris was ordered to go to the relief of Bergen with two thousand troops; the Lord Mayor of London was instructed to raise some of them by rounding up 'idle and loose persons' from the city streets.

None of this activity, of course, brought any relief to the financial difficulties. By the time the half-year accounts were made up to Michaelmas, 29 September, the 'chested treasure' had dwindled to £55,000, barely enough to meet the Queen's expenses for six weeks. The last instalment of the subsidy voted by Parliament was not due until November, and there was no alternative but to call another. Writs for elections were issued on 18 September for a new Parliament to assemble on 12 November.

6

One figure who was notably absent from all these discussions and preparations was the Queen's Lord Steward and Captain General, Robert Dudley, Earl of Leicester. Shortly after he and the Queen had watched the display by his stepson, the Earl of Essex, of his troops at St James, he was on his way to Buxton to take the waters. From Cornbury in Oxfordshire he sent the Queen his last letter, which she kept in a locked casket until the day of her death. There on 4 September he died.

He had few other mourners. His nephew Sir Robert Sidney came back from Edinburgh for his fairly lavish funeral in Warwick. Oxford University, of which he had been Chancellor for so many years, produced a conventional Latin ode. Thomas Cartwright, leader of the puritan movement, who had lived in Warwick under Leicester's protection, had good cause to regret the passing of his patron.

His followers were soon seeking other protectors. On 9 September, only five days after Leicester's death, Sir Francis Hastings, younger brother of the puritan Earl of Huntingdon, was urging the young Earl of Essex to follow in his stepfather's footsteps, 'that honourable, worthy gentleman whom God used so many times as a notable instrument for the good both of the Church and commonwealth.' Essex was particularly asked to bend the whole strength of his credit with the Queen 'to comfort and countenance the well-affected in religion and watchfully to foresee that the contrary sort be kept back'.

The death of such a controversial public figure brought the inevitable crop of rumours. His widow was suspected of poisoning him. Edward Croft, eldest son of Sir James Croft, the peace commissioner, was accused of having employed a conjuror to do away with Leicester, in revenge for having committed his father to prison; it is true that Leicester was present at a Privy Council meeting on 24 August at which Sir James's fate was decided. The rancour and muddle that had bedevilled Leicester's life continued for a while after his death, but he was soon forgotten. Edmund Spenser, his former secretary, wrote in a poem published a year later:

> He now is dead, and all his glory gone,
> And all his greatness vapoured to nought,
> That as a glass upon the water shone,
> Which vanish'd quite, as soon as it was sought:
>   His name is worn already out of thought.

It was a different matter with Richard Tarlton, the leading comic actor of the Queen's Men, who died the day after Leicester. He had first come to Court with Leicester's company of actors

> in favour to be with the Queen:
> Where oft he had made her grace for to smile
>   when she full sad was seen.

His obituary appeared in ballad form and his name was attached to popular ballad tunes.

> Commended he was, both of great and small,
>   wheresoever he did abide,
> In court or in city, in country or town –
>   so well himself he could guide.
>
> His looks and his gesture, his turns and his grace
>   each man so well did delight
> That none could be weary to see him on stage
>   from morning until it were night.

Jestbooks bore his name for generations and his portrait adorned the signs of inns and alehouses.

Richard Tarlton, playing pipe and tabor, from a jestbook of 1611

CHAPTER TEN

THE 'INVINCIBLE' ARMADA

Mendoza, nothing do you do. They only make me scoff –
Your poisons, weapons, and your brags; your zeal brings nothing off.
 This is, Mendoza, miscreant, the fruit of your deceit:
That you should be the greatest cause of haughty Spain's defeat.
 Hence you would do a deed for Spain, and please a Briton's heart,
If dangling on a rope you did your treacherous life depart.

(Trans. from Latin) *Answer to the Cologne Distich*

1

In June, when he had first received Cardinal Allen's *Admonition to the Nobility and People of England and Ireland*, Lord Burghley had written to Walsingham:

> For answer I could wish some expert learned man would feign an answer as from a number of Catholics that notwithstanding their evil contentment for religion should profess their obedience and service with their lives and power against all strange forces offering to land in this realm, and to advertise the Cardinal that he is deceived in his opinion to think that any nobleman in this land or any gentleman of possessions will favour the invasion of this realm.

A brief discovery of Dr Allen's Seditious Drifts had provided an immediate answer on similar lines. Meanwhile all suspected Catholics had been put safely in custody and any waverers warned by proclamation that treachery would be met with prompt reprisal. In the final paragraph of the narrative sent to Sir Edward Stafford in Paris, Burghley had claimed that Catholics had been as loyal as Protestants when their country was threatened with invasion.

Towards the end of August he had still not found a learned man expert enough to write the sort of pamphlet he had in mind. So in the midst of all his other cares and duties he began to write it himself. Burghley's literary style was prolix, even by the standards of the time. But he must be given credit for a version of events whose influence has lasted for four centuries.

There were three drafts, two of which survive in manuscript, the third having been sent to the printer. Internal evidence suggests that Burghley began to write his pamphlet around 26 August; it was ready for the printer by the beginning of September.

His reply to Allen was from the beginning conceived as a letter from an English Catholic to Don Bernadin de Mendoza, the arch-plotter against the Queen and her Council. The first draft, in Burghley's own hand, was primarily a reply to Allen's book, proclaiming the unity of the Queen's subjects, Protestant and Catholic alike, in the face of threatened invasion. Reflecting the receding anxiety about the return of the Armada that year, the second draft laid more emphasis on the preparedness and strength (grossly exaggerated) of England's defences, particularly of the navy, so as to discourage a further attempt at invasion next year; it is in the hand of Burghley's secretary, Henry Maynard, with so many alterations and additions by the author that it amounts to a third draft. A new introduction suggests a change of purpose. It was by now less important to answer Cardinal Allen than to discredit the Spanish ambassador in Paris, who was still busy rallying the forces of the Holy League against the King of France. With each version gibes against Mendoza were added and sharpened. By the final draft the pamphlet seems primarily intended to deal with the French situation; it was in fact first printed in French.

The final version began with an address on behalf of the English Catholics to Mendoza, who had 'had the principal managing hitherto of all our causes of long time both here and there in France'. For many years they had looked forward to an improvement in their condition to be brought about 'by the means of the devout and earnest incitations of the Pope's holiness, and the King Catholic [of Spain], and of other Potentates of the holy League, to take upon themselves the invasion and conquest of this realm'. Last spring Mendoza had sent word that all the King's preparations 'were now in full perfection, and without fail would this Summer come into our Seas with such mighty strength, as no Navy of England, or of Christendom, could resist or abide their force.' At the same time, the Duke of Parma had prepared for an invasion and speedy conquest of the realm.

'But, alas and with a deadly sorrow . . . we have seen in the space of eight or nine days in this last month of July . . . all our hopes, all our buildings . . . utterly overthrown.' Many good Catholics had therefore begun to wonder if 'this way of reformation intended by the Pope's holiness is not allowable in the sight of God . . . so as some begin to say that this purpose by violence, by blood, by slaughter, and by conquest, agreeth not with Christ's doctrine.'

The greatest harm had been done by 'the untimely hasty publishing abroad' of printed books notifying the people, 'that all the Realm should be invaded and conquered, that the Queen should be destroyed, [and] all the Nobility and men of reputation . . . should be with all their families rooted out, and their places, their honours, their houses and lands bestowed upon the conquerors.'

In fact there is no trace of such printed books until after the Armada had left Corunna and foreigners like Michael Eizinger began to threaten England and her allies with 'a Spanish yoke'. Cardinal Allen had stressed that the Spaniards were coming to deliver the English from the 'yoke of heresy' and expected most of his countrymen to support them. There is, however, ample evidence that the English government fostered such rumours. Burghley claimed that these threats had only inflamed the hearts of the people 'to venture their lives for the withstanding of all manner of conquest'. They were confirmed by

a new Bull lately published at Rome by the Pope's holiness, which I have seen, with more severity than other of his predecessors, whereby the Queen was accursed, and pronounced to be deprived of her Crown, and the Invasion and conquest of the Realm committed by the Pope to the King Catholic, to execute the same with his armies both by sea and land, and to take the Crown to himself, or to limit it to such a Potentate as the Pope and he should name.

And secondly there followed a large explanation of this Bull . . . printed in Antwerp even when the Navy of Spain was daily looked for, the original whereof was written by the reverend father Cardinal Allen in April last, called in his own writing the Cardinal of England; which book was so violently, sharply, and bitterly written, yea (say the Adversaries) so arrogantly, falsely, and slanderously, against the person of the Queen, against her father King Henry the eight, against all her Nobility and Council, as in very truth I was heartily sorry to perceive so many good men of our own religion offended therewith, in that there should be found in one accounted a father of the Church, who was also a born subject of this crown (though by the Adversaries reported to be very basely born) such foul, vile, irreverent, and violent speeches.

There were also 'other books printed in Spain and translated into French (as it is said by your Lordship) containing particular long descriptions and catalogues of Armadas of Castile, of Andalusia, of Biscay, of Guipusque, of Portugal, of Naples, of Sicily, of Ragusa, and other Countries of the Levant, with a mass of all kinds of provisions, beyond measure, for the said Armadas, sufficient in estimation to make conquest of many kingdoms or countries'.

All these printed books had only stimulated the Queen and her subjects, regardless of cost, 'to stir up their whole forces for their defence'. In the maritime counties from Cornwall to Lincolnshire, 'twenty thousand fighting men on horseback and on foot, with field ordnance, victuals, pioneers and carriages' were ready to be mobilized at forty-eight hours notice. It had been wrong to expect a foreign invader to find 'but a small number resolute to withstand the same, or to defend the Queen'. Nor could the invader have counted on the dwindling number of Catholics, for 'it hath appeared manifestly that for all earnest proceedings for arming, and for contributions of money, and for all other warlike actions, there was no difference to be seen betwixt the Catholic and the heretic.'

At the news of the arrival of the Armada in Corunna and of the preparations in Flanders, there had been a 'general murmur of the people' against the leading recusants, who had therefore been removed for their own protection to Ely, 'notwithstanding their offers of their service to the Queen; and so they do remain in the Bishop's palace there, with fruition of large walks about the same, altogether without any imprisonment, other than that they are not suffered to depart into the town or country.'

Burghley then went into a long digression about the treatment of Catholics in England, repeating the arguments of *The Execution of Justice* that they 'were never persecuted or brought into danger by their opinions in religion' but only for treason or disobedience to the laws.

Returning to his description of the English defence preparations, he then dealt with the navy, which at first, he explained, had been divided into three fleets, two in the east and one at Plymouth. But when it was confirmed that 'the great Navy of Spain was ready to come out of Lisbon, and that the fame thereof was blown abroad in Christendom to be invincible, and so published by books in print', the Lord Admiral had been ordered to join Sir Francis Drake in Plymouth, leaving Lord Henry Seymour 'with a good number of ships in the narrow Seas, upon the coast of Flanders, to attend the Duke of Parma'.

When the Armada came to the coast of England, the Lord Admiral and Drake brought fifty ships out of Plymouth and pursued the Spanish fleet of over 160 ships. The English, their number increasing to a hundred sail, had chased the Spaniards up the Channel for nine days, capturing three ships on the way. And in all this time, 'it is vaunted by our Adversaries, . . . the Spaniards did never take, or sink, any English ship or boat, or break any mast, or took any one man prisoner. A matter that indeed these Spaniards which are taken do marvel at greatly, and chafe thereat: so as some of them, in their anguish of mind let not to say that in all these fights, Christ showed himself a Lutheran.'

The Duke of Medina Sidonia was said (by Burghley) to have 'lodged in the bottom of his ship for his safety', while the Spanish commanders 'never would turn their ships, nor stay them, to defend any of their own ships that were forced to tarry behind'. In consequence, Don Pedro de Valdez was captured with his ship and crew, another galleon was spoiled by fire, Hugo de Moncada was slain in his galleass, and two galleons were left to be captured by the Dutch.

In future, Mendoza was advised, many more ships and much better planning would be required for a successful invasion of England. His main assumptions had proved baseless: the alleged weakness of the English navy, the supposed discontent of the English people with their Queen, and, most of all, the anticipated strong support of the English Catholics for the invader.

Next year the Enterprise would be even more difficult, for the English navy, already strong, was being augmented. The Queen had won the support of all her people. She had visited her army encamped in Essex and had gone among her soldiers without any escort, being 'generally saluted with cries, with shouts, with tokens of love, of obedience, of readiness and willingness to fight for her'. She had also been able to raise 'an army of about forty thousand footmen, and of six thousand horsemen, under the charge of Lord Hunsdon, Lord Chamberlain, . . . to be about her own person, without disarming the maritime counties'.

Burghley went on to describe the nobles who had brought their own bands of lances, light horsemen and other retainers to London, starting with the Catholic Viscount Montague. In the course of writing, he conceived the idea of answering Allen's *Admonition to the Nobility and People of England* by listing all the members of the nobility and the leading gentlemen, Protestant and Catholic alike, and describing the contribution of each to England's defence. He ended with the young earls of Rutland, Southampton, and Bedford, in his own wardship until they came of age, 'all three brought up in perverse religion', and the Earl of Arundel, 'in the Tower for attempting to have fled out of the Realm . . . yet I hear most certainly that he offereth his life in defence of the Queen against all the world.'

All the Spanish prisoners had confessed that they had expected the English

Catholics to rise in their support, but 'finding this report very false, many of these prisoners do by name curse you [Mendoza], as being the King's Ambassador, as him, they say, who . . . had these many years tempted the King their master . . . to attempt such a matter as this was.' The prisoners had also been told that the country was so weakly defended and the people so miserable that 'they thought the Conquest thereof had been of no more difficulty than the overcoming of naked Indians was at the beginning of the Conquest thereof by King Ferdinand.'

'Now, my Lord Ambassador,' Burghley's letter concluded, 'your Lordship may see, in the first part, our [the English Catholics'] present calamity, and miserable estate: in the second part, the state of the Queen, her Realm, her people . . . so far contrary to the expectation of the Pope's holiness, the King Catholic, and especially of you (my Lord).'

English Catholics would best be served by sending them, not invading armies, but 'discreet, holy and learned men', who would not meddle in affairs of state. They should also have a dispensation from the Pope allowing them to attend English church services, so relieving them of the need to pay fines, whence 'in process of time, the Catholic religion (by God's goodness) might with more surety be increased, to the honour of God, than ever it can be by any force whatsoever.'

The composition of the title was important. Books were sold sewn but not with covers, which were left to the discretion of the purchaser. The title page was therefore exposed to view and combined the functions of a modern dustjacket and publisher's blurb. Often the title gave an indication of the contents and the circumstances of publication. Burghley's pamphlet must have been completed shortly after the execution of the last six Catholics at Tyburn on 31 August because he used the name of the priest who had met his fate there.

2

This was not, in fact, the end of Burghley's long letter. About a week later, shortly after the second thanksgiving service at St Paul's on 8 September, he added a postscript. By this time he had further news of the Armada.

'But I for my part,' he wrote in his character of an English Catholic, 'wished them a prosperous wind to pass home about Ireland, considering I despaired for their return.' He described the demobilization of the English navy, followed by its rapid remobilization on the rumour that the Armada had revictualled in Scotland and was about to return. But eight or ten days later 'two or three Pinnaces that were sent out to discover where the Spanish Fleet was . . . certified that they were beyond the Orcades [Orkneys], sailing towards the West, in very evil case, having many of their people dead in those North parts, and in great distress for lack of masts, and also of Mariners.' The English fleet had again been disbanded, and Lord Howard, Lord Seymour, Lord Sheffield, and Sir Francis Drake, with all the captains except those of Lord Seymour's fleet, returned to Court.

And upon the return of these seamen to the City, there are spread such reports, to move the Noblemen, Gentlemen, Ladies, Gentlewomen, and all other vulgar

THE
COPIE OF A LET-
TER SENT OVT OF
ENGLAND TO DON BERNARDIN
MENDOZA AMBASSADOVR IN FRANCE FOR
the King of Spaine, declaring the ftate of England, contrary to the opinion of *Don Bernardin*, and of all
his partizans Spaniardes and others.

This Letter, although it was fent to Don Bernardin Mendoza,
*yet, by good hap, the Copies therof afwell in Englifh as in French, were
found in the chamber of one* Richard Leigh *a Seminarie Prieft,
who was lately executed for high treafon committed in the
time that the Spanifh Armada was on the feas.*

Whereunto are adioyned certaine late Aduertifements, concerning the
loffes and diftreffes happened to the Spanifh Nauie, afwell in fight with the
Englifh Nauie in the narrow feas of England, as alfo by tempefts, and con-
trarie winds, vpon the Weft, and North coafts of Ireland, in their
returne from the Northerne Ifles beyond
Scotland.

Imprinted at London by I. Vautrollier for
Richard Field.   1 5 8 8.

Title page of a late edition of Lord Burghley's *The Copy of a Letter*, incorporating *Certain Advertisements out of Ireland*, originally published separately

people of all sorts, into a mortal hatred of the Spaniards, as the poor Spanish prisoners were greatly afraid to have been all massacred: for that it was published, and of many believed, that the Lords of Spain, that were in the Navy, had made a special division among themselves of all the Noblemen's houses in England by their names, and had in a sort quartered England among themselves and had determined sundry manners of cruel death, both of the Nobility, and the rest of the people. The Ladies, Women, and Maidens were also destined to all villany . . . And to increase more hatred, it was reported, that there were a great number of Halters brought in the Spanish Navy, to strangle the vulgar people, and certain Irons graven with marks, to be heated for the marking of all children in their faces, being under seven years of age, that they might be known hereafter to have been the children of the conquered Nation. These were commonly reported by those that came from the English Navy, as having heard the Spaniards confess the same; so as for a time, there was a general murmur that these Spanish prisoners ought not to be suffered to live, as they did, but be killed, as they purposed to have done the English.

But wiser counsels had prevailed and the people had been contented by the display of captured Spanish banners, streamers and ensigns, 'brought to Paul's Churchyard, and there showed openly in the Sermon time, to the great rejoicing of all the people'. Just as in the previous July, the churches were filled 'all the day long from morning to evening, celebrating the return of the English Navy, the defeat of the Spanish Navy, news of disorders in Flanders and quarrels between the Spanish soldiers, their allies, and the Duke of Parma, wherein is remembered the great goodness of God towards England'.

At the beginning of his postcript, the writer had claimed to have put his letter into the hands of a 'very trusty and sound Catholic having perfect knowledge of the French tongue, who took it upon him to be put into French'. The truth was that the letter had been put in the hands of a very trusty and sound Protestant Huguenot living in London, to be translated and printed. The printer's name was Jaqueline Vautrollier, who had been forbidden by the Court of the Stationers Company, the previous March, to print 'any manner of book or books whatsoever'.

She was the widow of Thomas Vautrollier, who in 1583 had printed the French and Latin editions of Burghley's *The Execution of Justice in England*. Later Thomas had lived in Scotland, printing for the Scottish kirk, while his wife remained to look after the London side of the business. He died in the summer of 1587, shortly after his return to England. When his widow Jaqueline continued to operate the London press, the Stationers Company argued that she had not been admitted a member in her own right and in any case her late husband had forfeited his membership through his absence in Scotland. The court ruled that she was forbidden to print under the Star Chamber decree and must lose her husband's valuable monopolies, which included the exclusive right to print the works of Cicero, much used in grammar schools. She also lost the right to print music and music paper, assigned to her husband by William Byrd, and had to return his music type to Byrd's new printer. As a concession, the court of the Stationers Company allowed her to complete work in progress, 'provided always that she meddle not with the printing of anything else until she procure herself to be chosen and allowed to print according to the decree of the Star Chamber'.

It is not surprising, therefore, that when Lord Burghley's manuscript was placed in her hands, she did not go to Stationers Hall to register the copyright, where the watchful John Wolfe would undoubtedly have enforced the court's ruling. Fortunately Jaqueline Vautrollier had in her employ a former apprentice of her husband's called Richard Field, who had come up to London from Stratford-upon-Avon to serve his apprenticeship. Although he had no printing press of his own, he had been admitted a member of the Stationers Company. A doubtful legality was given to *The Copy of a Letter* by describing it as printed 'by J. Vautrollier for Richard Field'.

3

On Saturday 14 September, a few days after sending his *Copy of a Letter* to press, and less than a week after attending the second thanksgiving service at St Paul's, Lord Burghley received news that the Spaniards were landing in Ireland.

It had been the particular fear of the Privy Council, even before the Armada had sailed from Lisbon, that a Spanish invasion of Ireland was planned to coincide with the rising of the local population. That had been the plan of the ill-fated papal expedition under Nicholas Sanders in 1579, and Cardinal Allen's *Admonition* had been addressed to 'the Nobility and People of England *and Ireland*'.

Fewer than two thousand English troops protected the English colony in Dublin and the plantations in Munster from a largely hostile population which clung obstinately to its old religion. In Ulster to the north and Connaught to the west, Irish tribal chieftains ruled their own territories, and some were suspected of being in touch with Spain and Rome.

Earl Fitzwilliam had replaced the irascible Sir John Perrot as Lord Deputy of Ireland only in July. Soon after his arrival in Dublin he had spread it abroad (and perhaps believed himself) that the Lord Admiral was ready to land with ten thousand troops if there were any sign of trouble. The thought of such protection, he wrote to the Privy Council on 14 August, 'doth and will not only greatly encourage the poor and few number of the dutiful and faithful subjects, but likewise abate the pride of the traitorous and wicked sort, and by the goodness of God be a company sufficient to withstand the force and malice of the enemy after their landing.'

After that, Earl Fitzwilliam heard no news of the Armada for three weeks. But on 9 September he received a letter from the west coast of Ireland, 'in which appeareth nine great ships to be upon that coast, which we think to be a matter of weight'.

The news was confirmed by further letters. The governor of Limerick reported eleven ships in the river estuary. George Bingham described three Spanish ships making for the harbour of Killibeggs. Thomas Norris told of twenty-four Spaniards landing from three ships in the Bay of Tralee; they had been captured, interrogated, and then, though three had offered ransom, all executed 'because there was no way of safe keeping'. Earl Fitzwilliam felt that the situation called for ships to be sent from Bristol.

The Privy Council agreed that it was a matter of weight, but ordered Sir Walter Raleigh and Sir Richard Grenville to fit out an expedition of twenty-four ships and seven hundred men from Plymouth. They happened to be in Plymouth already, fitting out an expedition to relieve Raleigh's colony in Virginia.

A day or so later, the Privy Council received a summary of events from Sir John Popham, the Attorney General, who had gone over to Ireland shortly after receiving the news in Bridgwater of the Armada's arrival the previous July. There now seemed to be less cause for alarm.

> The advertisements are, that on Thursday last [5 September], and sithence that time, there arrived first a barque, which wrecked at the Bay of Tralee, another great ship being also now near that place; after that, two great ships and one frigate in the Blaskets in the Sound there; seven other sail in the Shannon, by Karryg-ni-Cowly, whereof two are taken to be of a thousand tons apiece, two more of 400 tons the piece, and three small barques; at the Lupus Head four great ships, and towards the Bay of Galway four great ships more. It is thought that the rest . . . are also about some other part of this island . . . The people in these parts are for the most part dangerously affected towards the Spaniards, but their forces are so much weakened there is no doubt here of any hurt.

Raleigh and Grenville were ordered to reduce the size of their expedition, now no longer required to repel an invasion but only to capture Spanish guns and treasure and to interrogate prisoners. One of the few of Mendoza's agents to have survived reported the intensive preparations in Plymouth but had no clue of their purpose or destination.

Surprisingly, the Privy Council even managed to keep the news for over a week from the Court. In the meantime, reports from Ireland daily lessened the prospect of invasion. The Spanish survivors who managed to reach the Irish shore were barely able to stand, let alone fight. A few had been helped by the local population, but the majority had been stripped of their clothes and jewellery and left to die of exposure. On one beach, where the survivors could hardly crawl, a Scottish 'gallowglass' or mercenary named McLaughlin McCabe had slain eighty of them with an axe.

It was impossible, however, to keep such news secret for long. One of the gentlemen pensioners arrived back from Ireland with a packet of letters and soon his stories of the plight of the Spaniards were circulating around London, together with a written summary of the numbers of Spanish ships and men lost. By 28 September a ballad had been entered in the Stationers Register of 'the late and wonderful distress which the Spanish Navy sustained in the late fight in the Sea, and upon the west coast of Ireland in this month of September 1588'. It was shortly followed by another 'of the valiant deeds of MacCab an Irish man'.

4

When he first received the news of the disasters of the Armada in Ireland, Lord Burghley was quick to see that it was an appropriate subject for another supplement to his *Copy of a letter . . . to . . . Mendoza*, which was already in the press. He could hardly continue in his rôle of an English Catholic, so this time his supplement was entitled 'From the Printer to the Reader'. It was not, of course, written by Jaqueline Vautrollier.

> Whilst I was occupied in the printing hereof, a good time after the letters were sent into France, there came to this City certain knowledge to all our great comfort, of sundry happy Accidents to the diminution of our mortal enemies in their famous Fleet, that was driven out of our seas about the last of July, towards the farthermost north parts of Scotland. . . .
> The particularities whereof are these. The Fleet was by tempest driven beyond the Isles of Orkney, about the first of August, which is now more than six weeks past, the place being about three score degrees from the North Pole: an unaccustomed place for the young Gallants of Spain, that never had felt storms on the sea, or cold weather in August. And about those North Islands, their mariners and soldiers died daily by multitudes: as by their bodies cast on land did appear. And after twenty days or more, having spent their time in miseries, they being desirous to return home to Spain, sailed very far Southwestward into the Ocean to recover Spain. But the Almighty God . . . ordered the winds to be so violently contrarious to his proud Navy, as it was with force dissevered on the high seas West upon Ireland: and so a great number of them, driven into sundry dangerous bays, and upon rocks, all along the West and North parts of Ireland . . . and there cast away: some sunk, some broken, some run upon sands, some burned by the Spaniards themselves.

He went on to give details of the number of ships reported lost in various places (he was keeping a tally in his copy of *La Felicissima Armada*) and of the Spaniards drowned or 'forced to come on land for succour among the wild Irish'. In the seven weeks between 21 July and 10 September, 'it is most likely that the said Navy had never good day, nor night.'

'These accidents,' he concluded, 'I thought good to add to the printed Copies of the letters of Don Bernardin: that he may see how God doth favour the just cause of our gracious Queen.'

The following week, further despatches arrived from Ireland, which Burghley began to summarize for yet another supplement to his *Copy of a letter*. But a few days later, reports of interrogations of Spanish prisoners began to come in, probably in the packet brought by the gentleman pensioner. Burghley realized, for once, that these reports would have more effect if they were printed verbatim, and bundled them all together under the title *Certain Advertisements out of Ireland*. The flavour is shown in this report of Emmanuel Fremoso, a Portuguese sailor who had been in one of the twenty-four ships under the command of Admiral Oquendo when the Duke of Medina Sidonia issued instructions in the north of Scotland for the Armada to sail home around Ireland. He was probably killed shortly after completing his statement.

> He saith that out of this ship there died four or five every day of hunger and thirst, and yet this ship was one that was best furnished for victuals; which he

knoweth, for out of four of the other ships, some people were sent to be relieved in this ship.

After this for a[bout] ten days, the whole fleet remaining held together, holding their course the best they could towards Spain. He saith that at the same time, which is now about 20 days or more past [i.e. about 22 August], they were severed by a great storm, which held from four of the clock in the afternoon of one day to ten of the clock in the morning of the next day, in which storm the admiral [Oquendo's flagship] came away with 27 sail, and that one of them was a galleass of 28 oars a side. What is become of the rest of the navy he cannot tell. He saith, also, that about ten days past they had another great storm with a mist, by which storm they were again severed, so as of these 27 sail there came into the coast of Dingle-i-cush but the admiral, another ship of 400 tons, and a barque of about 40 tons; and what is become of the rest of those 27 sail he knows not.

5

By this time *The Copy of a Letter* was already translated into French and probably printed, although perhaps not yet bound. Someone, probably Walsingham, decided that *Certain Advertisements out of Ireland* could not be delayed any longer for a French translation and must be published immediately in English. Jaqueline Vautrollier had it ready in less than a week, for on 30 September Walsingham sent a copy of it to Sir Edward Stafford in Paris.

> I do make this despatch unto you, to let you understand of such advertisements as we have lately received out of Ireland, which it is thought meet to send unto you, to the end that you may be able to satisfy such as shall be desirous to know thereof, which cannot be constructed to be delivered of any cunning on our part, considering that they are the confessions and testimonies of our adversaries themselves, and therefore it hath been thought convenient to commit them to the print. For the particularities I refer you to the printed book. We do look shortly to hear from thence of other ships to fall into the like distress, for the south-west winds have blown so hard, as in the judgement of our seamen it hath not been possible for them to return into Spain. It is likewise meant, that in a little while, the substance of the whole proceedings of the Spanish navy, shall be published in both French and Italian.

Stafford did not take Walsingham's advice but had his own French translation made and prefixed it with a letter from a Flemish merchant, 'a zealous Catholic', supposed to be residing in London. Probably Richard Hakluyt saw the pamphlet through the press, for it was published bound together with a French translation of a letter from Lord Hunsdon to Thomas Cavendish, who had just arrived back in England after repeating Drake's exploit of sailing round the world. On the way he had captured a valuable Spanish treasure ship off the Philippines. The whole packet made a convincing tribute to England's superiority at sea.

A D V E R T I S-
SEMENT CERTAIN
contenant les pertes aduenues
en l'armee d'Efpagne, vers le
Noeft, de la cofte d'Irlande, en
leur voyage intenté depuis les
Ifles du Nord, par delà l'Efcof-
fe enuers Efpagne.

Et du nombre des hommes &
nauires perdus .

Auec deux lettres, l'vne d'vn Flamen, Ca-
tholiqne zelé, demeurant à Londres, à vn
Seigneur Efpagnol , & l'autre de Mon-
fieur Candiche , qui a paffé le deftroit de
Magellan, pour aller aux Indes , & eft re-
tourné par le Cap de Bonne Efperance.

Sir Edward Stafford had his own translation of *Certain Advertisements out of Ireland* printed in Paris, together with a fictitious letter from a zealous Catholic in England and an account of Thomas Cavendish's recent circumnavigation of the globe

In the meantime, the Vautrollier edition in French of *Certain Advertisements out of Ireland* was coming off the press and copies were soon being sent into France, sometimes bound with *Copie d'une lettre . . . à . . . Mendoza*. French printers lost no time in bringing out their own editions, which must have sold well, judging by their number.

The primary purpose of these pamphlets was to give support to King Henry III of France, who at last was facing the long-delayed meeting of the Estates General at Blois. The description of the disasters suffered by the Spanish fleet and of the unity of the English, both Catholic and Protestant, provided strong ammunition against the machinations of the Holy League.

Another incident played into the King's hands just as the meeting opened. News arrived that the Duke of Savoy, a nephew of the King of Spain, had suddenly invaded and annexed the province of Saluzzo, the last remaining French possession beyond the Alps. The Duke of Guise was concerned that the incident would be used to rally French opinion behind their King, cutting across religious divisions, against Spain.

But when King Henry rose to address the assembly at Blois on 6 October, he made no reference to the Duke of Savoy's invasion, nor even to the English victory over the Spaniards. He merely asked for tolerance and the avoidance of civil war. He did go so far as to accuse the Holy League of fomenting division in France, but his call was for unity rather than recrimination.

While the King had temporized during September, the Duke of Guise's party had made sure of overwhelming representation at Blois. The Huguenots had refused to attend since no adequate provision had been made for safe conduct. The King's party, the *Politiques*, were outnumbered two to one. It therefore did not take long for the Holy League to enforce confirmation of the Edict of Union which the King had signed in July, of the appointment of the Duke of Guise as the King's Lieutenant General, and of the recognition of the Cardinal of Bourbon, rather than Henry of Navarre, as rightful heir to the throne. They were also able to ensure that, when the King's speech was printed in France, his adverse comments on the Holy League were omitted.

6

Just about the time that the first copies of *Certain Advertisements out of Ireland* began to issue from the Vautrollier press, the sad remnants of the Most Happy Fleet that the King had assembled in Lisbon began to limp into French and Spanish ports around the Bay of Biscay.

The first to arrive was the Duke of Medina Sidonia, who had followed his own instructions to the fleet to sail on a course which gave a wide berth to the coast of Ireland. Most of his crew were sick from plague or dysentery, while he himself, after three months at sea suffering continuously from seasickness, had to be carried ashore at Santander. He offered to come and report in person to the King of Spain, but Philip mercifully excused him and allowed him to return to his home to recover.

Captain Miguel Oquendo arrived a week later at Corunna, with seven ships out of his twenty-seven. Walsingham's correspondent in St Jean de Luz, the same who had had his windows smashed on the report of a Spanish victory, described with understandable glee how 'since their ships have come home to the Passage, they all hang down their heads like cur-dogs, and are ashamed of what they did.'

In Madrid, on 2 October the Venetian ambassador at last received the instructions sent by the Doge and Senate, six weeks before, to congratulate the King of Spain on his victory. He reported back that he felt justified in using his discretion to ignore the order. On 3 October King Philip informed the Spanish bishops that prayers for the Armada need no longer be said in churches.

By mid-September Count Olivarez, the Spanish ambassador in Rome, had come to realize that Don Bernardin de Mendoza's optimistic reports from Paris had been unfounded and that an invasion of England was unlikely to take place that year. Nevertheless he told the Pope that the King of Spain had 'fairly earned the million ducats; half a million was due immediately.' Even if the Pope had made no promise, he was still bound to come forward with assistance, considering what the King 'had done and spent in the cause of God'. He described the Pope's reaction in his despatch to King Philip:

> He listened without interrupting me, though he betrayed his impatience by twisting uneasily on his seat. When I had done he boiled over. He said he would keep his word, and more than keep it, but pressed he would not be, and so long as the Armada's fate was unknown he would not do a thing. From the symptoms

which have appeared in his Holiness during the last few days one would not credit him with that zeal for the extirpation of heresy and the salvation of souls which his position requires of him . . . Over against the benefit to Christendom, there has been set this grief at parting with money, and the fear and envy of your Majesty's greatness, and it becomes more clear every day that when he offered the million he did not believe that the enterprise would ever take place.

Three weeks later, still expecting the Armada to return and commence the invasion of England, Cardinal Allen went to see the Pope about joining the Duke of Parma in Flanders, so as to be ready to take up his position as Legate. 'The Pope treated him like a black,' Olivarez reported, 'and exhibited the greatest annoyance at his going, which, he signified, was not with his blessing until decisive intelligence of the result was received, and the certainty of convenience of his stay there.'

Eventually the Pope agreed to leave the date of Allen's departure to the discretion of the Spanish ambassador. But it was not long before Count Olivarez at last came to accept that the Armada had been defeated. On 19 October he reported his final attempt to get the Pope to agree to contribute some, at least, of the million ducats promised.

In one of my last discussions with the Pope on the money question, I reminded him how he would have repented of not sending the Legate if the affair had turned out as might reasonably have been hoped. He replied that if the enterprise had been ordained to succeed, the Legate would have been sent. He said this with great profundity, and although I replied that it would have required a very prophetic soul to have guessed it, he only cast up his eyes to heaven and said no more.

7

On 16 October Henry Killigrew, England's representative on the Council of the States, sent Lord Burghley another bull of the Pope that had been printed in the Netherlands. Unlike the 'roaring hellish bull' that Burghley had received four months before, this was a genuine bull of Pope Gregory XIII, renewed by Pope Sixtus V shortly after his accession, whose purpose was to declare Spain's war against the Turks a crusade. It had been translated into Dutch with a commentary, which almost submerged the text, by the Protestant polemicist, Philip de Marnix de Sainte Aldegonde.

A friend and supporter of William of Orange, Sainte Aldegonde had been one of the signatories of the letter to King Philip II of Spain in 1566 which had initiated the Netherlands war of independence. He was well known for his Protestant satire, *The Beehive of the Holy Roman Church*, which had been translated and frequently printed in England. But in 1585, a year after the assassination of his friend William, he found himself obliged to surrender the town of Antwerp to the victorious Duke of Parma.

He was allowed to go free, but his political career was at an end and he was living

The Holy Bull,

And Crusado of Rome: First published by the Holy father Gregory the riii. and afterwards renewed and ratified by Sixtus the fift: for all those which desire full pardon and indulgence of their sinnes: and that for a litle money, to sweete, for two Spanish Realls, vz. thirteene pence.

Very plainely set forth, and compared with the testimony of the holy scriptures, to the great benefite and profite of all good Christians.

2. Pet. 2. Verf. 18.

For when they speake the great swelling woords of Vanity, they entise through lusts, with the bayte of wantonnesse of the Fleshe, them that were cleane escaped from them, which are wrapped in errour: while they promise them liberty, whereof they them selues are the bond seruaunts of corruption.

Together

With a briefe declaration (set downe in the beginning) which was founde in the Armado of Spaine, of the prowde presumption of the Spaniard: which through the instigation of the aforesaide Bulle, hath taken in hand the setting forth of the inuincible Army (as they terme it) out of Portingale, towards England, and the Lowe countries, in which Army the saide Bulle hath been founde, with other like things. Which Armado is come to confusion through the hand of the Almighty.

Psalme 2. Verf. 15.

Behold he trauaileth with mischiefe, hee hath conceiued sorrow, and broughe forth Vngodlinesse.

Imprinted first
By *Richard Schilders* Printer to the States of Sealand: with consent of the States, Giuen at Middleborrowe, the rii. of September. 1588.
Subscribed
Ch. Roels.

And reprinted at London by Iohn Wolfe, dwelling in the Stationers Hall, 1588.

Title page of *The Holy Bull and Crusado of Rome* translated from the Dutch

but after that it was certenly understood that the Great Navy of Spayn was redy to come owt, and that the fame therof was blowen abrode in Cristendom to be invyncible and so published by books in prynt, the Q of E I am sure and all hir Council, war what so ever good Countenance they made greatly perplexed. She looked certenly for a fight uppon the seas, and therafter a landing and invasion.

But after that it was certainlie understood that the great navie of Spayne was ready to come owt from Lysbon *and that the fame thereof was blowen abroade in christendom to be Invincible, and so published by books in print, the Queene and all hir counsell were (whatsoever good countenance they made), I am sure not a litle* perplexed *as looking certainlie for a fight uppon the Seas, and after* that for *a landing, and Invasion:*

But after that it was certainely vnderstood, that the great Nauy of Spaine was ready to come out from Lisbone, and that the fame therof was blowne abroad in Christendome to be inuincible, and so published by bookes in print, the Quéene and all her Counsel I am sure (whatsoeuer good countenance they made) were not a little perplexed, as looking certainely for a daungerous fight vpon the Seas, and after that for a landing and Inuasion. Whereupon the Lord Admirall was commaunded to saile with the greatest ships, to the West of

Neither in the manuscript drafts (opposite) nor the printed version of *The Copy of a Letter* (above) was prominence given to the description of the Armada as 'invincible'

in semi-retirement on the island of Walcheren, though he seems to have maintained close touch with Henry Killigrew. He had been instrumental in supplying Killigrew in June with Cardinal Allen's *Admonition* and *Declaration*, smuggled out of Antwerp, but he had been unable to obtain copies for himself through his wife and other contacts there.

Perhaps that is why he turned to translating the bull of Pope Gregory XIII, adding a vigorous commentary which demonstrated that its reference to 'infidels and heretics' amounted to a licence to Spain to make war on Protestants. The final printed version also included a declaration claimed to have been found in the Spanish fleet and a list of indulgences issued by the Spanish Inquisition in April (after the Pope had refused to declare a jubilee). The book, *Heylige Bulle ende Krusado des Paus van Roomen*, was authorized at Middelburg on 2 September to be printed by Richard Schilders, printer to the States of Zealand.

There seems to have been a delay of over a month before it was printed, in the course of which a preface was added, which related stories attributed to Spanish prisoners too close to Burghley's *Copy of a Letter* to be coincidental. Possibly Sainte Aldegonde was the translator of one of the Dutch editions of Burghley's pamphlet from the Vautrollier French edition, available by the end of September.

As it happened, Lord Burghley had already seen a copy of Sainte Aldegonde's book. Sometime before 14 October he had authorized John Wolfe to have 'the pope's bull in Dutch with the answer thereto to be translated' on condition that 'no person shall print any part and parcel thereof to his hindrance.'

Burghley had every reason to wish the bull printed. A proclamation about a new bull of the Pope had been issued in July and there was a further reference to it in *The Copy of a Letter*, which was by now circulating widely in the English edition. The bull of Gregory XIII was harmless enough, had nothing to do with the Armada, nor, for that matter, with England, and moreover did not claim to depose the Queen or incite her subjects to rebellion. But it had been renewed by Pope Sixtus V and would serve to satisfy the curious.*

When John Wolfe's English edition of *The Holy Bull and Crusado of Rome* reached the public, what most caught their fancy was the reference on the title page to an ironic nickname which the Armada has never since lost. Three-quarters of the way down the long title occur the words 'the proud presumption of the Spaniard: which through the instigation of the aforesaid Bull, hath taken in hand the setting forth of the invincible Army (as they term it) out of Portingale, towards England.'

Though it was a direct translation of the Dutch *onverwinnelicke Armada*, it nevertheless seems to be Lord Burghley who deserves the credit for the invention. Even in the first draft of his *Copy of a Letter*, written in August, he had referred to the news 'that the Great Navy of Spain was ready to come out, and that the fame thereof was blown abroad in Christendom to be invincible and so published by books in print' (cf. p. 148 above). These 'books in print' were as fictitious as those which threatened to root out the English race.

The subsequent success of Burghley's epithet seems to have been accidental. It is not given emphasis in his manuscript draft or even in the first printing. Quite likely he did not expect to be taken literally. From the context, it is evident that he was thinking of *La Felicissima Armada* or of Mendoza's *Le vrai discours de l'armée*, neither of which published any such claim. But to Sainte Aldegonde (or his printer) is at least due the credit of giving the epithet prominence on the title page.

By the time John Wolfe came to print the Italian edition 'the Invincible Armada' had entered popular parlance. His translator may have been Petruccio Ubaldini, whose Italian was as convoluted as Burghley's English; he also seems to have been ready to make improvements in Burghley's text.

In the middle of the sentence in which Burghley claimed that the fame of the great navy of Spain 'was blown abroad in Christendom to be invincible', the Italian translator inserted the words: 'although that name was only allowed for that little space of time that it stayed in the port of Lisbon (say the Adversaries), for it was not long before the name was lost, through the losses suffered between there and Corunna.' Moreover at the end of the list of disasters in *Certain Advertisements out of Ireland* a triumphant coda was added: 'The end of the story of the unhappiness [*infelicita*] of the Spanish Armada, which was called INVINCIBLE, sent to conquer the most powerful Kingdom of most happy [*felicissima*] England.'

---

* Even William Camden was apparently confused enough to relate in his *Annales . . . regnante Elizabetha* (1615) that 'Sixtus Quintus . . . renewed the Bulls declaratory of Pius Quintus and Gregory the 13th, excommunicated the Queen, unthroned her, absolved her subjects from all allegiance, and published his Crusado in print, as against Turks and infidels, wherein out of the treasure of the Church he gave plenary indulgences to all that gave their assistance. Geoffrey Parker has advised me that the description *Invencible* appears obscurely in a long poem by Juan de Mena celebrating the departure of the fleet from Lisbon (C. Fernandez Duro, *La Armada Invencible*, Madrid 1884–5 II, 95). But there seems to be no trace of other 'books in print' and Dutch pamphlets only started to use the epithet after the publication of *Heylige Bulle*.

LA QVANTITA DELLE NAVI AFFONDATE, ET degli huomini annegati, & vccifi, o pigliati ne mefi di Luglio , & d'Agofto paffati, ne combattimenti, che fi fecero nello ftretto mare dell'Inghilterra, tra gli fpagnuoli, & gl'inglefi.

	Naui	Huomini.
Primieramente galere.	4	1612.
Vicinoad Edifton verfo Plemu a la prima fcaramuccia.	1	Il numero non fi fa.
Nello fteffo tempo la naue di don Pedro di Valdez fu feguitata, & pigliata.	1	122 } Amendue rimangon in Inghilterra.
Vna groffa naue bifcaina nel mede- fimo tempo offefa da fuoco , & pigliata.	1	289 }
La maggior delle galeazze di Na- poli fu dinanzi a Cales fpogliata.	1	686.
Vna groffa naue bifcaina s'affondò nella medefima battaglia.	1	Il numero non fi fa.
Il Galeone San Philippo.	1	532 } Quefte due furono me nate a Fleßinghe , ef- fendo ftate grauemen- te offefe dall'artiglieria inglefe.
Il Galeone San Matteo.	1	397 }
Vn bifcaino pigliato dinanzi Often- da.	1	La quantita non fi fa.
Due vinetiane affondarono due giorni dopo la battaglia.	2	843.
Vna groffa naue bifcaina, combat- tuta dalle naui della reina, fi per- dette inanzi il porto d'Haura di gratia in Francia.	1	Il numero non fi fa.

In tutte 1 5   4781.

Il numero d'amendue le perdite. 3 2   10775. De quali ci fono piu di mille prigionieri in Inghilter-

Oltre a molte altre , che fi tiene per fermo, fi fieno perdute, non oftante che di loro non fi fia infino a qui faputa cofa veruna di certo.

ra , & in Zelanda , oltre vna gran multitudine d'huomini non comprefi in quefto cal- culo, vccifi nelle fcarammuc- cie, o morti di difagi, come appare pergli rapporti de fo- pradetti effaminati.

Finifce il raccontamento dell'infelicità dell'Armata Spaniola , che IN- VINCIBILE fi diceua , mandata a conqueftare il potentifimo Regno della felicifima Inghilterra.

At the end of John Wolfe's Italian edition of *The Copy of a Letter* the ironic title 'invincible' was given prominence. The Armada suffered more losses than this early list indicates

Of course these additions may well have been made by Burghley himself, who had a collection of Italian books, including John Wolfe's, in his library.

Burghley's object seems to have been to print *The Copy of a Letter* and *Certain Advertisements out of Ireland* in the same languages as the *Relacion Verdadera* of the fleet assembled in Lisbon, omitting Spanish, just as the Spaniards had omitted English. The choice of printers was the same as for Burghley's *Execution of Justice in England* four years before (rather than Christopher Barker, the Queen's printer, whose imprint would have revealed its government source).

Translations into High and Low German were left to printers in the Netherlands. John Wolfe was the natural choice for the Italian edition; he had practised his craft in Florence before returning to London and becoming a member of the Stationers Company. He specialized in Italian books prohibited by the Index recently introduced by the Roman Catholic Church. Having started with the works of Machiavelli (which purported on the title pages to have been printed in Palermo or Piacenza), he was now engaged in printing the mildly pornographic books of Aretino in time for the Frankfurt Book Fair next spring. The title page of *Essempio d'una Lettera* did not bear Wolfe's name either, but 'Per Arrigo del Bosco' of Leyden, who must have been a new distributor, if indeed he existed.

For Jaqueline Vautrollier, Burghley's commission saved a business that had seemed doomed to failure. The two pamphlets were reprinted time and time again and the proceeds must have been enough to secure her financial future. The legal future of the business was secured by her marriage to Richard Field, probably thirty years her junior, who moved into the Vautrollier house with a garden at Blackfriars and whose name began to appear on the title pages as an accredited printing member of the Stationers Company.*

---

* It was in Blackfriars that William Shakespeare, a few years Field's junior at Stratford grammar school, came to set up house in London. It was Field who printed the first edition of his first published poem, *Venus and Adonis*. Though the poem was a popular success, he did not print the subsequent editions. He was probably a puritan and had, after all, married a Huguenot.

CHAPTER ELEVEN

ECCLESIASTICAL CAUSES

God's word with sword, and eke her crown,
  from foes she doth defend;
Yet pagan pope, that filthy sort of Rome,
  the devil doth legate send
    To spoil our Jewel brave.
But God will have no thing ill done;
he teacheth England how to shun,
and traitors to the gallows run –
    Elizabeth Lord save,
and still defend her with thy hand,
her happy days to pass the sand,
so shall this be a blessed land.

> Anon.: *Elizabeth Lord Save (A proper new ballad, wherein is*
> *plain to be seen how God blesseth England for love of our Queen).*

1

At the Old Bailey, on 4 October, three more Catholics were tried for treason. Neither Henry Garnet nor Robert Southwell were in London at the time. The only description of the trial and result comes from a pamphlet published by the Welsh printer, Richard Jones, a few weeks later, 'with the Speeches which passed between a learned Preacher and them: Faithfully collected, even in the same words, as near as might be remembered'. But there are signs that it was actually printed by the puritan Robert Waldegrave, who was still operating his secret press in East Molesey, assisted by the Welshman John Penry.

The first to be tried was John Weldon, a priest, who pleaded not guilty and benefit of clergy. The judge, Recorder Fleetwood, 'very gravely and learnedly' referred him to statutes made before the Reformation which allowed clergy to be tried before a lay jury for certain serious crimes such as treason. When Weldon refused to accept this exposition, the jury impatiently found him guilty. He was sentenced to be hanged, drawn, and quartered.

The second defendant was another priest, William Hartley. He had earlier been banished for smuggling Catholic books, such as Parsons' *Book of the Christian Exercise*, into the country, but had since returned to England. The star witness at the trial was Roger Walton, one of Walsingham's spies who had operated in France.* Walton

---

* For Hartley and his connection with Campion, cf. p. 9. Walton was also to be a principal witness in the trial of the Earl of Arundel, a prisoner in the Tower, who was alleged to have attended a mass praying for the success of the Armada.

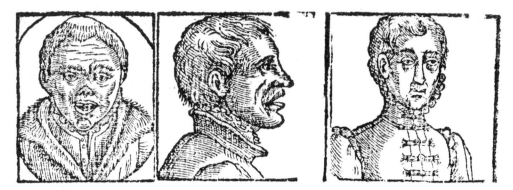

Caricatures of the villainous looking priests and effete schoolmaster from the pamphlet describing their trial and execution

testified that Hartley had sent a letter to seminary priests in Paris declaring his and his colleagues' intention to seize the Tower of London and set fire to the city 'immediately upon the landing of the Spaniards'. Hartley denied the charge, claiming that he was taken sick at the time, but his alibi was not accepted. The court was read part of his examination, 'taken before Master James Doulton and Master Richard Young and subscribed with his own hand'. It declared

> that if the Pope by his Apostolic authority, do deprive the Queen's Majesty, and do discharge her subjects of their obedience, and send an Army to restore the Catholic Roman Religion into *England*, he would not take her Majesty's part, but would pray that the Catholic Roman Army might prevail in that cause of Catholic religion: and in that faith he would spend (if he had them) ten thousand Millions of lives: and this he speaketh (as he saith) in the integrity of his soul.

Without further ado, Hartley was found guilty and awarded the same sentence as Weldon.

The third to be tried was Robert Sutton, a schoolmaster, who had been 'of late years reconciled to the Church of Rome and authority of the Pope, contrary to his former oath and allegiance'. He pleaded not guilty and confessed the Queen supreme governor within her dominions over all persons but not over all causes. In other words, he did not recognize her supremacy in the Church. His authority was 'a sentence of a father alleged (as he saith) by Campion, which he did not well remember'. The verdict and sentence were the same as the others.

The following day the three prisoners were put into the cart at Newgate and taken first to Mile End, where Weldon was to be executed. The executioner, however, had not yet arrived. In the meantime, the sheriff asked Weldon to prepare himself to die and to beg the Queen's forgiveness. The following dialogue ensued:

> 'Why' (quoth he) 'should I ask her forgiveness, whom I never offended?'
> 'No?' (said Mr Sheriff *Ofley*) 'hast thou not offended her? Wast thou not made

a Priest by authority, derived from the Pope at *Paris*? And afterwards camest thou not traitorously into this realm, to withdraw her Majesty's subjects from their obedience, is this no offence?'

'No' (quoth he) 'I came not willingly into this realm. I was drawn in against my will, and brought in by force.'

At these executions there was a 'learned and godly preacher present', who had also attended the trial, and who seems likely to have been the source of the eyewitness account subsequently published. The preacher revealed to the crowd surrounding the scaffold that in fact Weldon had first entered the country of his own free will, had been caught and sentenced, but had then been pardoned by the Queen and banished. He had once again returned to England, pretending to have been converted a Protestant, and had been helped with money. Afterwards he went into Flanders to attempt the assassination of the Earl of Leicester, but had been caught once more and brought back for trial. Weldon, however, was unrepentant:

'I have' (quoth he) 'done nothing but what a Roman Catholic priest ought to do, by the direction of our most holy Father the Pope being the head of the Church: who only hath authority over all persons, and in all causes Ecclesiastical . . . and in this Catholic Roman religion I will die, and willingly shed my blood.'

The executioner had still not arrived, so the preacher filled in the time with a lengthy sermon on the nature of the priesthood and of the false authority of the Church of Rome and the Pope, quoting numerous precedents from the Scriptures and the Church Fathers. He reminded Weldon that however he might hope to gain the name of martyr among the papists, it was 'not the punishment but the cause that maketh the martyr'. He implored him to repent and to pray, 'as a Christian should'.

Weldon, however, insisted on praying in Latin, whereupon the preacher '(seeing his obstinacy) willed the people to lift up their hearts in prayer', praying loudly himself in English. The executioner, who had at last arrived, then did his duty.

The procession moved on to 'Holywell, nigh to the Theater', with the preacher striving hard to persuade Hartley, the next victim, to repentance. On the scaffold, Hartley, like Weldon, maintained that he had committed no treason other than to exercise the function of a Roman Catholic priest. The preacher was not prepared to waste time arguing with him, but pointed out that although Hartley had been convicted of treason the Queen had mercifully commuted the sentence to hanging only. Hartley began to pray in Latin and the preacher in English, 'the people joining with him in great fervency', as the sentence was carried out.

The remaining prisoner, Sutton the schoolmaster, was then taken in the cart to Clerkenwell, with the preacher 'travailing still very earnestly to bring him to conformity'. Sutton was prepared to concede certain points and affirmed that he would fight in the Queen's cause 'against what pope or potentate soever'. He requested a stay of execution for a day or so in order to confer with the learned for a better settling of his conscience. The sheriff and officers 'very charitably' sent back to the Lord Chief Justice and the Attorney General for their opinion. The two law officers considered the request and were prepared to agree provided that Sutton would acknowledge the Queen supreme governor 'in all causes as over all persons'.

> [Sutton] stood for a while as it were in a doubt what he might do, and after said, that he durst not acknowledge that: because the church of Rome did not grant it: and I must (quoth he) remain in the unity of the Church, or else I cannot be saved, for so saith St *Augustine*. That is (quoth the preacher) in the unity of the Church of Christ, not of the Church of Rome: for the unity of wicked persons is no unity, but a conspiracy.

After another short sermon, the preacher accused Sutton of deliberately delaying matters and called upon the people to pray and to leave him to God. Finally he 'also made a godly prayer, after the which the prisoner persisting in his wilfulness was forthwith executed.'

2

The main concern of the Privy Council, including Archbishop Whitgift, was preparation for the new Parliament to be held in November. By statute, an election had to be held on the day of the next meeting of the county court after receipt of the writ of election issued on 18 September. County courts met on a set day once every four weeks, so that the elections were spread over the whole of October and even into early November. Two knights were elected from each English shire (only one in Wales) and two burgesses from each corporate town or other qualified borough.

There was seldom more than one nominee to a seat in Parliament and his election was normally carried by the acclamation of the assembled voters, from 'forty-shilling freeholders' upwards. In most cases even the nomination was a foregone conclusion; the leading landowner or his nominee was assured of a safe passage to Parliament. Thus Sir James Croft of Richards Castle, though still in prison, was as usual nominated and elected as senior knight for Herefordshire. (He was released from prison before Parliament assembled and resumed his seat on the Privy Council.)

Similarly, an important Court official who had held the seat in the previous Parliament could be certain of the nomination again; hence Sir Francis Walsingham became once again the senior knight for Surrey. High officials no longer eligible were entitled by custom to nominate their successors and might even go further. At the last Parliament, for example, Sir Christopher Hatton had been senior knight for Northamptonshire, with Sir Walter Mildmay as his junior. Now, as Lord Chancellor, he wrote on 5 October to the sheriff of his county, Sir Edward Mountague:

> I have thought fit, for divers good respects, to recommend to your choice therein my honourable good friend Sir Walter Mildmay, knight, a person well known unto you all both for his wisdom and great experience in the course of those affairs; as also my good friend Sir Richard Knightley, a gentleman so well affected to the good of his country as that I doubt not but to find yourself and the rest of our gentlemen very ready to yield unto them both your voices and

willing consents in that behalf, earnestly praying you to take the pains to move also your good friends, freeholders, tenants, and servants for the furtherance of their voices thereunto. Not doubting but that their travails and endeavours in every respect shall prove answerable to your expectations and to the full liking and contentment of you all.

Here he followed the convention that the nomination was decided by a consensus of the leading gentlemen of the county, whose 'friends, freeholders, tenants and servants' could be counted upon to endorse the candidate. Sir Walter Mildmay and Sir Richard Knightley were duly elected on 10 October.

Other high officials sought to advance members of their family. Only the day after the election writ was issued, Lord Burghley (who must have had a hand in the decision) wrote to the High Sheriff of Hertfordshire, of which he was Lord Lieutenant, about 'the parliament rumoured to begin about the 13th of November next':

If so it be that you have not made any earnest determination to grant your goodwill to some others, then I could be content to have your favourable allowance to favour my son, Robert Cecil, being already a Justice of the Peace in that shire and one that after me shall have a reasonable freehold in the same, that he might have the voices of your friends, to be one of the said two knights of the shire for the parliament to come.

Burghley's son was, of course, elected and held the seat until he became a peer.

On one occasion at least, in 1588, Court and local interests clashed. Sir Thomas Heneage, Vice-Chamberlain and a privy councillor, was nominated as senior knight for Essex. As Deputy Lieutenant of the county and holder of the seat in the last two parliaments, he was clearly a secure candidate. The other nominee was Sir Henry Gray, but his nomination was opposed by Lord Rich, an extremely wealthy landowner who could probably himself have commanded a majority of the freeholders and tenants. What was more, his cousin Robert Wroth (the same who had assisted Richard Rogers to regain his licence to preach) was the sheriff. Both were strong puritans and there can be little doubt that their candidate was likewise inclined.

Probably at the instance of Heneage, who supported Gray, the Privy Council wrote to the sheriff forbidding him to hold the election except at Chelmsford, the usual place (sheriffs had been known to arrange elections in a convenient location for their favoured candidate without informing the opposition). Two weeks later they wrote again, this time to Lord Rich himself, 'advising and requiring' him to abandon his rival candidate. The excuse given was that it was undesirable to bring together so large an assembly at that time and 'the worthiness of both the parties nominated for that place'. Since both Heneage and Gray were returned as members, it looks as if Lord Rich gave way and a contest was avoided.

Borough elections varied more in procedure. Boroughs were expected to meet the expenses of their burgesses while Parliament was sitting. Many of the smaller boroughs could ill afford this financial burden and welcomed the offer of representation by a gentleman wealthy enough to pay his own way; probably that is why Francis Bacon was returned unopposed for Liverpool. Other 'manorial boroughs' were wholly at the disposal of their owner. For example, it only required the nomination by Lord Howard of Effingham's bailiff to secure the election of Thomas Cockes as member for Bletchingley in Surrey (was he related to the Richard Cockes of Limehouse who was the only officer killed in the fight with the Armada?). The larger, financially independent towns were jealous of interference and managed their own nominations. In Exeter the Common Council discussed among themselves who were the 'most fit' to be proposed to the freeholders the next county court day and their nominees were duly elected without opposition.

Nevertheless, even if the result of election was a foregone conclusion, bands of freeholders and retainers were assembling outside shire halls all over the country to acclaim their masters' choice. Meanwhile the Privy Council was having second thoughts.

At the last parliament in 1587, the puritan faction, flushed with success at securing the execution of Mary Queen of Scots, had introduced 'a Bill and a Book'. The bill consisted mostly of a preamble outlining the progress in reformation of the Church since Henry VIII's time and describing the ideal, presbyterian Church 'approved by the general judgement and practice of all the best-reformed Churches'. The bill's two brief clauses authorized the sole use of the annexed Genevan Book of Common Prayer and rendered void all existing 'laws, customs, statutes, ordinances and constitutions' affecting the government of the Church and its services. The Queen had quashed the bill and eventually silenced debate by declaring that questions of religion were a matter for the royal prerogative.

While the 1587 Parliament was in session, John Penry, a young Welsh preacher, had arranged for the Oxford University press (which was under the Earl of Leicester's protection) to print a *Supplication* pleading for more educated ministers in his native Wales. He had been hauled before the High Commission and given a stern warning by Archbishop Whitgift. During the summer of 1588, Robert Waldegrave had secretly been printing a further series of pamphlets by Penry, which were this time addressed to the Governors of Wales, an oblique means of criticizing the High Commission. Penry not only pleaded for a learned ministry in his native country but also questioned the validity of the sacraments of the Church of England administered by clergy unqualified to preach but only capable of reading the Homilies. His campaign was taken seriously enough by the authorities for Dr Some to write a lengthy supplement to his *Godly Treatise* refuting his arguments, which was published in September by Christopher Barker, the Queen's printer.

Convocation met at the same time as Parliament and time was needed to prepare against further puritan attacks on the Church established. This may be why on 14 October a royal proclamation announced that 'for divers good causes and considerations' Parliament was prorogued from 12 November until 4 February.

Archbishop Whitgift used the breathing space to catch up on his administration. Puritans had been able to win sympathy and support from the more moderate members of parliament for their plea for a more learned ministry. During the last parliament they had presented surveys showing how many parishes lacked a minister competent to preach. As a result Whitgift had issued orders 'for the better increase in Learning in the inferior Ministers and for more Diligent Preaching and Catechising'.

On 5 November he instructed the bishops to send him returns on the admission of clergy and their educational qualifications according to the articles agreed in 1586, because 'it will be looked for at the next Parliament how the Articles have been used.' Returns should have been sent to him every year but apparently he could not find them.

The instructions were that every minister without licence to preach or a university degree was 'to provide a Bible, Bullinger's *Decades* of sermons in Latin or English, and a paper book'. Every day he was to read over a chapter of Holy Scripture, note the principal contents in his paper book, and every week he was to do the same with a sermon from the *Decades*, reporting once a quarter to a licensed preacher assigned for that purpose. Licensed preachers were instructed to preach twelve sermons a year in their diocese, eight to be in their own benefice.

It was not until 22 November that the Bishop of London called the attention of his archdeacons to these instructions. The Archdeacon of St Albans took until 20 December to render his returns.

3

The decision to postpone Parliament may also have been influenced by the appearance, in early or mid-October, of another product of Robert Waldegrave's secret press, called *A Demonstration of the truth of that Discipline which Christ hath prescribed in his word for the government of his Church, in all times and places, until the end of the world.* Fellow stationers could recognize by the typography that it was Waldegrave's work. The methodical arrangement of the main text, its careful, annotated progress from one logical premise to the next, and its debt to the doctrines of Thomas Cartwright, must have betrayed to students of his published sermons that it was written by John Udall, a curate of Kingston upon Thames who had been deprived of his licence to preach in June.

John Udall succinctly summarized the presbyterian position at the end, with references back to the nineteen chapters in which each point had been discussed in more detail:

Christ has prescribed unto us an exact and perfect platform of governing his church at all times and in all places, which is this:
[1] that there ought to be no ministers of the word but pastors and teachers, which are to be called by the people and ordained by the Eldership, are of equal authority in their several congregations, must with all faithful diligence employ themselves in the ministry of the word and sacraments;
[2] that there are to be in every congregation certain elders, whose office is to oversee the behaviour of the people and assist their pastor in the government of the church; also Deacons, who are to be employed only in receiving and bestowing the liberality and goods of the church to the relief of the poor and other necessary uses;

GODLY TREATISE

containing and deciding certaine
queſtions, mooued of late in London and
other places, touching the Miniſterie,
Sacraments, and Church.

Whereunto one Propoſition more is added.

After the ende of this Booke you ſhall
finde a defence of ſuch points as M. Penry
hath dealt againſt: And a confutati-
on of many groſſe errours broched
in M. PENRIES laſt
Treatiſe.

Written by Robert Some Doctor
of Diuinitie.

Epheſ. 4. verſe 15.
Let vs follow the trueth in loue, and in all things grow
vp into him, which is the head (that is) Chriſt, &c.

Imprinted at London by G. B. Deputie to Chri-
ſtopher Barker, Printer to the Queenes moſt excellent Maieſtie. 1588.

A DEMONSTRATION OF

the trueth of that Diſcipline which
Chriſte hath preſcribed in his worde for the
gouernement of his Church, in all times
and places, vntill the ende of the worlde.

¶ Wherein are gathered into a plaine
forme of reaſoning, the proofes thereof, out of
the ſcriptures, the euidence of it by the
light of reaſon rightly ruled, and the teſtimonies
that haue been giuen therevnto, by the courſe
o fthe Churche certaine hundreths of yeares after the Apoſtles time; and the generall con-
ſent of the Churches rightly reformed in
theſe latter times: according as they
are alleaged and maintained, in
thoſe ſeuerall bookes that
haue bin written con-
cerning the
ſame.

MATTH. 21. 38.
The husbandmen ſaid among themſelues, this is the heire; come
let vs kill him, and let vs take his inheritaunce.

LVKE. 19. 27.
Thoſe mine enemies which would not that I ſhoulde raigne ouer
them, bring hither, and ſlea them before me.

An official Government reply (left) to one of the pamphlets printed surreptitiously by Robert Waldegrave during the summer of 1588. The pamphlet by John Udall (right), also printed by Waldegrave, probably alerted the Privy Council to the likelihood of renewed puritan activity in the Parliament due to be held in November, but later prorogued

[3] Lastly, that there must be in every congregation an eldership of pastor, teacher (if they can have any) and elders, who are in common to see that the church be well governed, not only in maintaining the profession and practice of the word in general, but also in admonishing, reprehending, or separating from the Lord's supper them that walk offensively, and lastly in excommunicating them that by no other means can be reclaimed.

So that all and every government contrary or besides this, whether in part or in whole, swerveth from that order which Christ has set down in his word, and therefore is unlawful.

But the introduction to the pamphlet struck a different, more inflammatory note. It took the form of an address 'To the supposed Governors of the Church of England', who would be meeting in Convocation at the same time as Parliament.

It complained that 'certainly it is more free these days, to be a papist, anabaptist, of the family of love, yea any most wicked one whatsoever' than to be a believer in presbyterian reform. While papists went unmolested or were lodged in bishops' houses, puritans were kept in close confinement in prisons. The same complaint had been voiced in *The State of the Church of England* (see p. 38 above), to which the author of the Address referred as 'a *Dialogue* lately come forth against you, and since burned by you, [charging] that you care for nothing but the maintenance of your dignities, be it to the damnation of your own souls, and infinite millions more'.

This is an important clue that it was the author of the *Dialogue*, and not John Udall, who wrote the *Address to the supposed Governors*, which ended with the customary challenge to a disputation or public debate but appeared to threaten violence if the challenge were not taken up:

> We have sought to advance this cause of God by humble suit to the parliament, by supplication to your Convocation house, by writing in defence of it, and by challenging to dispute for it, seeing none of these means used by us have prevailed: If it come in by that means, which will make all your hearts to ache, blame your selves; for it must prevail, maugre the malice of all that stand against it, or such a judgement must overtake this land, as shall cause the ears that hear thereof to tingle, and to make us a by-word to all that pass by us.

It was the same author who was responsible for a pseudonymous pamphlet which began to circulate during the last two weeks in October: *An Epistle to the terrible Priests of the Confocation house* 'Compiled for the behoof and overthrow of the Parlous Fickers and Currats, that have learnt their Catechisms and are past grace: by the reverend and worthy Martin Marprelate gentleman'. He was a Warwickshire squire called Job Throckmorton, long-time friend of John Field and of Thomas Cartwright since his undergraduate days at Cambridge, who had been a member of the 1586–7 Parliament and taken an active part in the puritan campaign.

Probably to evade detection, the *Epistle* was printed in a 'dutch letter' (German blackletter type) which Robert Waldegrave had not used before. But the typography betrayed his hand in its composition.

The *Epistle* took the form of a mock petition to Convocation, which the author had expected would be meeting in November at the same time as Parliament:

> Most pitifully complaining therefore, you are to understand, that Dr Bridges hath written in your defence, a most senseless book, and I cannot very often at one breath come to a full point, when I read the same.

The ostensible target was a lengthy tome by the Dean of Salisbury, Dr John Bridges, published over a year before, entitled *A Defence of the Government Established in the Church of England for Ecclesiastical Matters*. It was an expansion, to the extent of 1,400 pages, of a sermon he had preached against a presbyterian manifesto, published clandestinely (and without the author's permission) by John Field in 1584. Dr Bridges' technique was to quote a sentence or two from the book (usually called *A Learned Discourse* from its running title) and then refute the arguments at length with copious references to the Bible, the Church Fathers, and continental theologians; it was a technique frequently used to refute Catholic treatises, apparently by sheer

Oh read ouer D. Iohn Bridges/for it is a worthy worke:

Or an epitome of the

fyrste Booke/of that right worshipfull vo=
lume/ written against the Puritanes/ in the defence of
the noble cleargie/ by as worshipfull a prieste/ Iohn Bridges/
Presbyter/Priest or elder/doctor of Diuilitie/ and Deane of
Sarum. Wherein the arguments of the puritans are
wisely preuented/ that when they come to an∢
swere M. Doctor/ they must needes
say something that hath
bene spoken.

Compiled for the behoofe and overthrow of
the Parsons/Fyckers/and Currats/that have lernt
their Catechismes/and are past grace: By the reverend
and worthie Martin Marprelate gentleman/and
dedicated to the Confocationhouse.

The Epitome is not yet published/ but it shall be when
the Bishops are at conuenient leysure to view the same.
In the meane time/let them be content with
this learned Epistle.

Printed ouersea/in Europe/within two fur=
longs of a Bouncing Priest/at the cost and charges
of M. Marprelate/gentleman.

Title page of Martin Marprelate's first pamphlet, usually referred to as the *Epistle* to distinguish it from
the later *Epitome*. It was in fact printed in East Molesey, not far from Hampton Court

weight of argument. Two puritan replies, one of them by Walter Travers, John Field's successor, had been printed in Middelburg by Richard Schilders and smuggled into England, but failed to create much of a stir.

Discussion of Dr Bridges' book in fact took up only about a fifth of the *Epistle*, which was mainly devoted to attacks on the dignities of the bishops and other higher clergy: 'They are petty popes, and petty Antichrists, whosoever usurp the authority of pastors over them, who by the ordinance of God, are to be under no pastors. For none but Antichristian popes and popelings ever claimed this authority unto themselves.'

Archbishop Whitgift, referred to as 'his Canterburiness' or 'John Cant', was accused of favouring papists and recusants over puritans and of persecuting printers like Waldegrave while dealing leniently with popish printers. But Martin Marprelate was careful to explain that he was not criticizing the Archbishop in his capacity of privy councillor (which would have been a treasonable offence).

Other targets included Bishop John Aylmer of London, for playing bowls on Sunday and for deceiving some weavers out of stolen cloth, the allegedly bigamous Bishop of St Asaph ('sir Ass'), and the Archdeacon of Surrey, bribed by a usurer to have John Udall deprived of his licence to preach.

Martin Marprelate evidently had access to the surveys which John Field had collected for his parliamentary campaigns to reform abuses in the Church: 'what a perilous fellow M. Marprelate is: he understands all of your knavery, and it may be he keeps a register of them: unless you amend, they shall come into the light one day.' If Convocation failed to meet his demands, he threatened to 'place a young Martin in every diocese, which may take notices of your practices' and to publish more books, such as *Martin's dream, Of the lives and doings of English popes*, my *Itinerarium, or visitations*, my *Lambethisms*. Interspersed with all this inconsequential jocularity and gossip were serious arguments for reform of the Church according to the Calvinist Discipline.

Martin Marprelate explained and justified his technique in a later pamphlet:

> I saw the cause of Christ's government, and of the Bishops' Antichristian dealing to be hidden. The most part of men could not be gotten to read any thing, written in the defence of the one and against the other. I bethought me therefore, of a way whereby men might be drawn to do both, perceiving the humours of men in these times (especially those who are in any place [of public office]) to be given to mirth. I took that course. I might lawfully do it. Aye, for jesting is lawful by circumstances, even in the greatest matters.

The immediate success of Martin Marprelate's *Epistle* at Court, where copies were passed surreptitiously from hand to hand, owed as much to snobbery as to Martin's jokes. Courtiers enjoyed his irreverence towards bishops because they were lords by virtue of office rather than by honour of blood. But the puritans were less enthusiastic; while they were accustomed to expressing their contempt for the Church hierarchy at private meetings, it was another matter to bring it into the open and to discuss such serious matters in so frivolous a vein.

Moreover Martin's jocularity lost the qualified support to the puritan cause given by clergy and others who recognized the need for reform in the Church though not the radical reorganization demanded by the Genevan Discipline. In an 'Epistle Dedicatory' (to Thomas Cooper, Bishop of Winchester) of an Accession Day sermon, John Prime of New College, Oxford, lamented Martin Marprelate's 'late most false, shameless, and unchristian libelling' and concluded:

> The corruption of Patrons, the inability of Ministers [to preach], their requisite diligence and some like matters of importance to be looked into and provided for, by the strength of best authority, for mine own part I do greatly desire. But this *Gentleman's* humour hath, I know not what other vagrant and hungry conceits. I crave pardon in respecting this man as he came in my way, I have stepped aside.

4

Mrs Elizabeth Crane, the owner of the house in East Molesey where Waldegrave's secret press had been operating since April, was becoming concerned. She had already asked John Penry to find another hiding place and he in turn, the previous September, had approached Sir Richard Knightley about using a room in his house at Fawsley in Northamptonshire. Sir Richard, besides being a strong puritan, was Deputy Lieutenant of the county and a member of parliament (recently renominated by none other than Sir Christopher Hatton, the Lord Chancellor).

Towards the end of October, one of Sir Richard Knightley's tenants arrived with a cart at East Molesey to collect a load from Mrs Crane's house, which he then took to Fawsley and left in the keeping of Sir Richard's caretaker. When Mrs Crane inspected her house on 1 November she found no one there and not a sign of a printing press.

She was just in time. Martin Marprelate's *Epistle* had earned the disapproval of the Queen and her Privy Council. On 14 November Sir Christopher Hatton and Lord Burghley sent a letter to the Archbishop of Canterbury, advising him that 'her Majesty hath understanding of a lewd and seditious book lately printed as it should seem in a secret manner, and as secretly dispersed by persons of unquiet spirits.'

> Your grace, with the advice of some other of the Bishops your brethren, should use all privy means, by force of your Commission ecclesiastical or otherwise, to fetch out the authors hereof and their complices, and the printers and the secret dispersers of the same; and to cause them to be apprehended and committed.

This authority brought the full weight of the government to bear. Richard Bancroft, former chaplain and speechwriter to Sir Christopher Hatton, had already been investigating the puritan movement and was a member of the ecclesiastical High Commission. Now he could employ the services of pursuivants and government agents like Anthony Munday (cf. p. 10) and Roger Walton, previously engaged in searching out Catholics. Munday had actually succeeded in obtaining entry as a student to the English College in Rome, while a Richard Walton (perhaps the same) was eventually to discover the secret Martin Marprelate press.

A very portable booke, a horſe may cary it if he be not too weake.,

The Epitome of the firſt booke, of this worthye volume, written by my brother Sarum, Deane John, Sic fœliciter incipit.

In the promised *Epitome*, Martin Marprelate began to use satirical headings (above), marginal notes, and even pseudo-errata (below) to draw attention to his points

Errata, or faults eſcaped.

1 Wherſoeuer the prelats are called my Lords, either in the epiſtle to the confocatiou houſe, or in this Epitome, take that for a fault. Becauſe they are none of M. Martins Lords, neither ſhal any prieſt of them all be my Lord. For I tell thee true, I think foul ſcorne they ſhould be my Lords, or the Lords of any of my ſonnes.

2 There is nothing ſpoken at all, of that notable hypocrite Scambler, Biſhop of Norwich. Take it for a great faulte, but vnleſſe he leaue his cloſe dealing againſt the truth, ile beſtow a whole booke of him. And let the reſt of you hypocrits take heede of perſecuting.

3 But the greateſt fault of all is, that I coulde ſay againſt our vngodly prieſts, but vnleſſe they mend, iſe fullie amende this fault, and I can doe it with a ſmall warninge. And I would deuiſe them not to perſecute men for my worſhipes booke as they doe.

It was about this time that a man turned up with his servant at Sir Richard Knightley's house at Fawsley and said he had come to sort out Sir Richard's title deeds. The newcomer was Robert Waldegrave.

Sir Richard Knightley's house was in a remote valley with a good view of any approach roads a pursuivant might use. Robert Waldegrave's printing press was installed in an upper room and he was soon engaged in printing the second of Martin Marprelate's pamphlets, the promised *Epitome* of Dr John Bridges' heavy tome. An epitome was a crib used by university students who could not be bothered to read the full text of the books on which they were to be examined.

In his preface Martin boasted of the reception of the *Epistle*: 'I have been entertained at the Court: Every man talks of my worship. Many would gladly receive my books, if they could tell where to find them.' But he conceded that those whose cause he was championing were less enthusiastic: 'The Puritans are angry with me, I mean the puritan preachers. And why? Because I am too open. Because I jest. I jested because I dealt against a worshipful jester, Dr Bridges, whose writings and sermons tend to no other end, than to make men laugh.'

The searchers of the Stationers Company, after a number of wild goose chases, were still none the wiser about Waldegrave's whereabouts. At the end of November, as copies of the *Epitome* began to arrive in London from Northamptonshire, they carried out another raid on Waldegrave's premises in St Paul's Churchyard, breaking down a wall to gain entry. They found nothing.

The Privy Council was having little more success. On 6 December, as a result of their order to round up the usual suspects, Giles Wigginton, formerly vicar of Sedbergh in Yorkshire, found himself being conveyed in a boat to Lambeth Palace by Anthony Munday to be examined by Archbishop Whitgift. Unlike the Archbishop, Wigginton had already seen Marprelate's second pamphlet, but he was an old hand at interrogation and would not even admit that he had read the *Epistle*.

> I understand by hearsay . . . that many Lords and Ladies, and other great and wealthy personages of all estates, have had and read it, if I have done either or both. And in my simple judgement it would be more for your credit if you would examine indifferently all sorts about, and not poor folks as you use to do.

5

Towards the end of October the reinforcements to the Jesuit mission which Henry Garnet had so anxiously awaited in July arrived off the coast of Norfolk, after a rough crossing of three days. They were Edward Oldcorne and John Gerard, who were accompanied by two seminary priests. They were landed by boat after nightfall between Yarmouth and Cromer and waited until daylight before going their separate ways.

Oldcorne was lucky enough to fall in with a group of sailors who were making their way along the coast to London. They took him along with them without suspicion, although he reprimanded them from time to time for swearing; perhaps they thought he was a puritan.

John Gerard set out across country, pretending to anyone he met that he was a falconer who had lost his hawk. That night he stayed in a village inn where he bought a horse. On his way to Norwich, the next morning, he rode straight into the watch guarding the entrance to a village. They questioned him and insisted that he come before the constable and officer of the watch, who was at Sunday morning service. Arriving at the church, Gerard refused to enter, giving as his excuse that he had to watch his horse, though the real reason was that he was forbidden to enter a heretical assembly. Eventually the officer came out and began angrily to interrogate him on his name, his occupation, his residence, the reason for his journey, and whether he carried any letters. Gerard managed to satisfy him and volunteered to be searched. The officer said that it would be necessary to take him before a justice of the peace, but Gerard pleaded that he was in a hurry to return to his master. Finally the officer relented, with the words: 'You've the look of an honest fellow. Go on then in God's name. I won't hold you back any longer.'

In Norwich, Gerard managed to get in touch with a wealthy Catholic who gave him shelter for a few days and then provided a horse and servant for his journey to London, where he arrived in December. He was soon united with Edward Oldcorne and Henry Garnet; Robert Southwell had been sent out of London in November for a seven weeks tour of the country.

There had been no more executions of Catholics since those of Hartley, Weldon and Sutton at the beginning of October. Probably the authorities found that the public execution of young men in their twenties, clearly prepared to die for their faith, had not always made the desired impression on the spectators.

It was only in publications intended for foreign consumption that English Catholics were claimed to have been as forward as Protestants in offering their services to the Queen. In practice, suspicion continued much as before. The leading recusants confined at Ely Castle in Wisbech since July had been induced to sign a declaration of loyalty to the Queen as a condition of release. On 1 December the warden of Ely Castle was ordered, in view of their 'very dutiful protestation of their allegiance toward her Majesty', to bring them up to London and before the Archbishop of Canterbury, who would direct where they were to live 'in some convenient places within ten miles of London'. When they came before the Archbishop they found that they would also be required to enter a bond of £2,000 each for their good behaviour.

The Queen's clemency towards those who recanted was as usual demonstrated publicly. On 1 and 8 December respectively, there appeared at Paul's Cross during the sermon time, William Tedder and Anthony Tyrell, 'sometime two Seminary Priests of the English College in Rome, and now by the great mercy of almighty God converted unto the profession of the Gospel of Jesus Christ'. The recantations were printed in a pamphlet shortly afterwards.

On his second appearance at Paul's Cross that year, 'not of any compulsion', he claimed, 'or for fear of any temporal punishment', Tyrell abjectly apologized for his previous behaviour:

Considering the notorious and outrageous trespass, after so many merciful remissions, that not many months past, I publicly committed at this place (right honourable, worshipful and well-beloved) in the dispersing of certain infamous Libels, to the great dishonour of almighty God, contempt of true Religion, displeasure of my Prince, scandal and offence unto all good and godly Christians, rejoicing of God's enemies, and my own eternal rebuke and infamy: I was afeared lest that my name for ever had been blotted out of the Book of life, and that no place had been left me in this world for true repentance.

But behold, . . . such hath been the great favour showed me, in the toleration of my lewd and heinous fact, such hath been the exceeding clemency of my gracious Prince and Sovereign: but above all, such hath been the infinite mercy of almighty God, in the renewing and perfecting this act of my conversion, that I do not only inwardly feel an assured hope of God's everlasting pardon and forgiveness, but outwardly also, I seem to see almost comfortable resemblance that all you, which have had just cause to hate and contemn me, will yet be moved with compassion.

CHAPTER TWELVE

THE WONDERFUL YEAR

Was die Armada, ausgesant
Vom Spannier wieder Engellandt,
Verrichtedt hab, weiss jederman:
Kein macht ohn Godt gewinnen kan.

What the Armada underwent,
When from Spain to England sent,
Everyone has heard the tale:
No might without God can prevail.

German broadside

1

'The Queen had intended to go to St Paul's to give public thanks for the victory', wrote one of Mendoza's informants, anxious to provide news that would please his paymaster, but she had been dissuaded by the Privy Council 'for fear that a harquebus might be fired at her'. There was such a state of alarm and terror in London, he continued, 'that there is no sign of rejoicing among the Councillors at the victories they have gained. They look rather like men who have a heavy burden to bear . . . The Queen is much aged and spent and is very melancholy. Her intimates say that this is caused by the death of the Earl of Leicester' but the real cause was fear of assassination and the burdens of state.

On the day this despatch was written, the Queen moved from St James's Palace to Greenwich, her favourite residence, where she had been born. There was no sign that she was off her usual form. 'All irresolutions and lacks', wrote Burghley to Walsingham, 'are thrown upon us two in all her speeches to everybody. The wrong is intolerable.'

In spite of the almost continuous series of sermons and victory celebrations, practically every Sunday for nearly three months, she even found fault 'that there hath as yet been no Public Prayer and General Thanksgiving ordained for so rare benefits'. On 3 November the Archbishop of Canterbury and the Dean and Chapter of York (whose archbishop had died the previous July) were instructed by the Privy Council to order a special day of thanksgiving in their respective provinces. On the following day, Archbishop Whitgift passed the word on to his bishops 'that on the 19 day of November, being Tuesday, there shall be a general concurrence of all the people in the Realm in repairing to their Parish Churches, and giving public thanks.'

They should tell 'all Preachers in their Sermons upon that day to declare unto the people the wonderful mercies of God in the said overthrow of our enemies; the particulars whereof they may understand by such pamphlets as have been published of late touching the success [*sic*] of the Spanish Navy.' Archdeacons were to arrange for 'those Preachers who have no special charge' to officiate in parishes with no preaching minister. In every parish there was to be a 'general ringing of Bells, singing of Psalms and all other external signs of joy and thanksgiving'.

These were prosperous days for members of the Stationers Company. Members lucky enough to have secured the printing rights of government inspired pamphlets, like *The Copy of a letter . . . to . . . Mendoza, Certain Advertisements out of Ireland*, and *The Holy Bull and Crusado* had a guaranteed sale, not only to the public, but to preachers gathering material for their sermons.

John Wolfe, whose printing presses were by now installed in Stationers Hall itself, printed a translation of a Dutch pamphlet on the examination of Don Diego Pimentelli, captured by the Dutch, while another printer published the *Orders set down by the Duke of Medina, Lord General of the King's Fleet, to be observed in the voyage toward England*. No more than Don Pedro de Valdez did Don Pimentelli say anything about the intention to root out the English race, nor did the Duke of Medina Sidonia's orders. But of course it was by now far too late to subvert the efforts of the ballad singers and preachers.

Maurice Kyffin, a young Welsh poet, had prepared a supplement to his poem 'The Blessedness of Britain' to celebrate the Queen's Accession Day on 17 November, 'Containing the late Accidents and Occurrents of this year 88':

> Where Tyrants triumph, Mischiefs must ensue:
> No spare of hoary Age, or Infants small:
> Matrons and Maids, their shameful Rape shall Rue:
> Slaughter and Slav'ry, shall be serv'd on all:
>> Huge Storms, and streams, of wasteful wrack and woe,
>> The Cities, Towns, and Fields, shall overflow.'

'What shall I say,' wrote James Aske, 'the book-binders' shops, and every printer's press are so cloyed and clogged with books of these and such like matters, that they were good for nothing (as they say) but to make waste-paper.' He was referring to his poem, 'Elizabetha Triumphans', which described in blank verse 'the Damned practices that the devilish Popes of Rome have used ever sithence her Highness first coming to the Crown, by moving her wicked and traitorous subjects to Rebellion and Conspiracies'. After recounting the various plots on the Queen's life, he came to the Pope's famous bull of 1588, deduced from the proclamation against it:

> In this same year of eighty-eight, the King
> Catholic hath (unto the end he may
> In England hear the credit of the Pope
> Renew again) had from his Holiness
> Both money, men, with many of his Bulls,
> In which he sings the Cuckoo's song (all one)
> Except this clause, 'He hath both dispossessed

> Our royal Queen of this her happy seat
> And all her Nobles and grave Councillors
> Which shall alliant be unto our Queen.'

He went on to describe 'how her excellency was entertained by her Soldiers in her Camp Royal at Tilbury . . . and of the overthrow had against the Spanish Fleet', placing the visit to Tilbury, for dramatic effect, before his account of the naval battle which had taken place two weeks beforehand. Aske may have been present at Tilbury, but the despised ballad writers were more accurate reporters.*

He claimed to have written his poem immediately afterwards and even prepared it for the press, but a quarrel with the printer held things up for ten weeks. The 'commonness of Ballads, with books to this purpose' almost persuaded him to throw his pamphlet on the fire, 'but the entreaty of divers of my dearest friends stayed my determinate purpose.' His friends succeeded in convincing him that the books and ballads did not do his subject justice, and that it was better to publish his work 'than to let such broken tales, told in plain ballets, express the unspeakable acts and wondrous overthrows had against the Pope by this our Royal Queen and her (by this made famous) Island'. With this excuse for the action of a gentleman in committing his verse to vulgar print, he managed to get out his book just in time for the Christmas trade, dedicating it to Dr Julius Caesar, Chief Justice of the Court of Admiralty, whose star was rising with the Lord Admiral's.

2

There was a good deal of speculation in London about when the Queen would come to the city in person for a service of thanksgiving in St Paul's. Her Accession Day, 17 November, was the most likely choice, if not 19 November, the day appointed for thanksgiving for the victory, which happened to be St Elizabeth's Day.

The printers started their preparations in good time. Henry Carre registered two ballads about the overthrow of the Spaniards on 3 November. The following day the wary John Wolfe entered 'A song wherein is contained the treachery of the wicked and is made to be sung on the Coronation Day or any other day'. On 8 November the matter seemed to be cleared up at last. The new Lord Mayor of London, Martin Calthrop, sent a letter to all the livery companies revealing that 'the Queen's most excellent Majesty intendeth to come in her Majesty's most royal person, on the eighteenth day of the present month, from Somerset House to Paul's to hear a sermon.'

Special stands were to be erected along the processional route for the members of each company, 'strong and well-railed, the forerail to be covered with a fair blue

---

* His version of the Queen's speech to the troops, obviously invented on classical models, has been cited as evidence that Dr Sharpe's version is a forgery. Another version may be found in Christopher Ocland's *Elizabetheis*, Book II of which, describing the events of 1588 in Latin hexameters, was published in 1589. He has the Queen reciting Psalm 56. Ocland's Virgilian poem had been ordered by the Privy Council into the school curriculum as an antidote to Ovid and other heathen poets.

cloth'. All members were to attend dressed in their best livery. Each company was also to provide 'whifflers in coats of velvet and chains, ten at the least', to keep the way clear.

But the date was not to be 18 November after all. On 10 November Philip Gawdy wrote to his brother: 'The Queen cometh to Somerset House upon friday, and upon Tuesday next [19 November] she is appointed to hear a sermon at Paul's.'

The Queen did not come to Somerset House on Friday. The Lambeth churchwardens' accounts show that the bells were rung for her arrival on Saturday. It was still not certain when she would go to St Paul's, for on 14 November John Wolfe, in desperation, left the date open when he registered 'a joyful ballad of the Royal entrance of Queen Elizabeth into the City of London the   Day of November 1588 and of the solemnity used by her majesty to the glory of God for the wonderful overthrow of the Spaniards'.

A good deal of the ballad was probably already written by then. The Lord Chamberlain had drawn up the order of procession, a tricky task involving specialized knowledge of whether an earl's son should take precedence over a bishop etc.; in fact he simply used his old files, neglecting to omit the Archbishop of York, who was dead and not yet replaced, and the Comptroller of the Queen's Household, Sir James Croft, who was in the Fleet prison. The list was published and all the arrangements were known except the date, so that it did not require an eyewitness to write the introductory verses:

> Among the wondrous works of God
> For safeguard of our Queen
> Against the heap of traitorous foes
> Which have confounded been,
> The great and mighty overthrow
> Of Spaniards proud in mind
> Have given us all just cause to say
> The Lord is good and kind.
>
> And that we might not thankless be
> Unto our Gracious God
> That hath in mercy cast away
> His grievous scourging Rod
>
> . . . .
>
> Our noble Queen and peerless prince
> Did make a straight decree
> That through the land a solemn day
> Unto the Lord should be.
>
> . . . .
>
> Therefore to lovely London fair
> Our noble Queen would go
> And at Paul's Cross before her God
> Her thankful heart to show.

As it turned out, even this bit of anticipation did not prove to be entirely correct. After her arrival at Somerset House from Greenwich on Saturday 16 November, the Queen decided that she would attend the service at St Paul's neither on Sunday the 17th, her Accession Day, nor on the following Tuesday, the solemn day of thanksgiving decreed throughout the land. She would go on the following Sunday, 24 November.

There was yet more speculation about this change of plan. One of Mendoza's agents was convinced that it was all due to an argument with the French ambassador. Claude de l'Aubespine, Sieur de Chateauneuf, was in any case disgruntled because he was anxious to be home by Christmas but had been forbidden by King Henry to leave England. The Queen invited him to attend the thanksgiving service with her, but he refused on the grounds that he had no instructions from his sovereign. The Queen argued that she was only going to render thanks to God for reigning thirty years, but the ambassador insisted that he could not go on a day when there would be bonfires and other victory celebrations. So, according to Mendoza's informant, the Queen's visit was eventually postponed to 24 November.

That may have been the Court gossip. But perhaps the real cause was simply the one suggested by a story that was current. Preparing for one of the Queen's journeys, a carter in her service was told about yet another change of plan, the third that day. He slapped his thighs and said, 'Now I see that the Queen is a woman, as well as my wife.' The Queen overheard him from a window above the courtyard, called out 'What a villain is this!' and threw him three gold coins.

3

On Accession Day, 17 November, the Queen undoubtedly watched the traditional jousting in the tiltyard at Westminster. It is equally certain, though not recorded, that the Earl of Essex and the Earl of Cumberland, dressed in expensive but outdated armour, demonstrated their status and prowess at horsemanship, as they had done at St James, three months before, watched by a large, admiring public.

All the London livery companies, however, had to go in their best livery to hear a sermon at Paul's Cross, preached by Thomas Cooper, Bishop of Winchester. No record of his sermon has survived, but perhaps he tried out some material which he published in a book two months later, condemning the scurrilous attacks on the Queen's Church Established in the very hour of triumph. It will serve to show the kind of thing a captive, mainly puritan London audience listened to on a cold November day:

> Oh my good Brethren and loving Country men, what a lamentable thing is this, that even now, when the view of the mighty Navy of the Spaniards is scant passed out of our sight: when the terrible sound of their shot ringeth, as it were, yet in our ears: when the certain purpose of most cruel and bloody conquest in this Realm is confessed by themselves, and blazed before our eyes: when our sighs and groans with our fasting and prayers, in show of our repentance, are fresh in memory, and the tears not washed away from the eyes of many good

men: when the mighty works of God, and his marvellous mercies in delivering us, and in scattering and confounding our enemies, is bruited all over the world, and with humble thanks renowned by all them that love the Gospel: when our Christian duty requireth for joy and thanksgiving, that we should be seen yet still lifting up our hands and hearts to heaven, and with thankful minds setting forth the glory of God, and with Moses and the Israelites singing praises unto his Name, and saying, The Lord hath triumphed gloriously, the horse and the Rider, the Ships and the Sailors, the Soldiers and their Captains he hath overthrown in the Sea: the Lord is our strength, the Lord is become our salvation, &c. That even now (I say) at this present time, we should see in men's hands and bosoms, commonly slanderous Pamphlets fresh from the Press, against the best of the Church of England, and that we should hear at every table, and in Sermons and Lectures, at private Conventicles, the voices of many not giving praise to God, but scoffing, mocking, railing, and depraving the lives and doings of Bishops, and other of the Ministry, and contemptuously defacing the state of Government of this Church, begun in the time of that godly and blessed Prince, King Edward the Sixth, and confirmed and established by our most gracious Sovereign. . . .

The London companies had to turn out again in their best liveries on the following Tuesday, the decreed day of thanksgiving. There were bonfires and processions all over London, with dancing and ringing of bells, as well as more jousts in the tiltyard. But it was the following Sunday that everyone was looking forward to. By the end of the week all the preparations had been completed, the stands erected for the spectators, and the stages for pageants and tableaux, while the performers had learned and rehearsed their lines.

4

On the morning of Sunday 24 November the Masters, Wardens, Assistants and liverymen of the city companies assembled at their respective halls by eight o'clock, once again dressed in their best liveries and apparel. Then each company went to take up its allotted position, designated by its coat of arms, along the north side of Fleet Street, opposite the gentlemen of the Inns of Court, who waited on the south side.

> And from Temple Bar unto Paul's Church
> Along one side the way,
> The Citizens in their liveries
> Each one in rich array
> With streamers fair and little flags
> In order due did stand,
> Wherein their arms were richly drawn
> To make each trade discerned.

The Lord Mayor's instructions had been carried out punctiliously. The companies were standing within their railings covered with blue cloth. The whifflers were there to keep the crowds in order.

> And every Company by themselves
> As in their rails they stood
> Had youngmen stored in velvet coats   [equipped]
> And chains of gold all good,
> And each of them, to clear the way
> As they did waiting stand,
> Did still avoid the multitude   [disperse]
> With walking staves in hand.

Along the route, no one was allowed to look out from the windows of houses where the Queen was to pass unless the householder was prepared to stake his life and goods on his trustworthiness. 'However, there were persons who vouched for me,' wrote Henry Garnet, Superior of the Jesuit mission, 'for they believe I have the Queen's safety more at heart than her own Calvinist ministers.'

> The streets were hung with tapestry
> Of colours fresh and bright
> And everything provided fit
> For such a glorious sight.
> The Lord Mayor and his brethren,
> In scarlet rich arrayed,
> Upon their steeds at Temple bar
> For their Dread Sovereign stayed.

At about eleven o'clock, the procession set out from Somerset House, headed by 'gentlemen riding two and two with a very comely grace', followed by civil servants and law officers, judges and bishops, knights and noblemen, in ascending order of rank. Reports differ about who took part. The clerk of the Drapers Company who described 'her Majesty's coming to Paul's to hear a sermon there' (Henry Garnet said to hear a *Te Deum*) listed many of the dignitaries by name but did not mention the bishops or Archbishop. But the Archbishop was certainly there, in a place of honour, next to Sir Christopher Hatton.

> The Noble Lord High Chancellor
> Nigh gravely rode in place,
> The Archbishop of Canterbury
> Before her Royal Grace.

Scarlet, the royal colour, was most predominant among the robes of the judges, privy councillors, and the Archbishop, who rode directly before the Queen. There was one striking exception:

> The Lord Ambassador of France
> And all his Gentlemen
> In velvet black among the Lords
> Did take his place as then.

M. de Chateauneuf had not been enthusiastic about joining the procession in the first place, but the Queen had insisted. Nevertheless he could show that for him, at least, it was an occasion for mourning rather than celebration.

> Then came Her Royal Majesty,
> Most virginlike in sight,
> And gloriously attired was
> In cloth of silver white,
> And eke the chariot where she sat
> Of silver cloth did shine,
> And milk white steeds did bear the same
> All trapped rich and fine.

The Queen's chariot was ornamented with four pillars, which bore the silver canopy, gathered under a golden globe, high above the gilded chair on which she sat, and draped behind her, leaving the front and sides open to the public view. Two smaller pillars stood in front, on which were the Lion of England and the Dragon of Wales, the supporters of the Royal Arms. Henry Garnet, less euphoric than most, described the milk white steeds that drew the carriage as 'two grey horses, royally caparisoned'. The draper, with a professional eye, described them as being 'all whited with caparisons of white velvet spangled'.

As the procession drew up to Temple Bar, which marked the boundary of the City of London, the Lord Mayor dismounted to greet the Queen. Bareheaded and on bended knee he offered her a sceptre, which she accepted and then returned to him again, saying that he had well begun and should so continue his term of office. The sword-bearer stood by with the jewelled sword which the Queen herself had presented to the city as the symbol of corporate status. There were other presentations and speeches, as well as music from the city waits, playing their trumpets and hautboys from a platform erected over the gates at Temple Bar. Then the procession re-formed to continue to St Paul's, the Lord Mayor, bearing the sceptre, joining it directly in front of the Queen. The aldermen were placed nearer the front of the procession.

The Gentlemen Pensioners, on foot, surrounded the royal chariot. Directly behind rode the handsome and youthful Earl of Essex, Master of the Queen's Horse, with the Queen's personal mount on a leading rein. Behind him rode his rival, Sir Walter Raleigh, commanding the escort to the ladies-in-waiting, the Yeomen of the Guard,

> Attired in their coats most rich
> All wrought with glistering gold,
> Which was a most delightful sight
> And joyful to behold.

> And so to Paul's she rode along
> A mild and softly pace,
> The people crying joyfully
> Lord Jesus save your Grace.

From time to time the procession stopped, while the Queen watched pageants performed on stages along the route and listened to congratulatory verses. It was therefore not until about noon that she arrived at St Paul's Churchyard.

> The ground before the gates of Paul's
> With tapestry was spread
> Of purpose for her Royal Grace
> When she did light to tread.

At the Great West Door of St Paul's, the Queen was greeted by the Bishop of London and some fifty clergy of the Church of England, each one dressed, whatever his private views about popish vestments, in ecclesiastical robes befitting his station. To Henry Garnet it seemed a ridiculous charade:

> They looked silly in the eyes of all, dressed up as they were in Catholic copes: copes which heretofore they had burned or cut up in pieces and used for profane purposes. They had been forced to fetch them, in mutilated condition, from the Queen's chapel or from an old armoury in the Tower.

The Queen alighted from her chariot and knelt to pray, in full view of the people of London, at a table set up before the Great West Door. Then she entered the cathedral and walked up the west aisle, while the clergy sang the Litany. After the communion service, she was brought to a closet newly constructed out of the old chantry chapel of the Duchy of Lancaster, one of many that lined the apse. In the north wall of the cathedral, at the end of the chapel, new windows had been inserted, which opened onto the churchyard near the open air pulpit of Paul's Cross.

Probably she stepped out of the windows onto a balcony to hear the sermon preached by the Bishop of Salisbury. From time to time in the course of the sermon, we learn from Henry Garnet, 'she applauded the preacher in a loud voice when he was either praising the Queen's clemency or asserting that she was anxious before all else to establish peace.' No copy has survived of the sermon, though it was entered in the Stationers Register a year later. The bishop must have given a satisfactory performance, for he was created Archbishop of York the following February.

After the sermon was over, an interesting scene was described by the ballad writer, who must have had an informant inside the cathedral:

> The Earl of Oxford opening then
> The windows for her Grace
> The Children of the Hospital
> She saw before her face.

The Queen is sitting in the newly constructed balcony to listen to the sermon from Paul's Cross. The Bishop of Salisbury is preaching from the open pulpit on the left

The Earl of Oxford was there in the chantry chapel in his capacity as hereditary Lord Great Chamberlain. Some years before, he had rather ostentatiously become a Roman Catholic. He had also been notoriously unfaithful to his wife, Lord Burghley's daughter, who had died the previous summer. Such behaviour did not endear him to the Queen, despite his personal charm. It seems likely that he would use the opportunity to gain the Queen's favour.

He was perhaps responsible for the fact that William Byrd, a fellow Catholic and a Gentleman of the Chapel Royal, set to music a poem the Queen had recently composed on the theme of thanksgiving. The words survive both in a manuscript copy and in a printed book, both attributing them to the Queen, while the music only survives in the form of an arrangement for lute, made many years later; originally it was probably set for solo voice accompanied by a consort of viols, the last line of each verse repeated as a chorus sung by the boys of Christ's Hospital:

> Look and bow down thine ear, O Lord,
> From thy bright sphere behold and see
> Thy handmaid and thy handiwork,
> Amongst thy priests, offering to thee
> Zeal for incense reaching the skies,
> Myself and sceptre sacrifice.
>
> My soul ascend to holy place.
> Ascribe him strength and sing him praise,
> For he refraineth princes' spirits
> And hath done wonders in my days.
> He made the winds and waters rise
> To scatter all my enemies.
>
> This Joseph's Lord and Israel's God,
> The fiery pillar and day's cloud,
> That saved the saints from wicked men
> And drenched the honour of the proud
> And hath preserved in tender love
> The spirit of his turtle dove.

After this graceful compliment, the Queen returned through the cathedral to emerge from the Great West Door and cross the courtyard to the Bishop of London's palace, directly opposite, for dinner. Meanwhile, officers and liverymen of the city companies adjourned to their respective halls for a dinner at the companies' expense, returning to their places in Fleet Street at three o'clock. By the time dinner was over at the Bishop's palace, dusk was falling.

> And dinner being ended then
> In order as she came
> She did return unto the Court
> With all her noble train,
> Delivering the sword again
> Into the Lord Mayor's hand.
> A thousand torches burning bright
> Along the way did stand.
>
> Thus went our noble Queen away
> Unto her Highness' Court,
> Where multitudes of people did
> Continually resort,

> Desiring God for evermore
> Her Grace to keep and save
> That long unto her subjects' joy
> Her presence we may have.

It was a scene similar to the one vividly recalled by Bishop Goodman, over sixty years later, of a December evening in 1588 when he was a schoolboy living in the Strand, near St Clements church.

> I was told, 'If you will see the queen, you must come quickly.' Then we all ran, and when the court gates were set open . . . there we stayed an hour and a half, and the yard was full, there being a great number of torches, when the queen came out in great state. Then we cried 'God save your Majesty' and the Queen turned to us, and said, 'God bless you all, my good people.' Then we cried again, 'God save your Majesty.' Then the Queen said again to us, 'You may well have a greater prince, but you shall never have a more loving prince,' and so looking upon one another for a while the Queen departed.
>
> This wrought such an impression upon us, for shows and pageants are ever best seen by torchlight, that all the way long, we did nothing but talk what an admirable queen she was, and how we would adventure our lives to do her a service. Now this was in a year when she had most enemies, and how easily might they have gotten into the crowd and multitude to have done her a mischief.

5

Preachers were giving little credit for the victory to the prowess of the Lord Admiral's fleet in gunnery, Drake's skill in tacking, or the manoeuvrability of Hawkins's ships. In his sermon preached at St Mary's, Oxford, on the Queen's Accession Day, John Prime, a protégé of Thomas Cooper, Bishop of Winchester, declared the true victor over the Armada:

> At their coming we had warning of them, at their entry we had a good beginning, in their passage we gained the wind, or rather God gave it us, and when they were rooted over-right us, they were displanted again. In these things he that seeth not the finger of God to have been, and to be with Queen *Elizabeth*, seeth nothing and the brightness of God shining upon her, and by her upon us, doth dazzle his sight, that he cannot see.

Such sentiments were echoed by Protestants in Europe, who had regarded the well publicized might of the Spanish assault on England as a rehearsal for Armageddon. The King of Spain's pious motto, *Non sufficit orbis* (The world is not enough), was gleefully interpreted as evidence of his greed and ambition, on which God had passed judgement. But the news of the disasters to the Spanish fleet which swept through Europe depended almost entirely on *Certain Advertisements out of Ireland*, quickly followed by Lord Burghley's *Copy of a Letter*, both of which were frequently reprinted on the Continent.

As usual, first with the news of the English success was the European banking fraternity. Sir Horatio Palavicino had borrowed money to defray the Queen's expenses at the maximum allowed interest rate of 10 per cent, but had arranged to be repaid in foreign currency. Because of the increase in the value of the English pound he found himself being reimbursed at a loss. No one at Court had much sympathy. Sir Horatio gained some comfort, however, by composing an account of his own part in the fight against the Armada for circulation (in manuscript and in Italian) among his banker friends, who were no more likely than he to be able to tell port from starboard.

Another who related his adventures was Sir William Harborne, the Queen's ambassador to the Sublime Porte in Constantinople, but who depended on the Turkey Company for his salary. He had set out on an overland return to England on 28 July, bearing a message (in Latin) from Sultan Murad III to 'most shining Elizabeth, Queen of England and Prince of the magnanimous followers of Jesus, Guide of all affairs of the multitude and family of the Nazarenes'. Her ambassador had informed him, he said, of her four years' war with the King of Spain and how Portugal had been snatched from Don Antonio, and he regretted that the Persian war had prevented him from sending 'triremes' against Spain.

On reaching Poland by the end of September Sir William had merely been given a message to the Queen by the Chancellor. But by 12 October when he reached Elbing on the Baltic Sea he was being 'most friendly welcomed by the Senate of that City' and on the 27th at Danzig 'was courteously received by one of the Burgermasters accompanied by two others of the Senate, and a Civil doctor their Secretary'. On through Pomerania he visited each of the Hanseatic ports, invariably meeting with a friendly reception, being presented with their best wine and fresh fish, and on each occasion given 'a long discourse, congratulating, in the names of their whole Senate, her Majesty's victory over the Spaniard, and my safe return, concluding with offer of their ready service to her future disposing'.

His success seems to have been commemorated in a poem or ballad later attached to a play:

> The Turk admires to hear her government,
> And babies in *Jewry*, sound her princely name,
> All Christian Princes to that Prince hath sent,
> After her rule was rumour'd forth by fame.
> The Turk hath sworn never to lift his hand,
> To wrong the Princess of this blessed land.

Théodore Bèze, Calvin's successor at Geneva, and at nearly seventy still full of vigour (he had just got married again), summed up the Protestant view in a Latin sonnet, published throughout northern Europe, 'To the Most Serene Elizabeth, Queen of England':

Strewing the sea with ships, the Spaniard strove
  To join the British kingdom with his own.
What cause provoked all this? Ambition drove
  These pridesick men, by Greed their sails were blown.
How well the wind has sunk your vain desire
  And swollen waters o'ercome swollen pride.
How well have those who craved the world entire
  Been justly swallowed by the boundless tide.
Now you, the whole world's ornament, the Queen
  On whose behalf both winds and oceans fight,
Rule on with God, far from ambition seen,
  And succour still the pious with your might,
That England you, you England long hold dear,
  Whom good men love as much as wicked fear.

The poem was printed in London on a broadside together with versions in English, Dutch, Spanish, Hebrew, Greek, Italian and French.*

The Queen, whose Church was under siege from Geneva's puritan allies, must have regarded these tributes with mixed feelings, just as she did the medals struck in her honour by the Dutch, who, like the Hanseatic ports, continued to trade with Spain despite her efforts to impose a blockade. One medal, depicting the fire-ships at Calais and the Armada in confusion, was inscribed *Dux foemina facti* (A woman was general of the exploit), but the dies of another were borrowed to strike a commemorative medal in England. This was the one which showed the Spanish fleet encircled by the words *Flavi et dissipati sunt* (I blew and they were scattered). The reverse depicted the Church on a rock surrounded by waves, with the motto *Allidor non laedor* (I am struck at, not harmed).

Early in November the Privy Council heard that the Duke of Parma had retired from the siege of Bergen-op-Zoom to Brussels. The credit for the victory was due to Lord Willoughby, the governor of the English garrison, rather than Sir John Norris, who had not arrived in time to have any material effect on the action. It was the first time Parma had retreated and was taken as a demonstration of England's prowess on land as well as sea. Norris returned to London to recommence preparations for the Portugal expedition with Sir Francis Drake, who in the meantime had been made a freeman of the City of London and provided with a house, while books of his exploits against Spain in the Indies and at Cadiz were being hurriedly reprinted.

---

*The very free English version included these lines, not to be found in the original Latin:

Now if you ask what set this king on fire,
To practise war when he of peace did treat,
It was his *Pride*, and never quench'd desire,
To spoil that Island's wealth, by Peace made great:

This medal commemorating the victory over the Armada was struck in England from Dutch dies

Archbishop Whitgift issued a fund-raising letter:

It is more necessary that the Clergy should show themselves above all others most forward in furthering so holy and necessary a cause, when besides the removal of the Gospel amongst us, we should also look into the great and barbarous cruelty that was meet to have been used against all the religious and well affected subjects of the realm. The Bishop is enjoined speedily to assemble such of the Clergy as are most fit and able to persuade others to contribute to the good cause, and to appoint some to collect the benevolence of the Clergy with as little cost as may be. Sir Francis Drake doth promise, that if the journey prosper the money shall be repaid again with advantage.

The flotation of the company to finance the expedition was going well. Drake himself supplied £2,000 and some of his friends £6,000 more. Friends of Sir John Norris were expected to subscribe £20,000. The Lord Mayor of London appointed a committee who raised £10,000 in the city and £5,000 from merchants of Leadenhall. Don Antonio, the pretender to the Portuguese throne, offered bonds to the value of £10,000, redeemable after the victory. The Earl of Northumberland, Lord Rich, and many others contributed. Shortly before Christmas the Dutch promised to provide a siege train. But the main financial burden was to fall on the Queen, who was having to sell land and resort to further forced loans to meet her mounting expenses.

There are signs that the Privy Council was prepared to use the popular stage to reconcile the Queen's subjects to the need to pay more taxes for their benefits. *The Life and Death of Jack Straw* was mainly concerned with the irresponsibility of rebellion and displayed the courage of an ancestor of Martin Calthrop, the new Lord Mayor, in defending Richard II against those who had been incited by the 'naughty and seditious' John Ball. But the following comment of the Archbishop of

Canterbury, betraying a contemporary concern of Lord Burghley, could hardly have been included without prompting of some kind:

> Lord Treasurer, it seemeth strange to me,
> That being won with reason and regard,
> Of true succeeding Prince, the common sort,
> Should be so slack to give or grudge the gift,
> That is to be employed for their behoof,
> Hard and unnatural be the thoughts of theirs,
> That suck the milk, and will not help the well.

6

The real drama of 1588, however, was not to end without further excitement. Since King Henry III of France had capitulated to the Holy League at the meeting of the Estates General at Blois it had seemed that little could be hoped from him. Like the Dutch, he had been asked to 'help impeach all those they shall find laden with grain, or any kind of victual, from repairing [to Spain], of what nation soever they be.' On 10 December Walsingham wrote to Sir Edward Stafford from the Court at Greenwich that the Queen was 'greatly contented with the King's friendly answer touching the restraint [of corn]' but expressed surprise that the King had accepted 'so quietly the wrong' committed by the Duke of Savoy in occupying Saluzzo. 'The present diseases of France will not be cured with that temporising course that he now holdeth.'

But four days later, which was Christmas Eve in France, Stafford wrote an account of the dramatic manner in which King Henry had at last sought to assert himself. He had lured his persecutor, the Duke of Guise, into his private apartments in his palace at Blois and had him assassinated. The following day the Cardinal of Guise met the same fate. The Cardinal of Bourbon, Henry of Navarre's uncle and the Holy League's candidate for the throne of France, was taken into custody. It seemed that the King would acknowledge the Protestant King of Navarre as heir to the throne and that the alliance of France would become a reality.

This meant further effort to discredit the Spanish ambassador in Paris. Lord Burghley wrote to Walsingham on 30 December: 'I send you, translated out of the Spanish, lies which I have termed a Pack of Spanish Lies . . . with the discovery of the same pack in English. I mean to have the same printed in Spanish for the comforting of Don B. Mendoza.' His technique was to print in parallel columns first the lies from Spain and then 'A condemnation of the Spanish lies. From England.' There were also lively footnotes, not written in Burghley's ponderous style, but he may have been responsible for this one on the 'Relation' printed in Chapter Nine:

> [The Duke of Medina Sidonia] can tell the King, with great grief, that he never had fortunate day, from his coming to the Groyne [Corunna], till he returned with the loss of as many ships, men, victuals, treasure, and ordnance, as might have made a good army by sea. And great pity it is for Christendom, that both that which is lost, and that which remaineth, had not been used by the King

A Packe of SPA-NISH lyes.	*A condemnation of* the SPANISH lies.
From Spaine.	*From England.*

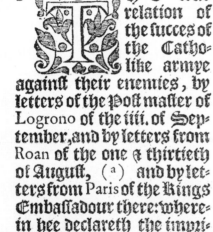

1 THE true relation of the succes of the Catholike armye against their enemies, by letters of the Post master of Logrono of the iiii. of September, and by letters from Roan of the one & thirtieth of August, (a) and by letters from Paris of the Kings Embassadour there: wherein hee declareth the imprisonment of Francis Drake, and other great Nobles of Englande, and howe the Queene is in the fielde with an armie, (b) and of a certaine mutinie which was amongst the Queenes army, **with**

1 IT is wel knowen to all the worlde, how false all this relation is, and either falsly coloured by the Letters remembred, or els both the post Master of *Logrono*, and the writers from *Roan* ought to be waged as Intelligencers for the deuill the father of lyes, whom they haue herein truely serued: and if they so continue in mayntenance thereof against the knowen trueth, their damnation is certaine, and hell is open for them.

(a) The Letters from the kings Ambassadour, whose name is *Mendoza*, agreeable to their Masters name, being the reporter of *mendacia mendacissima*, & considering that hee hath written that *Francis Drake* is imprisoned, and many Nobles of England, if *Mendoza* will stand to his Letters, so as he would gage, and
A 2 **by**

Catholic against the Infidels, and not, with ambition, to employ such kind of forces to invade Christian countries therewith; who, if he would live in peace with them, would be ready to join their forces with his, to dilate the fines [spread the boundaries] of Christendom, and forbear spending of Christian blood amongst Christians.

The pamphlet was printed in English by Christopher Barker, the Queen's printer, and translated into the same languages as the Spanish *Relacion Verdadera*. One trusts it was not sent to the Turkish Sultan. The full title was *A Pack of Spanish Lies, sent abroad in the World: first printed in Spain in the Spanish Tongue, and translated out of the Original. Now ripped up, unfolded, and, by just Examination, condemned, as containing false, corrupt, and detestable Wares, worthy to be damned and burned.*

7

It was Martin Marprelate who provided the first dateable reference to 1588 as 'the wonderful year'. In the preface to his promised *Epitome*, published towards the end of November, he declared: 'And bishops, I would I could make this year 1588 to be the wonderful year, by removing you all out of England.'

If there had been one thing clear about the Latin verses of Leovitius, by now universally attributed to Regiomontanus, it was that in the *mirabilis annus* of 1588 none would be spared. *Totus malus occidet*, total catastrophe had been the theme, as Maurice Kyffin had pointed out in his supplement to *The Blessedness of Britain*, which went to press in October:

> The fatal year of fearful Eighty Eight,
> Forethreatening fall of Empires, Realms, and Kings:
> Out-breathing Bale, to every Earthly wight,
> By pestering Plagues, and Dreadful dreary things:
>   Is Now nigh spent, and yet our Realm and Queen,
>   Through God's great Pow'r, secure in Safety seen.
>
> Whereby appears, Men's prophecies be vain,
> When God decreeth a Contrary Success:
> Fraud is the fruit of Man's unstable brain
> Out-stray'd from Truth, in Error's wide excess:
>   Who trusts Untroth must needs downslip and slide:
>   Men are but Men, God is the certain Guide.

One might have expected the famous prophecy of 1588 to have been consigned to oblivion with the same derision that had met Richard Harvey's *Astrological Discourse* in 1583. But as the news of the disasters suffered by the Spanish fleet spread across Europe, the 'fatal year of fearful Eighty Eight' became a 'wonderful year' for Protestants. In a Latin ode, a poet in Calvinist Heidelberg felt Regiomontanus thoroughly vindicated:

Annus hic obvius
Miraculum certe exhibuit ratum,
Quod astra portendere; de quo
Vaticinans cecinit vir ingens
De MONTE gestans nomina REGIO.

This year now come to pass
Assuredly has shown the marvel true,
Portended by the stars; concerning which
A great man in prophetic verse foretold,
Bearing the titles of a REGAL MOUNT.

The puritan lecturer, Henry Smith, back in his pulpit at St Clement Danes, reproved his congregation in the first of a series of sermons on Jonah's Punishment:

I would there were not many worse than Jonah among us. Will you know what I think of you? I think you are worse than infidels, Turks, or pagans, that in this wonderful year of wonderful mercies are not thankful, believe not in God, trust not in Him, glorify not His name: but like Pharaoh's sorcerers, who, seeing the great works of God which Moses wrought passing their skill, confessed, saying, *This is the finger of God* (Exod. viii 9): for you confess it is the great work of God (as you must needs) but where are the fruits it hath brought forth in you? The captain saith, I have done nothing; the soldier saith, I stirred not; but the Lord sent out a mighty tempest upon them, and after that they had escaped our hands, the Lord stretched out his mighty arm against them, and Pharaoh is drowned in the sea; so that he never attained the Land of promise, which he gaped for, and made full account to possess.

As the Queen and her subjects celebrated the twelve days of Christmas and gave each other New Year's gifts, at least they were not disturbed by prophecies of the year to come worse than the usual threats of high winds and the warnings of plague. On 3 December the Queen had issued a proclamation recognizing that 'by the diligent foresight of our loving subjects Richard Watkins and James Robertes many fantastical and fond prophesyings . . . are now left unprinted notwithstanding that divers yet yearly come to their hands in written Copies to be printed.' By letters patent they were granted for twenty-one years the exclusive right to print almanacs and prognostications, all others being forbidden on pain of being fined 12d. a copy. Watkins and Robertes were provided with long and profitable printing runs and the censors were saved a good deal of work.

TIME TO FINISH THE GAME

> In Eighty Eight how she did fight
>   Is known to all and some,
> When the Spaniard came, her courage to tame,
>   But had better have stay'd at home:
> They came with Ships, fill'd full of Whips,
>   To have lash'd her Princely Hide;
> But she had a Drake made them all cry Quake,
>   And bang'd them back and side.
>
> Anon.: *Upon the Death of Queen Elizabeth*

1

On the night of 1 January, according to John Stow, 'a great wind in the north-east untiled many houses, overturned trees, and otherwise did great harms both by land and seas.' Few other expectations of 1589 came to fruition.

In a sermon at Paul's Cross, on the first Sunday of the Parliament, Richard Bancroft, Hatton's chaplain and now a member of the High Commission, lumped Martin Marprelate and his adherents together with anabaptists and separatists as heretics and traitors. Though Martin continued to elude his pursuers and to provide entertainment in several more pamphlets his impudence had divided the puritan movement and provided the authorities with an excuse for suppression. He was finally silenced in August 1589. For their complicity, Sir Richard Knightley was heavily fined, John Penry was executed, and John Udall died in prison, but the real author, Job Throckmorton, the Warwickshire squire, was never charged. The deaths of their protector, the Earl of Leicester, and their principal organizer, John Field, left the puritans in disarray and apart from a few brave spirits they did not emerge into the open again until the reign of James I, when Robert Waldegrave, who had fled to Scotland and become the King's printer, returned to London in triumph in 1603.

In the Parliament of 1589, Sir Christopher Hatton condemned Pope Sixtus V for renewing the bull of Pius V, 'fraughting the same with most villainous slanders', and attacked papists and puritans alike as subverters of the state. The loyalty of Catholics remained suspect and they were subjected to more persecution. The work of the seminary priests was also hampered by internal dissensions and lack of leadership, particularly after the death of Cardinal Allen in 1594.

King Henry III of France procrastinated as usual and it was not for three months that he signed an alliance with Henry of Navarre, recognizing him as his successor. In August he was himself assassinated by a fanatical friar while their united forces were besieging Paris. The intervention of the Duke of Parma in 1590 saved Paris from capitulation to the new King Henry IV but the diversion of his resources also saved the Dutch Republic. It was not until 1593 that King Henry renounced his Protestant faith ('Paris is well worth a mass') and began to gain the united support of his country against Spanish interference.

The Portugal expedition was plagued with delays and did not set sail until April 1589. The cost rose to £80,000, of which the Queen supplied a quarter. Once distanced from the Queen, the English commanders ignored her instructions to destroy the remnants of the Armada, now virtually unprotected in Spanish ports. Instead they sacked Corunna, where their crews got drunk on the local wine and caught the plague. They then moved on to Lisbon, where the supporters of Don Antonio had been safely locked up and the defences of the city were well prepared. The Dutch had failed to supply a siege train so that all the expedition could accomplish was to lay waste the countryside. They arrived back in England in July in almost as sorry a state as the Armada the previous year, with little to show for the vast expense. A pamphlet was produced claiming a victory, which Don Bernardin de Mendoza in Paris had the satisfaction of refuting. Having lost the confidence of the Queen, Drake retired to the life of a country gentleman until his last voyage.

Although his resources were now overstretched by wars in both the Netherlands and France, King Philip of Spain managed to fit out three more Armadas to invade England, but all were driven back by storms before they reached the English coast. His reconstruction of the Spanish navy protected his Indies treasure fleet from English privateers such as Sir Richard Grenville and the Earl of Cumberland, but failed to save him from bankruptcy. Queen Elizabeth's treasury, drained by wars in the Netherlands, France and Ireland, fared little better, while plague and a series of poor harvests undermined her popularity and the prosperity of her realm, nurtured by thirty years of careful housekeeping.

2

After King James VI of Scotland came to the throne as King James I of England and 'our dread sovereign' became 'Good Queen Bess', Englishmen continued to celebrate Queen Elizabeth's Accession Day to annoy the Scottish king, particularly when he was trying to restore diplomatic relations with Spain. Armada Year became one of the highlights of her 'glorious reign' in what came to be regarded as a Golden Age.

A ballad (see Appendix III), first printed in 1630 and described as 'an old song', seems to recall ballads sung in 1588, including some that have been lost, and demonstrates the early burgeoning of the story of the thrashing of the Invincible Armada while the Queen was at Tilbury. The tune, 'Eighty-eight', was popular throughout the seventeenth century.

Lord Burghley's *The Copy of a letter . . . to . . . Mendoza* had a much longer history as a source for 1588. At the time of its publication it seems to have been recognized at Court as Burghley's work, for one of Mendoza's agents wrote to him from London about 'a little tract in French which they, in their usual cunning way, pretended to have been written by a Catholic to your lordship. It was done by the Lord Treasurer,

The Army of 20000 Souldiers laid along ÿ Southern Coast of England.

The Army of 1000 horse, and 22000 Foot, which ÿ Earle of Leicester comanded when hee Pitched his Tents att Tilbury

The Ld. Hen: Seymor wth 40 Englifh and Dutch Ships keeping the Coast of the Netherlands to hinder ÿ Prince of Parma's coming forth.

Severall ftrange Weapons taken from the Spaniard which were provided to deftroy ÿ Englifh

Anti-Catholic propagandist playing cards produced *c*. 1679 at the time of the 'Popish Plot'. The descriptions owe much to Burghley's *The Copy of a Letter* and other propaganda dating from 1588 and they sent a great number of copies to France.' But Burghley's authorship was soon forgotten. As early as 1601, Jean le Petit incorporated it as a genuine letter into his *La Grande Chronique*.

The pamphlet was reprinted in 1641 and 1746, but its widest circulation was in the second volume of *The Harleian Miscellany* of tracts in the library of Edward Harley, second Earl of Oxford, edited by his former secretary, William Oldys, assisted by Samuel Johnson. The collection was first published in 1744 and reprinted in 1752, 1808, and 1809. In his summary, Oldys clearly accepted the letter as genuine:

> The author, a Papist, and in the Spanish interest, informs the King of Spain, that the hopes of a foreign invasion did not only depend on a large army to be transported, but on a strong party ready in England to join the foreign forces at their landing . . . He shows the error of the Popish states, who confide on the numbers of those that profess Popery in England; and clears the laws of the land from the imputation of punishing any priest, or Jesuit, or other recusant, for his religion only.

Sir Walter Scott, who reprinted the pamphlet in his edition of the Somers collection of tracts (1809–12), was more circumspect, describing the letter as 'supposititious'. But about this time Burghley's letter entered a rôle that would have surprised him. During the campaign for Catholic emancipation, it was cited as proof of the loyalty of Catholics to Queen Elizabeth; in many school textbooks for over a century it was even stated that Queen Elizabeth had appointed a loyal Catholic, Lord Howard of Effingham, as commander-in-chief of her naval forces.

Burghley's authorship was rediscovered, appropriately enough, by the Jesuits, and published in *The Month* in 1911, but was generally ignored for another half century.

3

> For swift to east and swift to west the ghostly war-flame spread,
> High on St Michael's Mount it shone; it shone on Beachy Head,
>
>   . . . .
>
> Till Skiddaw saw the fire that burned on Gaunt's embattled pile,
> And the red glare on Skiddaw roused the burghers of Carlisle.

With Macaulay's poem describing how the beacon warning of the arrival of the Armada spread from Cornwall to Carlisle overnight, we are entering the realm of nineteenth century legend, to be followed by Sir Henry Newbolt's *Drake's Drum*.

But it was the eighteenth century William Oldys who was chiefly responsible for the one incident that everyone remembers about Armada year: Drake's game of bowls at Plymouth Hoe. To account for it we must investigate how the story of the defeat of the Spanish Armada got into the history books.

The first full narrative was written by the Florentine refugee, Petruccio Ubaldini, in Italian, based on notes provided by the Lord Admiral Howard of Effingham, probably in October 1588, when he was being criticized for his failure to capture or sink more Spanish ships. Sir Francis Drake was the hero of the hour, preparing to carry the war to Spanish waters in the Portugal expedition. Considering that he had not been given full credit for his contribution to the victory, Drake too provided Ubaldini with notes, from which a second narrative was compiled, also in Italian. The two were bound together in a copy dated April 1589, just as Drake was setting out for Spain and Portugal. Ubaldini left it to the reader to decide which version he preferred.

By the time Drake returned in disgrace after the failure of the Portugal expedition, the Lord Admiral had recovered his position, and distributed manuscript copies of Ubaldini's first narrative to his friends as 1590 New Year's gifts. It was translated into English and printed in 1590, apparently without Ubaldini's permission, for he complained of receiving no payment.

This English version was the basis of the account of the year 1588 in John Stow's *Annals of England, Scotland and Ireland* (1592, 1598, and 1605) and the principal source for William Camden's account of the naval action in his *Annals of Queen Elizabeth's Most Happy Reign* which was first printed, in Latin, in 1615. Camden's Annals were translated into French (printed by Richard Field in 1624), from which an English translation was made. By that time Howard's original notes had been transmuted through five editors and translators and three languages besides English in less than forty years.

The other popular account of the Spanish Armada was also written by a foreigner, the Dutch historian Emanuel van Meteren for his *History of the Low Countries*. It was translated into English and published by Richard Hakluyt in his *Principal Navigations* (1598) and provides a useful summary of the mixture of fact and fiction absorbed by someone who lived through the events.

In 1615, the same year as Camden's *Annals*, a fourth edition of Stow's *Annals* appeared. Since Stow's death, his papers had been acquired by an antiquary called Edmund Howes, who almost completely discarded Stow's narrative of the events of 1588, based on Ubaldini, and substituted another, which may have drawn on Stow's notes.

Howes certainly made his own contributions, such as quoting the 'prophecy of Regiomontanus' in Thomas Rogers' translation. Some of his information, like the story that Howard was ordered to send back four Queen's ships from Plymouth, just before the Armada arrived, is otherwise only found in Camden. We cannot therefore be wholly confident that Howes relied on contemporary sources when he described the mood in Plymouth in July 1588 when the English thought the Armada had been driven back to port by storms:

> June and July being almost spent, and no appearance of the enemy, the English thought the Spaniards would not come; some ships being better victualled than the rest, made out unto the Irish coast, others took harbour in the West country; their captains, officers, and others kept revels on the shore, dancing, bowling, and making merry, even at the instant of the foe's approach.

This first reference to the English captains amusing themselves at bowls fails to specify exactly where any game took place. Nor is 'instant' the same thing as 'announcement'.

A few years later Thomas Scott, rector of St Saviour's, Norwich, created a considerable stir by an anonymous pamphlet attacking Gondomar, the Spanish ambassador to England, and the proposed marriage treaty with Spain. Scott retreated to the Netherlands and took up the position of preacher to the English garrison in Utrecht, where in 1624 he published another pamphlet on the same theme, called *The Second Part of Vox Populi or Gondomar appearing in the likeness of Machiavelli in a Spanish Parliament*. An account of a supposed meeting of the Cortes described the Spaniards' pretence of peace negotiations in Flanders as the Armada approached, 'while their Commanders and Captains were at bowls upon the hoe of Plymouth'.

Scott's pamphlets would have remained in obscurity had they not been reprinted in 1732 in a collection, edited by Joseph Morgan, called *Phoenix Britannicus*, to which William Oldys contributed a 'Dissertation on Pamphlets'. Four years later, Oldys brought out a new edition of Sir Walter Raleigh's *History of the World* to which he prefixed *The Life of Sir Walter Raleigh from his Birth to his death on the Scaffold*. He acknowledged his debt to *Phoenix Britannicus* in the following account (otherwise based on Camden) of the events of 19 July 1588:

> The Queen had received such assurance they [the Spaniards] were so disabled from coming this year by storm, that she made Secretary Walsingham send for four of her first-rate Ships to be brought home to Chatham. But their Return was prevented by the Intelligence, which Captain Thomas Fleming brought into the harbour the 19th of July, that he had discovered the Enemy approaching from the Lizardpoint in Cornwall. The Captains and Commanders were then it seems at Bowls upon the Hoe at Plymouth; and the Tradition goes, that Drake would needs see the Game up, but was soon prevailed to go and play at the Rubbers with the Spaniards.

Oldys' *Life of Raleigh* was reprinted several times, usually in abridged form. But this anecdote, adding the unsubstantiated 'tradition' that Drake wanted to finish a game of bowls interrupted by Captain Fleming's news of the Armada's approach, took another century to find its way into the history books.

Certainly it is not found in David Hume's *History of England* (1759), where the account of the Armada battle is based mainly on Stow and Camden, but also on the reminiscences of Sir William Monson, written some thirty years after he took part in the battle at the age of eighteen. It was from Monson's confusion with another sailor of the same name that Hume got his description of Captain Thomas Fleming as a 'Scottish pirate'; Fleming was, in fact, related by marriage to Sir John Hawkins and his *Golden Hind* was one of the London ships.

Nor is there is any sign of the tradition in Richard Sheridan's spoof of an Elizabethan play at the end of *The Critic* (1779), set at Tilbury Fort, where Sir Walter Raleigh and Sir Christopher Hatton await the arrival of 'The famed Armada, by the Pope baptised, with purpose to invade these realms'.

It is to a compatriot of David Hume that we owe the next appearance of the game of bowls. Patrick Fraser Tytler won some renown with his first book, *The Life of the Admirable Crichton*. His friend Sir Walter Scott encouraged him to write a History of Scotland. While engaged on this task, he turned out a number of pot-boilers, among which was a *Life of Sir Walter Raleigh*, first published in 1833. Tytler acknowledged his debt to William Oldys, whose life of Raleigh had been reprinted by the Oxford University Press in 1829 as an introductory volume to Raleigh's collected works. There cannot be much doubt that Tytler used this edition, which altered Oldys' text to 'Drake . . . was soon prevailed on to play out the rubbers with the Spaniards.' It also gave *Phoenix Britannicus* as the source in a footnote. Tytler failed to mention either source for the following passage:

> on the 19th of July [the Armada] entered the British Channel, and at sunset was observed off the Lizard by Fleming, a Scottish pirate or rover, who brought the intelligence to Plymouth. At the moment this notice was given, the captains and commanders were engaged in playing bowls on the Hoe; and Sir Francis Drake, it is said, insisted, in the true spirit of a sailor, that the match must be played out, as there was ample time both to win the game and beat the Spaniards.

Nevertheless, the story, now further embellished, did not immediately gain popular currency, or it surely would have been included in Lady Callcott's *Little Arthur's History of England* (1836), a compendium of memorable history on the level of Raleigh and his cloak, Alfred and the cakes, and Bruce and the spider. Nor did it appear in Charles Dickens's *A Child's History of England* (1852–4). But it was soon to become a favourite Victorian illustration of English sang-froid.

Sir John Barrow could not resist quoting the anecdote in *The Life, Voyages, and Exploits of Admiral Sir Francis Drake, Knt* (1843), giving Tytler, whose reputation he clearly respected, as his source. But Sir John Barrow was Secretary of the Admiralty with access to the archives, and so regarded the story as 'very improbable' since Lord Admiral Howard himself had written of the haste with which they warped the ships out of Plymouth harbour.

On the other hand Sir Edward Creasey in *The Fifteen Decisive Battles of the World* (1851) began his account of the defeat of the Spanish Armada by describing the distinguished assembly on the Hoe at Plymouth, who included Drake, Hawkins, Frobisher, Howard, and Sir Walter Raleigh (who must have been there because he was commander of Plymouth). While they were playing bowls, Fleming, 'the master of a Scotch privateer', arrived to announce that he had seen the Armada that morning off the Cornish coast.

> At this exciting information the captains began to hurry down to the water, and there was a shouting for the ships' boats; but Drake coolly checked his comrades, and insisted that the match should be played out. He said there was plenty of time both to win the game and beat the Spaniards.

Creasey did not give his source, but the wording and the presence of Sir Walter Raleigh both indicate Tytler. Raleigh was in fact at Court in Richmond, as Captain of the Queen's Guard, for he was mentioned in Burghley's *Copy of a letter* as one of the courtiers who left to join the fleet at Dover. Creasey's book was popular enough to give new life to the legend, but its healthy growth was assured, four years later, by the publication of Charles Kingsley's best-selling historical novel, *Westward Ho!*.

Kingsley also described the gathering of admirals and captains, including, of course, Sir Walter Raleigh, as 'Jack Fleming', the old sea-dog, risked a hanging to come and tell them of the arrival of the Armada. Howard wished to prepare for battle immediately, but Drake refused to be hurried, and insisted on having a drink with his old crony. Howard and the others departed, while Drake remained behind to continue the game of bowls and to discuss strategy with John Hawkins:

> Does he think we are going to knock about on a lee-shore all the afternoon and run our noses at night – and dead up-wind, too – into the Dons' mouths? Let them go by, and go by, and stick to them well to windward, and pick up stragglers, and pickings, too, Jack – the prizes, Jack!

In fact, as Sir John Barrow had appreciated, the English ships escaped from Plymouth harbour as quickly as they could, and ran their noses the following night up-wind and round behind the Spaniards. But several generations of children were brought up on Kingsley's version. A famous picture of the scene by Seymour Lewis was exhibited at the Royal Academy in 1880.

Drake at bowls on Plymouth Hoe as depicted by a Victorian artist

Just as the story was becoming an established part of English folklore, W.H.K. Wright, a Plymouth librarian, traced it back through Morgan's *Phoenix Britannicus* (which had vanished from the footnotes since 1829) to Thomas Scott's *The Second Part of Vox Populi* of 1624. By this circular argument, the story of Drake and his bowls was claimed to have been current within living memory of the Armada battle. In everyone's imagination, of course, it included all the later embellishments such as Drake's famous remark.

In its final 'authenticated' form, the story appeared in the life of Drake by 'J.K.L.' in the *Dictionary of National Biography* (1888):

> An old and apparently well-founded tradition relates that when the news of the Armada being off the Lizard was brought to the lord high admiral, he and the other admirals and captains of the fleet were playing at bowls on the Hoe; that Howard wished to put to sea at once, but that Drake prevented him, saying, 'There's plenty of time to win this game and to thrash the Spaniards too.' (cf. J. Morgan, *Phoenix Britannicus*, p. 345).

4

This account was published at the tercentenary of the Armada battle, when Britain still ruled an empire, protected by sea power, on which the sun never set. The Armada myth, embellished by Victorian poets such as Lord Macaulay on the Armada beacons and Sir Henry Newbolt on Drake's drum, survived uncritically as a foundation of Britain's power in the world.

But only seven years later, J.K.L. or Sir John Knox Laughton edited the *State Papers relating to the Defeat of the Spanish Armada* for the Navy Records Society, followed by Martin Hume's Calendar of the Spanish state papers for the Public Record Office. Historians, professional or amateur, were no longer dependent on Camden or Hakluyt, and a considerable Armada industry developed.

By 1988, the quatercentenary, Britain was no longer a world power, and the Armada had become a media event to attract tourism. Queen Elizabeth II visited Plymouth Hoe and then sailed off to visit a King of Spain who had rescued his country from a regime as oppressive as that of Philip II. Meanwhile, an actress took the part of Queen Elizabeth I at a pageant at Tilbury, while a popular history magazine claimed that the speech she gave was a seventeenth century forgery. A chain of 500 beacons carried the 'war-flame' from Cornwall to Durham, while a Devon professor expressed doubt that they had ever been lit in 1588. In the Maritime Museum at Greenwich, an exhibition with contributions from both Spain and the Vatican was careful to avoid chauvinistic celebration; some visitors expressed bewilderment about who had actually won. Naval historians continued to wrangle over what had actually happened, but generally agreed that the naval engagements had been indecisive (as Drake and Hawkins had thought at the time).

It is hard to resist the conclusion that the victory was of the pen rather than of the sword.

ARMADA BALLADS

It is often asserted, following a statement by Miller Christy in an article in *English Historical Review* XXXIV (1919), 43–61, that of twenty-four Armada ballads only four have survived. In their original broadside form, this is true, but a further two survive in manuscript copies, while two more can be identified more doubtfully. Some of the entries in the Stationers Register were probably never printed. The survival rate, 6–8 out of a maximum of 24, is not below par. For tunes see Claude M. Simpson *The British Broadside Ballad and Its Music*, Rutgers, New Brunswick, N.J. 1966 [BBB].

BALLAD ENTRIES IN THE STATIONERS REGISTER 1588 RELATING TO THE SPANISH ARMADA

29 June   A Dyttie of Encouragement to English men to be bold to fight in Defence of prince and countrey

9 July   a ballad of Encouragement to English soldiours valyantly to behave themselves in Defence of the true religion and their Cuntrey

3 Aug   an excellent newe songe of prayer and prowesse

Possibly 'An Exhortation to all English Subjects to join for the defence of Queen Elizabeth and their native country'. No tune indicated. Not broadside. STC7582

4 Aug   a Joyfull sonnet of the Redines of the shires and nobilitie of England to do her majesties service

10 Aug   a ballad of th obteyninge of the galeazzo wherein Don Pedro de Val[d]ez was Chief

'A joyful new Ballad, Declaring the happy obtaining of the great Galleazzo, wherein *Don Pedro de Valdez* was the chief, through the mighty power and providence of God, being a special token of his gracious and fatherly goodness towards us, to the great encouragement of all those that willingly fight in the defence of his gospel and our good Queen of *England*' (by Thomas Deloney). Tune: Monsieurs Almain [BBB 495]. STC6557

10 Aug   the quenes visitinge the camp at Tilberye and her enterteynement there the 8 and 9 of August 1588

'The Queen's visiting of the Camp at *Tilsbury* with the entertainment there' [by Thomas Deloney]. Tune: 'Wilson's Wild' [BBB 791]. STC6565

10 Aug   A joyfull song of the Roiall Receaving of the quenes majestie into her Campe at Tilbery: the 8 and 9 of August 1588

'A joyful song of the royal receiving of the Queen into the camp at Tilbury' [by T.J.]. Tune: 'Triumph and Joy' [BBB 270; Greensleeves?]. STC14067

18 Aug   a ballad intytuled the Englishe preparacon of the Spaniardes navigacon
[probably about the fireships]

23 Aug   An excellen[t] songe of the breaking up of the campe

28 Aug   A proper newe ballad briefely shewinge the honorable Companyes of horsmen and footemen whiche dyverse nobles of Englande broughte before her majestie &c

31 Aug   a ballad intytuled, a ballade of the strange whippes which the Spanyardes had prepared [for] the Englishemen and women

'A new Ballet of the strange and most cruel Whips which the Spaniards had prepared to whip and torment English men and women: *which were found and taken at the overthrow of the Spanish Ships*, in July last past, 1588' (by Thomas Deloney). Tune: 'The valiant Soldier' [BBB 392 Jog On?]. STC6558

7 Sept   the martiall showes of horsemen before her majestie at Sainct James

28 Sept   A Ballad intytuled, the late wonderfull dystres whiche the Spanishe Navye sustayned yn the late fighte in the Sea, and upon the west coaste of Ireland in this moneth of September 1588

30 Sept   A ballad intituled of the valiant deedes of MacCab an Irishe man

7 Oct   A Ballad of thankes gyvinge unto God, for his mercy toward hir majesty begynnynge Rejoyce England

3 Nov   A new ballad of the glorious victory of Christ Jesus, as was late seene by th overthrowe of the Spanyardes

3 Nov   A ballad of the most happie Victory obtained over the Spaniardes and their overthrowe in July last 1588

4 Nov   A songe wherein is Conteyned the Treacherie of the wicked and is made to be songe on the Coronacon Daye or any other tyme

14 Nov   a Joyfull ballad of the Roiall entrance of Quene Elizabeth into her cyty of London the Day of november 1588 and of the solemnity used by her majestie to the glory of God for the wonderful overthrowe of the Spaniardes

'A joyful ballad of the Royal entrance of Queen Elizabeth into the City of London, the 24th of November in the thirty-first year of Her Majesty's reign, to give God praise for the overthrow of the Spaniards' (no tune indicated). MS copy

14 Nov   A Dytty of th exploit of Th erle of Cumberland on the Sea in October 1588 and of th overthrowe of 1600 Spaniardes in Ireland

21 Nov   a new ballad of Englandes Joy and delight, In the back Rebound of the Spanyardes spyght

Possibly 'A proper new ballad, wherein is plain to be seen how God blesseth England for love of our Queen'. Tune: 'Tarleton's Medley' [BBB 678 The Spanish Pavan?]. MS copy

25 Nov   a thinge Intytuled A Joyefull Songe or Sonett of the royall receavinge of the queenes majestye into the cyttye of London on Sondaye the 24th of November 1588 all along Flete Streete to the Cathedrall church of Sainct Paule &c

26 Nov   an excellent dyttie of the Queenes comming to Paules Crosse the 24th
          Daie of November 1588
27 Nov   A ballad Intituled, The joyfull Tryumphes performed by diverse christian
          princes beyond the Seas for the happines of England and the overthrowe
          of the Spanishe Navye, shewinge also the Justinge at Westminster on the
          Coronacion Daie in the xxxjth yere of her majesties reigne

Possibly the speech at the end of *The True Tragedy of Richard III* (first printed 1594).

HENRY SMITH'S ADVICE TO HEARERS

Henry Smith ('silver-tongued Smith' Nashe called him) was a popular and successful preacher because he studied his audience. The following is an extract from a sermon probably delivered shortly after the restoration of his licence to preach. (From *The Sermons of Master Henrie Smith, gathered into one volume. Printed according to his corrected copies in his life time.* 1592, 646–8). Both spelling and punctuation have been modernized.

Some come unto the service to save forfeiture[1] and then they stay the Sermon for shame. Some come because they would not be counted Atheists. Some come because they would avoid the name of papists. Some come to please their friends; one hath a good man to his friend, and lest he should offend him he frequents the Preachers, that his friend may think well of him. Some come with their Masters and Mistresses for attendance. Some come with a fame, they have heard great speech of the man, and therefore they will spend one hour to hear him once, but to see whether it be so as they say. Some come because they be idle; to pass the time they go to a Sermon, lest they should be weary of doing nothing. Some come with their fellows; one saith, 'let us go to the Sermon;' 'content,' saith he, and he goeth for company. Some hear the sound of a voice, as they pass by the church, and step in before they be aware. Another hath some occasion of business, and he appoints his friend to meet him at such a sermon, as they do at *Pauls*.[2] All these are accidental hearers, like children which sit in the market,[3] and neither buy nor sell. But as many foxes have been taken when they come to take, so they which come to spy, or wonder, or gaze, or scoff, have changed their minds before they went home, like one which finds when he doth not seek.

As ye come with divers motions,[4] so ye hear in divers manners. One is like an Athenian,[5] and he hearkeneth after news: if the Preacher say anything of our Armies beyond sea, or council[6] at home, or matters of Court, that is his lure. Another is like the Pharisee, and he watcheth if any thing be said that may be wrested to be spoken against persons in high place that he may play the Devil in accusing of his brethren; let him write that in his tables[7] too! Another smacks of eloquence, and he gapes for a phrase, that when he cometh to his ordinary,[8] he may have one figure more to grace and worship his tale. Another is malcontent and he never pricketh up his ears till the Preacher come to gird against some whom he spiteth, and when the sermon is done, he remembereth nothing which was said to him, but that which was spoken against other. Another cometh to gaze about the Church; he hath an evil eye, which is still looking upon that from which Job did avert his eye.[9] Another cometh to muse, so soon as he is set, he falleth into a brown study; sometimes his mind runs on his market, sometimes of his journey, sometimes of his suit,[10] sometimes of his dinner, sometimes of his sport after dinner, and the sermon is done before the man think where he is. Another cometh to hear, but so soon as the Preacher hath said his prayer, he falls fast asleep, as though he had been brought in for a corpse, and the Preacher should preach at his funeral.

1. Fine for non-attendance at church. 2. St Paul's Cathedral was a common meeting-place for lawyers, merchants, tradesmen etc. and their clients, even while services were in progress. 3. cf. Matt. 11:16. 4. Motives. 5. cf. Acts 17:21. 6. Privy Council, i.e. the Government. 7. Tablets on which many churchgoers (and playgoers) took notes so as to give an account of the performance to their friends. 8. Bishop. 9. Ogling girls. Cf. Job 31:1. 10. Lawsuit or petition.

'AN OLD SONG ON THE SPANISH ARMADO IN '88'

(Reprinted from 6th edition of *A banquet of jests or a change of cheare* first printed in 1630, when not attributed to Archie Armstrong but anon. in *Archie Armstrong's Banquet of Jests*, Edinburgh 1872.) The last line of each verse is repeated.

Some years of late, in eighty eight
  As I do well remember,
It was some say, nineteenth of May,
  But some say in September.

The *Spanish* train launch'd forth amain,
  With many a fine Bravado,
Their as they thought, but it prov'd not,
  Invincible Armado.

There was a little man that dwelt in Spain
  Who shot well in a Gun-a,
Don Pedro hight, as black a wight,
  As the Knight of the Sun-a.

King Philip made him Admiral,
  And bid him not to stay-a,
But to destroy both man and boy,
  And so to come his way-a.

Their Navy was well victualled
  With biscuit, Pease, and Bacon:
They brought 2 ships full fraught with whips,
  But I think they were mistaken.

Their men was young, munition strong,
  And to do us more harm-a,
They thought it meet to join their fleet,
  All with the Prince of Parma's.

They coasted round about our land,
  And so came in by *Dover*:
But we had men, soon set on them,
  And threw the rascals over.

The Queen was then at *Tilsbury*,
  What could we more desire-a?
And sir Francis Drake, for her sweet sake,
  Did set them all on fire-a.

When straight they fled by sea and land,
  So that one man kill'd three score-a,
And but that they all ran way,
  O' my Soul he had kill'd more-a.

Then let them neither brag nor boast,
  But if they come again-a
Let 'em take heed they do not speed,
  As they did they know when-a.

SOURCES AND NOTES

I have not attempted to list every book scavenged nor such standard authorities as J.B. Black, Christopher Hill, and A.L. Rowse, to whom my debt is particularly to their footnotes.

The only specific study is Conyers Read: 'William Cecil and Elizabethan Public Relations' in *Elizabethan Government and Society (Essays presented to Sir John Neale)*, 1961, 21–55. Christopher Morris, *Political Thought in England, Tyndale to Hooker*, Oxford, 1953, is one of the few books to recognize the essentially propagandist nature of most sixteenth-century theological treatises; concise but based on wide knowledge of texts. J.P.R. Lyell's unpublished thesis (see below) is useful on bibliography. For anti-Spanish propaganda see W.S. Maltby, *The Black Legend in England*, Durham N.C. 1971.

Printed media have received most attention, e.g. Frank Mumby, *Publishing and Bookselling*, 1949, ch.IV, M.A. Shaaber, *Some Forerunners of the Newspaper in England, 1476–1622*, 1929, and F.S. Siebert *Freedom of the Press in England 1476–1776*, Urbana 1952, but in practice I have not found such general studies useful. On ballads see Hyder E. Rollins, *An Analytical Index to the Ballad-Entries (1557–1709) in the Registers of the Company of Stationers of London*, Univ. of North Carolina 1925, reprinted 1967, Hatboro, Penn. Claude M. Simpson, *The British Broadside Ballad and Its Music*, New Brunswick 1966, has comprehensive bibliography. On iconography see Roy Strong, *Portraits of Queen Elizabeth* and *Gloriana*, Oxford 1963 and 1987. There is probably a lot more manuscript material, such as private newsletters, tucked away unnoticed in local archives.

Garrett Mattingly's outstanding *The Defeat of the Spanish Armada*, 1959, was the first account, other than Froude's, to place the naval battle in the political and ideological context of sixteenth-century Europe. Naturally there have since been new discoveries of which the best account is given by Colin Martin and Geoffrey Parker in *The Spanish Armada*, 1988. The Official Catalogue to the Armada Exhibition at the National Maritime Museum 1988 contains a very full bibliography but is not reliable on pamphlets discussed in this study.

Some books are cited for further reading, some have useful bibliographies. The notes refer to the numbered sections within each chapter. A reference back to the full title is indicated not by *op. cit.* but by chapter and section, e.g. [II 3]. A semicolon separates alternative texts; (brackets) indicate previous source cited by the author, not necessarily consulted by me. Place of publication is London unless otherwise indicated. The following abbreviations have been used for works frequently cited:

APC: *Acts of the Privy Council*, ed. J.R. Dasent, New Series XVI, 1897.
Book of Homilies: Certain Sermons or Homilies appointed to be read in Churches in the time of Queen Elizabeth, SPCK 1908.

Boynton: Lindsay Boynton, *The Elizabethan Militia 1558–1638*, 1967.

Camden: *History*; William Camden, *The History of the most renowned and victorious Princess Elizabeth late Queen of England.* Selections ed. by W.T. MacCaffrey, Chicago 1970.

Caraman: *Garnet*; Philip Caraman, *Henry Garnet 1555–1606 and the Gunpowder Plot*, 1964.

CRS: Catholic Record Society.

CSP: *Calendar of State Papers*, HMSO.

CSPD: Domestic 1581-1590 ed. R. Lemon and M.A.E. Green, 1865.

CSPDAdd: Domestic Addenda 1580–1625 ed. M.A.E. Green, 1872.

CSPF: Foreign 21/1 June 1586–June 1588 ed. S.C. Lomas, 1927; 21/4 January–June 1588 (Holland and Flanders) ed. S.C. Lomas and A.B. Hinds, 1931; 22 July–December 1588 ed. R.B. Wernham, 1936.

CSPIre: Ireland 1588–92 ed. H.C. Hamilton, 1885.

CSPSpan: Spanish IV 1587–1603 ed. M.A.S. Hume, 1899.

CSPVen: Venetian VIII 1581–1591 ed. H.F. Brown, 1894.

Deloney: *Works*; F.O. Mann ed., *The Works of Thomas Deloney*, Oxford 1912.

Devlin: *Southwell*; Christopher Devlin, *The Life of Robert Southwell, Poet and Martyr*, 1956.

Eliz. Stage: E.K. Chambers, *The Elizabethan Stage*, 4 vols., 1923.

Froude: J.A. Froude, *The Reign of Queen Elizabeth*, Dent Everyman 1912.

Gawdy Letters: I.H. Jeayes ed., *Letters of Philip Gawdy 1579–1616*, 1906.

Hardwicke Papers: P. Yorke ed., *Miscellaneous State Papers from 1501 to 1726*, 1778.

Harleian Misc.: W. Oldys ed., *Harleian Miscellany of Tracts*, 1809.

HMC: Historical Manuscripts Commission: Calendars of Beaulieu, Foljambe, Montague, Rutland and Salisbury manuscripts.

Hughes and Larkin: P.L. Hughes and J.F. Larkin eds., *Tudor Royal Proclamations* III The Later Tudors (1588–1603), Yale 1969.

Laughton: J.K. Laughton ed., *State Papers relating to the Defeat of the Spanish Armada*, Navy Records Society, 2nd ed., 1895.

Lyell: J.P.R. Lyell, *A Commentary on Certain Aspects of the Spanish Armada* (B.Litt. thesis 1932; Bodleian MSS Lyell empt 64–5).

Meyer: A.O. Meyer, *England and the Catholic Church under Queen Elizabeth* (trs. J.R. McKee), 1916.

Naval Misc. IV: G.P. Naish ed., 'Documents illustrating . . . the Spanish Armada' in *Naval Miscellany IV*, Navy Records Society 1952.

Read: *Burghley*; Conyers Read, *Lord Burghley and Queen Elizabeth*, 1965.

Read: *Walsingham*; Conyers Read, *Mr Secretary Walsingham and the Policy of Queen Elizabeth*, 3 vols., 1925.

Rogers Diary: M.M. Knappen ed., *Two Elizabethan Puritan Diaries by Richard Rogers and Samuel Ward*, 1933.

Somers Tracts: Walter Scott ed., *A Collection of Scarce and Valuable Tracts . . . particularly . . . of the late Lord Somers*, 2nd ed., 1809.

SR: E. Arber ed., *A Transcript of the Registers of the Company of Stationers of London 1554–1640 A.D.* II, 1875.

St Albans Archdeaconry: H.R.Wilton Hall ed., *Records of the Old Archdeaconry of St Albans 1575–1637*, St Albans and Hertfordshire Architectural and Archaeological Society 1908.

STC: *A Short-Title Catalogue of Books Printed in England, Scotland, and Ireland and of English Books Printed Abroad 1475–1640*, 2nd ed. rev. by W.A. Jackson, F.S. Ferguson, and K.F. Pantzer, 1976, 1986.

Strype: *Annals*; J. Strype, *Annals of the Reformation . . . during Queen Elizabeth's happy reign* III ii, Oxford 1824.

Strype: *Whitgift*; J. Strype, *Life and Acts of John Whitgift*, Oxford 1822.

Prologue (pp. 1–16)

Verse on Campion cit. Meyer, 244 (W. Allen, *A Briefe historie of the glorious martyrdom of twelve reverend priests*, ed. J.H. Pollen 1908, 46). Martin Haile [Marie Hallé], *An Elizabethan Cardinal William Allen*, 1914. Patrick McGrath, *Papists and Puritans Under Elizabeth I*, 1967. S.T. Bindoff, *Tudor England*, Harmondsworth 1950.

1. Feria's report: Conyers Read, *Mr Secretary Cecil and Queen Elizabeth*, 1965, 118 (trs. by P.F. Tytler); in full in Camden Miscellany XXVIII 1984.

2. *Book of Homilies* I (On Obedience) Pt 3, 120. T. Norton, *A Disclosing of the Great Bull* (STC18679); *Harleian Misc.* VII 535.

3. P. Renold ed., *Letters of William Allen and Richard Barrett*, CRS 1967, 277–81, 284–9. Robert M. Kingdon ed., *The Execution of Justice in England by William Cecil and A True, Sincere and Modest Defence of English Catholics by William Allen*, Cornell 1965; the former in *Harleian Misc.* II.

4. Geoffrey Parker, *The Dutch Revolt*, 1985, 305, 318. Camden: *History*, 189. *A Declaration of the Causes* (STC9189); Somers Tracts I 410–20.

5. G. Mattingly, 'William Allen and Catholic Propaganda in England', *Travaux d'Humanisme et Renaissance* XXVIII, Geneva 1957, 326ff. J.H. Elliott, *Europe Divided*, 1968, 321. L. von Ranke, *The History of the Popes*, Bohn 1913, III 137. Froude V 338. W. Allen, *Letter concerning the rendering of Daventrie* (STC370), 29. F. Hicks ed., *Letters and Memorials of Father Robert Parsons SJ*, CRS 1942, I 306–7. CSPSpan 132.

Chapter One (pp. 17–32)

German verse: Leovitius q.v. (my translation).

1. Cyprianus Leovitius, *Ephemeridum novum . . . 1556 usque in 1606*, Augsburg 1557, fol.228v. *Prognosticon ab Anno Domini 1564* [n.d.]. T. Rogers trs., *Of the ende of this world* (STC11803a–7). R.

Harvey, *An Astrological Discourse* (STC12909.7–11.5) fol.19. On extent of literacy see D. Cressy, *Literacy and the Social Order*, Cambridge 1980. Francis Bacon: 'Of Prophecies' in *Essays* 1597 etc. Camden: *History* 280. Hughes and Larkin II No. 694. SR 30 Oct and 10 Nov 1587. Walter Gray, *An Almanacke and Prognostication* (STC451). J. Harvey, *A Dyscoursive Probleme concerning Prophesyes* (STC12908).

2. *Gawdy Letters* 21. *Eliz. Stage* IV 103. R. Wilson, *The Cobbler's Prophecy* (STC25781); Malone Society 1914. CSPSpan 191.

3. *Eliz. Stage* I 222 n.2. G.B. Harrison, *Elizabethan Plays and Players*, Ann Arbor 1956, ll (S. Gosson, *The School of Abuse*, ed. E. Arber, 1906, 40). Read: *Burghley* 421.

4. CSPSpan 166–7. Laughton i 49. Hughes and Larkin No. 697. *Book of Homilies* II (Against Excess of Apparel) 326–7.

5. *Gawdy Letters* 34. CSPF 462. Froude V 374. T. Hughes, *The Misfortunes of Arthur*, ed. J.W. Cunliffe in *Early English Classical Tragedies*, Oxford 1912, 217–96. G.M. Logan, *Hughes' use of Lucan in The Misfortunes of Arthur*, Review of English Studies New Series 20 (1970), 22.

6. CSPF/21/4 129.

Chapter Two (pp. 33–41)

Some: *A Godly Treatise* (STC22908).

1. Millar McClure, *The Paul's Cross Sermons 1534–1642*, Toronto 1958. Devlin: *Southwell* 159. Strype: *Annals* III ii 433.

2. *Rogers Diary* 77. Patrick Collinson, *The Elizabethan Puritan Movement*, 1967, 327–8. SR II 27.

3. J.E. Lievsay, 'Silver-Tongued Smith,' *Huntington Library Quarterly* XI. Penry's *Exhortation* (STC19605.5); D. Williams ed., *Three Treatises concerning Wales*, Cardiff 1960. *The State of the Church of England* (STC24505); ed., E. Arber,

1879. SR 13 May.

4. Robert Some, *A Godly Treatise* (STC22908) Aiii, 15–16. *A Buckler against a Spanish Brag* in *Two fruitful exercises* (STC20571), 165, 170.

5. Caraman: *Garnet* 65.

Chapter Three (pp. 42–54)

Edmond Harris, *Sermon . . . at Brocket Hall* (STC12803) fol.A4.

1. Boynton 132ff.

2. Read: *Burghley* 418–20. *American Historical Review* ii (1896) 93–8 (Cotton MSS Vespasian C viii f.12ff.).

3. CSPDAdd 248. HMC Foljambe 32. Laughton i 124.

4. Laughton i 97–107. CSPSpan 258. 'Colchester Archdeaconry Visitations 1588' *Essex Review* XXXII 1929, 134. CSPSpan 240.

5. T. Wright, *Queen Elizabeth and her Times*, 1838, ii 361. CSPD 474. A.H. Johnson, *The History of the Worshipful Company of Drapers of London*, Oxford 1915, II 148–50.

6. CSPF/21/4 193–4, 242, 338, 368, 384. Read: *Burghley* 402–4.

7. CSPF/21/1 609–11, 637. J. Bruce ed., *Letters of Queen Elizabeth and King James VI of Scotland*, Camden Society 46 (1849), 48. CSPF/21/1 470. *Naval Misc. IV* 54.

Chapter Four (pp. 55–71)

Luis de Gongora y Argote: *On the Armada that sailed for England 1588* (my translation from Spanish).

1. CSPVen 344–5. CSPF/21/1 508. Baron Hübner, *The Life and Times of Sixtus the Fifth* (trs. H.E.H. Jerningham) 1872, II 181. CSPSpan 232.

2. Philip II to Medina Sidonia cit. A. McKee, *From Merciless Invaders*, 1973, 22.

3. Allen's *Admonition* (STC368). *Declaration* (STC22590); Charles Dodd, *Church History of England* (ed. M.A. Tierney) 1839–43, Appx. XII.

4. CSPSpan 236–7, 264, 287–9. Joseph Lefèvre, *Correspondance de Philippe II*, Pt 2 III (1585–91) Brussels 1956, 292–5, 302–3.

5. CSPSpan 273 etc. R.H. Motley, *The United Netherlands* I 486ff. De Lamar Jensen, *Diplomacy and Dogmatism: Bernardin de Mendoza and the French Catholic League*, Harvard 1964, 139, 143–4. Ibid, 'Franco-Spanish Diplomacy and the Armada' in

From the Renaissance to the Counter-Reformation, ed. C.H. Carter, 1966.

6. CSPSpan 284, 294–5. A. Alvarez, *La Felicissima Armada*, Lisbon 1588. C. Martin and G. Parker, *The Spanish Armada*, 1988, 279.

7. L. Stone, *An Elizabethan: Sir Horatio Palavicino*, 1956, 22. CSPF/24 640. CSPSpan 317, 333, 362. *Naval Misc. IV* 23–4. Martin and Parker [6] 279. Lyell Nos. 46–51 (*Relacion Verdadera*, Alonso Gomez, Madrid; *Le vray discours de l'armée*, Guillaume Chaudière, Paris; V. Accolti, Rome; Nicolas Korrn, Nürnberg (6 August N.S.); Gottfried von Kempen, Köln) and W.P.C. Knüttel, *Catalogus van de Pampfletten-Verzameling*, The Hague 1889, No. 832 (*Die wonderlijke groote Armade*, Hans van Salenson, Ghent).

8. CSPF/21/4 461, 531. CSPF/22, 2.

Chapter Five (pp. 72–90)

An Exhortation (STC7582)

1. CSPF/21/4 425–6, 453, 465–6. R.H. Motley, *The United Netherlands* I

2. Read: *Burghley* 426. HMC Foljambe 42. CSPF/21/4 485. *Gawdy Letters* 38

3. Read: *Walsingham* 308. CSPF/21/4 492, 528. CSPF/22, 33.

4. S. Haynes and W. Murdin eds., *Collection of State Papers . . . left by William Cecil, Lord Burghley* 1740–59, 627–9. E.G.R.Taylor ed., *The Original Writings of the Two Richard Hakluyts*, 1935, II 381. HMC Salisbury iii 329. Bruce: *Letters of Queen Elizabeth* [II 7], 50, 53.

5. Hughes and Larkin No. 699. CSPD 493. William Averell, *A mervaillous combat of contrarieties* (STC981), D4.

6. Devlin: *Southwell* 167. Transcript of ARSJ Fondo Gesuitico 651, fol. 67. J.H. Pollen ed., *Unpublished Documents relating to the English Martyrs*, CRS 1908, I 151.

7. Read: *Burghley* 427. CSPSpan 345. Strype: *Whitgift* 526–7. *A fourme of prayer* (STC16519); Strype: *Annals* III ii 15–16. St Albans Archdeaconry 63. William Averell [5] E2–3.

8. Allen's *Letter concerning Daventrie* (STC370). Devlin: *Southwell* 154. G.D. *A brief Discovery of D. Allen's Seditious Drifts* (STC6166) 81, 124. W.W. Greg, *A Companion to Arber*, Oxford 1967, 147–8. CSPSpan 354. For John Stubbe see Read: *Burghley* 566 n.86.

9. SR 9 and 23 March, 24 April, 15 May. W. Chappell ed., *The Roxburghe Ballads* 1871–97, VI 285. *An Exhortacion to als English Subjects* (STC7582) fol. A2v–3. Read: *Walsingham* 310. Laughton ii 173. Read: *Burghley* 406–7, 425. Laughton i 285.

Chapter Six (pp. 91–101)

Deloney: *Works* 469.

1. Emmanuel Green, *The Preparations in Somerset against the Spanish Armada*, 1888, 110–14. Boynton ch. V. E. Spenser, *The Faerie Queene*, I xi 14.

2. *Discours Véritable* see VII 2. APC 169–77. O. Pigge *Meditations Concerning praiers* (STC19916), 8. Broadside prayer (STC12576). Deloney: *Works* 468.

3. F.H. Mares ed., *The Memoirs of Robert Carey*, Oxford 1972, 9. Laughton i 304. *Rogers Diary* 79. E.M. Tenison, *Elizabethan England*, Leamington Spa 1933–60, VII 288; Froude V 405. CSPD 213, 227. Deloney: *Works* 470. APC 200.

4. Deloney: *Works* 471. CSPF/22?, 92. R.R. Sharpe, *London the Kingdom*, 1894–5, I 538. Anthony Marten in *Harleian Misc.* I 177.

5. APC 205. HMC Rutland 253. R.R. Sharpe [4] I 539, 542. Ubaldini in *Naval Misc.* IV 63. Laughton i 354–6. R.W. Kenny, *Elizabeth's Admiral – Charles Howard*, Johns Hopkins 1970, 158. APC 218.

Chapter Seven (pp. 102–12)

Deloney: *Works* 482.

1. *Le vray discours de l'armée*, G. Chaudière, Paris 1588.

2. CSPVen 373. Meyer 336 n.4. CSPF/22 121. HMC Rutland I 258. P.R.O. Roman Transcripts 31/9/83ff. 225–8 (Francia vol. 22, 83ff.); *Discours véritable de ce qui s'est passé entre les deux armées de mer d'Angleterre et d'Espagne* [Paris?] 1588. Anr. version [La Rochelle?] 1588; a related MS copy in HMC Rutland I 254–5. CSPSpan 386.

3. CSPSpan 386. CSPF/22, 122.

4. From *A Packe of Spanish Lies* (STC23011); Harleian Misc. III 391–3 slightly modified according to Spanish document in Lyell. Froude V 448; CSPDAdd 255.

5. CSPVen 381–2. CSPSpan 466. Meyer 337.

Chapter Eight (pp. 113–28)

Deloney: *Works* 474.

1. Deloney: *Works* 470. Laughton i 340–1, 360, 364.

2. Laughton i 341. R. Wilson, *Three Lords and Three Ladies of London*, Dodsley's Old Plays VI, 450. *Rogers Diary* 80. Read: *Burghley* 429.

3. Tilbury ballads by T.D[eloney] (STC6565) in *Works* 474–8 and by T.I. (STC14067) in *Roxburghe Ballads* [V 9] VI, 390–7. Hughes and Larkin No. 701 (On Price of Victuals). Queen Elizabeth's speech from *Cabala sive Scrinia Sacra* 1654. On authenticity see J.E. Neale, *Essays in Elizabethan History*, 103–6. HMC Salisbury iii 346. Read: *Burghley* 430. 'Return journey' in *British Museum Quarterly* X (1935–6), 166. *Rogers Diary* 80.

4. Read: *Burghley* 429. Leonel Sharpe in *Somers Tracts* I reprinted from *Cabala* 1691, 343. Don Pedro's actual examination in Laughton ii 27. Ubaldini in *Naval Misc.* IV 60. CSPSpan 421.

5. Read: *Burghley* 425, 430. Boynton 163. Stow: *Annales*.

Chapter Nine (pp. 129–44)

David Gwynn (STC12556) A7.

1. HMC Salisbury iii 342–3. Bruce, *Letters of Queen Elizabeth* [V 4] 171.

2. *The Copie of a letter* (see Ch. X). Laughton ii, 145, 49. CSPD 532. APC 273. Boynton, 169. Hughes and Larkin No. 703. Lost sermon by Adam Hill SR 21 November; R. Watt, *Bibliotheca Britannica*, Edinburgh 1824, 496t. CSPSpan 418–9.

3. APC 236. 'Execution of Justice' in *Harleian Misc.* II, 153. Devlin: *Southwell* 172. *A briefe Treatise* (STC24215) (N.B. 'A warning to all false Traitors' in J.P. Collier *Broadside Blackletter Ballads*, 1868, 57–62, is not genuine). CSPSpan 420. Pollen [V 6] V, 327.

4. Read: *Burghley* 431. Stow: *Annales*. 'Psalm and Collect' in Strype: *Annals* III ii 28. R. Humston (STC13969) fol. 24r. *A true Discourse of the Army* (STC22999), 5, 14. Cologne Distich in Nürnberg edition of *Warhaftige Zeytung* [IV 7] translated from Spanish in Cologne. Replies in Latin, fol. E4 of *A true Discourse*; English translations in *Holy Bull* (STC12354).

5. Anthony Marten, *An Exhortation to stirre up the Minds of all Her Majestys faithfull Subjects*

(STC17489); *Harleian Misc.* I 171. APC 291. R.B. Wernham, 'Queen Elizabeth and the Portugal Expedition of 1589', *English Historical Review* No. 258 1951, 7, 197; ibid. *Before the Armada*, 1966, 404.

6. Collinson [II 2] 444. APC 236, 249. Spenser, *The Ruines of Time*, lines 218–22. 'Willie and Peggie' in *Shirburn Ballads*, ed. A. Clarke 1907, 351. SR 26 September.

Chapter Ten (pp. 145–64)

Distichon Coloniensis (STC22999) fol. E4 (my translation from Latin).

1. Read: *Burghley* 426, 431–3. *The Copie of a Letter* (STC15412 etc); *Harleian Misc.* II; BM Lansdowne MS 103 ff. 134–63v.

2. For Thomas and Jaqueline Vautrollier see Colin Clair in *Gutenberg Jahrbuch* (1960) 233–8; A.E.M. Kirkwood, 'Richard Field, printer (1589–1624)' *The Library* IV xii 1–39; Greg and Boswell, *Records of the Court of the Stationers Company*, 26–7.

3. CSPIre 5, 27–9. Laughton ii 218. APC 277, 281. CSPSpan 493, 462. Froude XII 509. Lost ballad SR 30 September.

4. Fremoso in *Certaine Advertisements out of Ireland* (STC15412 Pt 2), *Harleian Misc.* III, and Laughton ii 221.

5. Walsingham to Stafford 30 Sept in Hardwicke Papers I 364. *Advertissement Certain, contenant les pertes advenues en l'armée d'Espagne . . . Avec deux lettres* [Guillaume Auwray? Paris 1588] Henry III's speech at Blois in G–J. de Mayer, *Des Etats généraux*, Paris 1788–9, XV 350–1.

6. CSPDAdd 255. CSPVen 399. Froude V 452. CSPSpan 471, 474.

7. CSPF/22 267–8. I have been unable to trace *Copije van een Brief uit Engelandt*, Delft 1588 36 pp. mentioned in Mattingly's notes to ch. XXIX of *The Defeat of the Spanish Armada* but suspect Ste Aldegonde was the author. *Heylige Bulle ende Krusado von Paus des Room*, R. Schilders, Middelburg 1588. *The Holy Bull and Crusado of Rome* (STC12354). Lyell 181–3. Kirkwood, *Richard Field* [2].

Chapter Eleven (pp. 165–80)

F.J. Furnivall and W.R. Morfill eds., *Ballads from Manuscripts*, 1873, II ii 93.

1. *A True Report of the inditement . . . and Execution*

of John Weldon, William Hartley, and Robert Sutton (STC25229). A second edition dated 24 Oct was printed by Richard Jones.

2. J.E. Neale, *The Elizabethan House of Commons*, 1963 (Chs. 4 and 5 give accounts of two 1588 elections). HMC Montague 21. Hughes and Larkin No. 705. Strype: *Whitgift* 531–2. *St Albans Archdeaconry* 66–8.

3. Udall, *Demonstration of Discipline* (STC24499); ed., E. Arber 1880, 82–3. Marprelate's *Epistle* (STC17454), *Hay any worke for Cooper* (STC17456), 14; Scolar Press facsimile, *The Marprelate Tracts*, Menston 1967. See R.B. McKerrow, *The Works of Thomas Nash* V 1910 for good brief survey of Marprelate controversy, L.H. Carlson, *Martin Marprelate, Gentleman*, San Marino 1981 for exhaustive study of authorship.

4. John Prime, *The Consolations of David* (STC20368), A2v–A3r. E. Arber, *An Introductory Sketch to the Martin Marprelate Controversy*, 1880, 107–8, 160. *The Epitome* (STC17454).

5. John Gerard, *The Autobiography of an Elizabethan*, trs. Philip Caraman 1951, 9–16. Strype: *Whitgift* 528. APC 370. *The Recantations . . . by William Tedder and Anthony Tyrell* (STC23859), 36.

Chapter Twelve (pp. 181–99)

German verse cit. Meyer 342 (my translation) (Bodleian, Sutherland MS 122).

1. CSPSpan 481. *Lambeth Churchwardens Accounts*, Surrey Record Society XVIII 1941. APC 334. *St Albans Archdeaconry* 66. Don Pimentel (STC19935). M. Kyffin, *The Blessednes of Brytaine* (STC15097) D2v. J. Aske, *Elizabetha Triumphans* (STC847); J. Nichols, *Progresses and Processions of Queen Elizabeth*, 1823, II 546, 561. C. Ocland, *Elizabetheis, Liber secundus* (STC18776) G1v. APC XIII (1581–82) 389–90.

2. SR 3 and 4 November. Nichols, *Progresses* 537–41. *Gawdy Letters* 42. *Lambeth Churchwardens Accounts* [1] fol. 126v. SR 14 November. CSPSpan 493. Transcript of 'A Joyfull ballad of the Royall entrance of Quene E. into the City of London' in A.M.W. Stirling *Life's Little Day* 1924, 277–81; B.M. Ward, *The Seventeenth Earl of Oxford*, 1928, 293–4. T. Birch, *Memoirs of the Reign of Queen Elizabeth*, 1764, I 154–5.

3. SR 27 November. Strype: *Annals* III ii 27. T.

Cooper, *An Admonition to the People of England* (STC5681) ed. E. Arber, 1882 (R.B. McKerrow, *An Introduction to Bibliography*, Oxford 1927, 227 shows this section was added at last moment).

4. *Royall entrance of Quene E.* [2]. Caraman: *Garnet* 82–3 includes practically all Garnet's letter in MS Fondo Gesuitico 651, f. 7. The draper in A.H. Johnson [III 5], 152. Sir William Segar, *Honor Military and Civil*, 1602, IV 244–5. Nichols, *Progresses* III 539. Philip Brett ed., *The Byrd Edition*, Vol. 16 1976, 197–8. Song attr. to Queen Elizabeth in *Naval Misc. IV* 84. G. Goodman, *Memoirs of the Court of King James I*, 1839, I 163.

5. John Prime, *The Consolations of David* (STC20368) B3v. Palavicino: Stone [IV 7] 155–6; Laughton ii 203–9. Harborne: HMC Salisbury XIII 378, CSPD 404, R. Hakluyt, *Principal Navigations*, Glasgow 1894, VI 58–9. *The True Tragedy of Richard III*, Malone Society, lines 2208–13. Beza, *Ad Serenissimam Elizabetham Angliae reginam* (STC1998); my translation – the contemporary English translation is much more free. *St Albans Archdeaconry* 65. Strype: *Annals* III 194. *Jack Straw* (1594) Act I Sc.2.

6. E.P. Cheyney, *A History of England . . . to the Death of Elizabeth*, 1914, I 158–9. Stafford's despatch is in Hardwicke Papers I 266–96. Wernham, *Portugal Expedition* [IX 5]. *A packe of Spanish lyes* [VII 4]; *Harleian Misc.* III 391.

7. M. Kyffin [1] C3v. N. Eleutherius, *Triumphalia de Victoriis Elizabethae* [Heidelberg? 1588], 27 [not John Wolfe as in Lyell, 137] (my translation).

Henry Smith, *Works*, ed. Thomas Fuller, 1866, II 224. SR II 817–9 (3 December misdated 1589); W.W. Greg, *A Companion to Arber* 1967, 44.

Epilogue (pp. 200–8)

Furnivall and Morfill, *Ballads from Manuscripts* [XI] II ii 98.

1. J.E. Neale, *Elizabeth I and her Parliaments*, 1965, II 195ff. R. Bancroft, *A Sermon preached at Pauls Cross* (STC1346). R.B. Wernham [IX 5] and *After the Armada*, Oxford 1984, which gives a detailed account of events in the Netherlands and France. Winston Graham, *The Spanish Armadas*, 1972.

2. J.E. Neale, in 'November 17th' in Essays in Elizabethan History. *Archie Armstrong's Banquet of Jests*, Edinburgh 1872, 87–90. Boynton 152. *Harleian Misc.* II 142. Devlin: *Southwell* 351 n.6 (J.H. Pollen, 'An Anti–Catholic Forgery' *The Month* 1911, 300).

3. P. Ubaldino, *A Discourse concerninge the Spanishe fleete invadinge Englande 1588*, 1590 (STC24481); *Harleian Misc.* I. John Stow, *Annales* (ed. Howes 1615) 744. Oldys and Birch, *The Works of Sir Walter Ralegh Kt*, Oxford 1829, 194–5 (refers to *Phoenix Britannicus*, 1731, 346). David Hume, *The History of England*, Dublin 1772, V 360. P.F. Tytler, *Life of Sir Walter Raleigh*, 3rd ed., Edinburgh 1840, 80. John Barrow *op.cit.* 1843, 286. D.N.B.: Drake.

4. *History Today* Vol. 38 (May 1988) 38, (September 1988) 59.

INDEX

Page numbers given in italic refer to illustrations.